GW01090423

Secret Ingredients

SECRET INGREDIENTS

RACE, GENDER, AND CLASS AT THE DINNER TABLE

SHERRIE A. INNESS

SECRET INGREDIENTS
© Sherrie A. Inness, 2006.

First published in 2006 by
PALGRAVE MACMILLAN™
175 Fifth Avenue, New York, N.Y. 10010 and
Houndmills, Basingstoke, Hampshire, England RG21 6XS
Companies and representatives throughout the world.

PALGRAVE MACMILLAN is the global academic imprint of the Palgrave Macmillan division of St. Martin's Press, LLC and of Palgrave Macmillan Ltd. Macmillan® is a registered trademark in the United States, United Kingdom and other countries. Palgrave is a registered trademark in the European Union and other countries.

ISBN 1–4039–7008–4

Library of Congress Cataloging-in-Publication Data

Inness, Sherrie A.
    Secret ingredients : race, gender, and class at the dinner table / Sherrie A. Inness.
        p. cm.
    Includes bibliographical references and index.
    ISBN 1–4039–7008–4
    1. Cookery—Social aspects. 2. Social norms. I. Title.

GT2855.I66 2005
394.1'2—dc22   2005047572

A catalogue record for this book is available from the British Library.

Design by Newgen Imaging Systems (P) Ltd., Chennai, India.

First edition: January 2006

10 9 8 7 6 5 4 3 2 1

Printed in the United States of America.

Transferred to digital printing in 2007.

For Debra Mandel
and Margaret E. Murray

Contents

Acknowledgments

My work has benefited from the input of friends and colleagues. I would like to thank the people who have read drafts of my entire book or chapters of it before its completion, including Brandon Derrow and Julie Hucke. I wish to thank everyone at Palgrave Macmillan who helped make this book possible, including Amanda Johnson, Paige Casey, Debra Manette, Erin Ivy, and Petrina Crockford.

I appreciate the kindness and support of family members and friends. My parents, Irene Gammel, Ann Gleig, Pia Maria Lange, Gillian O'Driscoll, Charlotte Rice, Heather Schell, Lisa Somer, and Liz Wilson deserve deep gratitude. My Miami University colleagues, especially Paul V. Anderson, Mark Christian, Kelli Lyon Johnson, Pete Martin, Diana A. Royer, Carol Shulman, and Whitney Womack, provided invaluable support and encouragement during the process of writing this book, I also appreciate the work of other food scholars, including Janet Theophano, Amy Bentley, Anne L. Bower, Carole Counihan, Barbara Haber, Lisa Heldke, Lucy M. Long, and Jessamyn Neuhaus. Their work has inspired me and sharpened my thinking.

Finally, I want to thank the libraries and special collections that made this book possible including Miami University, Radcliffe University, the Library Company of Philadelphia, and the University of Pennsylvania. They were always happy to help with even the most arcane queries. This book is dedicated with love to my dear friends, Debra Mandel and Margaret E. Murray.

Introduction:
Recipes for Revolution

When I was a child, my family's cookbooks were crowded in a single row in a kitchen cabinet near the stove. We did not own many; nevertheless, our small collection is ingrained in my memory as I often turned to the books because I cooked regularly. In addition, we had a few dozen *Sunset* magazines that contained unusual recipes, such as Chinese pot stickers and meat pies flavored with chile. There was also Mom's battered green metal file, crammed with recipes from relatives, neighbors, and friends. My mother would let me try out whatever recipe I wanted—I remember one ambitious attempt to prepare baked Alaska at age eight—so I would thumb through the books for inspiration and new recipes. I turned to *The Joy of Cooking*, stained, coverless, and smelling faintly of cinnamon, when making anything from biscuits to brioche, lentil soup to lasagna, macaroni and cheese to meatloaf, chocolate-chip cookies to chocolate cake. I also read the book out of curiosity. How did someone cook a moose? Although I did not have a moose to cook, it was fascinating to read such a recipe and other unusual ones, imagining who would eat such exotic fare. *The Peanuts Cookbook* was a small Scholastic paperback filled with cartoons and recipes, including ones for pumpkin cookies and Lucy's lemon squares, both popular in my home. *The Good for Me Cookbook*, a children's illustrated book, included recipes for healthy dishes such as stir fries, muesli, granola, and homemade whole-wheat bread. I remember *The Chinese Cookbook*, with its detailed pictures and bright red cover, chiefly for its lemon chicken and spicy shrimp, two dishes that I requested for my birthday celebration—a time when my mom would make me any dinner that I desired; without fail, I would always ask for the most elaborate ones possible. *The Swedish Cookbook*, *The Betty Crocker Cookbook*, *The Walter Hayes Cookbook*, *Diet for a Small Planet*, and a few others rounded out this small collection, similar to ones in millions of

American households. Almost every home has a shelf or two filled with cookbooks, some of the most omnipresent books in many women's (and sometimes men's) lives.

Cookbooks are one of the most popular forms of literature in the United States. Any major bookstore's cooking section is filled with books; Italian, Korean, Indian, French, Hungarian, Chinese, Thai, Vietnamese, Russian, and German cookbooks pack store shelves. There are books that focus solely on cheese, chocolate, candy, or caviar and others that discuss how to prepare food for every diet from Atkins to The Zone. Each year the section on cookbooks expands, with new selections, new trends, and new chefs. American society possesses an insatiable appetite for information about food and cooking that is found not only in books, but also in many other sources. Every bookstore is stocked with culinary magazines: *Gourmet, Food & Wine, Saveur, Vegetarian Journal, Everyday Cooking, Cooking Light,* and *Fine Cooking,* to name a few. The bookstore is not the only place to find information on the culinary arts. On television, cooking is well represented with numerous shows, not to mention a whole network devoted entirely to food and cooking twenty-four hours a day; if someone desires to learn how to make a hazelnut torte at 3 A.M., she can switch on the television. Similarly, the Internet is filled with websites dedicated to food. Some describe every region's cuisine; others devote themselves to recipes from professional and amateur chefs; yet other sites discuss countless variations for any recipe. Clearly, reading about cooking and food fascinates our society. However, even though culinary culture fills books, magazines, television shows, and Internet sites, little scholarly attention has been paid to what messages have been conveyed by culinary culture over the last half century, although this has gradually begun to change over the last few decades. Despite the prevalence of cookbooks, mainstream society disregards them as culturally unimportant, except for the messages they convey about cooking. One reason for this attitude is because of their connection to women; the stereotype that female concerns are insignificant has long been part of American society. It is common to think of women's hobbies and pursuits, especially those that take place in the domestic realm, as less significant than men's interests.

Cookbooks have been marginalized because cooking, especially daily domestic cooking, has long been stereotyped as trivial, while in fact nothing could be further from the truth. Cookbooks and other cooking literature are rich, complex texts that reveal a great deal about a society and its changing mores, not just culinary ones.[1] Because of their long association with women, cookbooks are particularly revealing about society's views of gender and the roles that men and women are expected to adopt; cookbooks provide recipes for masculine and feminine behavior as well as for meat-loaf.[2] In addition, cooking literature teaches lessons about race, class, and ethnicity; none of these issues is absent from a cookbook, including one that might appear to be nothing more than a collection of recipes. Even recipes raise questions about a culture: which recipes are included or excluded? Who is supposed to cook or eat them? What ingredients are used and who is able to afford them? For anyone interested in exploring cultural change, cookbooks are a valuable resource, since like any other genre, cookbooks need "a context, a point, a reason to be," as Susan J. Leonardi observes in her influential essay, "Recipes for Reading: Pasta Salad, Lobster à la Riseholme and Key Lime Pie" (1989).[3] No text, including cookbooks and other cooking literature, exists in a vacuum but in a cultural context that infuses it with meaning.

Over the last few decades, a number of scholars, many influenced by feminism, have turned to thinking about cookbooks, recognizing that they might contain more important messages about women's lives than society has assumed. For example, in her book, *Eat My Words: Reading Women's Lives Through the Cookbooks They Wrote* (2002), Janet Theophano suggests that since their beginning, American cookbooks have provided a place for women to express their ideas about society. She writes, "For hundreds of years, women of diverse backgrounds have found the homely cookbook a suitable place to record their stories and thoughts as well as their recipes" (1). She argues for considering cookbooks as "worthy objects of serious textual analysis. We ordinarily focus on contemporary cookbooks for their utilitarian or aesthetic purposes, but . . . [we should] shift our attention to their expressive potential" (5).[4] Theophano recognizes that cookbooks have been slighted as "women's work" so that, at least in the past, scholars have not studied them with the same care as "serious" texts; she suggests that cookbooks contain more lessons about women's experiences rather than just their kitchen tasks. She and others are rewriting how society thinks about literature on cooking and how it shapes American culture, especially in relation to issues of gender.

Owing to the cookbook's long association with women and their domestic roles in the kitchen, some people argue that such works are innately conservative. It is not uncommon for culinary writers to focus primarily on how literature on cooking has perpetuated socially conservative and traditional roles for women and men.[5] For example, in her book, *Manly*

Meals and Mom's Home Cooking: Cookbooks and Gender in Modern America (2003), Jessamyn Neuhaus writes about cookbooks' restrictive role in the early twentieth century:

> The recipes, language, and illustrations in these books reiterated a powerful set of social norms. Throughout the modern era, cookbooks uniformly advocated very specific gender roles: via the medium of food preparation, they joined a much larger chorus of experts and pundits who insisted that, despite the many changes facing American society in the twentieth century, families could continue to depend on mom's home cooking. (4)

Although she makes a number of astute observations about cooking literature's frequently conservative roles, Neuhaus does not focus in sufficient depth on how it can also be transgressive. Likewise, my previous book on women and cooking, *Dinner Roles: American Women and Culinary Culture* (2001), examines how cooking literature from the first half of the twentieth century played a conservative part in keeping women in the kitchen by informing them that cooking—except for outdoor grilling, barbecuing, and preparing steak and game—was their "natural" responsibility. The popular media reinforced the idea that women, not men, belonged in the kitchen, which helped reaffirm traditional gender roles during a time of great change. *Dinner Roles* focuses on one significant message that cooking literature conveys, but this is not the *only* one; like all texts, cookbooks pass on a multitude of lessons, some conservative, some not. *Secret Ingredients* explores a different issue in cooking literature: how it functions as a venue for social and political change. Cooking literature plays more political roles than we might assume, and we should recognize these roles in order to understand how this literature accomplishes something more than just supporting traditional gender roles for women and men.

Many fail to understand that, today and in the past, cooking literature has served different political purposes: promulgating certain agendas, while undermining others. A political agenda can most easily be noticed in cookbooks that explicitly support a particular cause or movement. For example, cookbooks supported the temperance movement, including the *Massachusetts Woman's Christian Temperance Union Cuisine* (1878) and the *W.C.T.U. Cookbook: Health and Comfort for the Home* (1889). Other cookbooks supported suffrage, including Hattie A. Burr's *The Woman's Suffrage*

Cook Book (1886), Linda Deziah Jennings's *Washington Women's Cook Book* (1909), and Mrs. L. O. Kleber's *The Suffrage Cook Book* (1915). The dedication of Jennings's book reveals that such cookbooks conveyed passionate lessons about women's issues: "To the first woman who realized that half the human race were not getting a square deal, and who had the courage to voice a protest; and also to the long line of women from that day unto this, who . . . braved misrepresentation, ridicule, calumny and social ostracism. . . . To all those valiant and undaunted soldiers of press, we dedicate our labors" (n.p.). While suffrage and temperance were recurring political themes, cookbooks included numerous other movements. In her book, *A Thousand Years Over a Hot Stove: A History of American Women Told through Food, Recipes, and Remembrances* (2003), Laura Schenone writes, "The American cookbook . . . [was] a . . . vehicle for women who wanted to politely call for social reforms, ranging from labor-saving kitchens to women's education, temperance, suffrage, and the politics of the Civil War" (107). Many cookbooks have political agendas, even if they are not described openly. For example, Southern cookbooks not only pass on recipes, but they also convey lessons about Southern identity, history, and culture.[6] Community cookbooks from churches, women's groups, schools, and other organizations pass down a group's beliefs, even if not stated explicitly.[7] Culinary historian Anne Bower in her book *Recipes for Reading: Community Cookbooks, Stories, Histories* writes that in community cookbooks, "silenced women [make] a place to express some part of who they are, singly or as a part of a group. The texts . . . provide a space in which women assert their values" (47). She continues, "Fund-raising cookbooks are ideologically motivated . . ." (7). As she notes, all community cookbooks carry political messages about their writers and potential readers. Similarly, Hispanic cookbooks convey not only recipes, but also spread pride in Hispanic culture and its accomplishments.[8] Jewish cookbooks share recipes and keep traditions alive.[9] While cookbooks teach lessons about how to cook, they also convey political messages that are not always conservative but, instead, radical, questioning dominant American beliefs and sometimes calling for widespread social reform.

Whether Southern, Hispanic, Jewish—or from a different regional, socioeconomic, ethnic, or religious group—women have used cooking literature to voice the need to change society. This is intriguing because, as mentioned earlier, people tend to view cookbooks as preservers of the status quo. After all, they often pass down the recipes of earlier generations, help to retain traditional gender roles, and perpetuate the notion that women are "naturally" the ones who cook. But, in actuality, cookbooks are also about change. Although cookbooks pass down conservative lessons about gender roles, they convey more subversive messages about other issues, including ones involving gender, race, class, and different concerns that impact women's lives. Sometimes these lessons are anything but conservative. In *Can She Bake a Cherry Pie? American Women and the Kitchen in the Twentieth Century* (2000), Mary Drake McFeely writes, "Reading between the lines of the recipes and surrounding texts of cookbooks reveals much about societal expectations and how they change. Women may have been trapped in the kitchen by cultural demands, but they have also found ways to resist them" (4). As she observes, women might have been confined to the kitchen, but they discovered ways to use that gender-stereotyped space to question society's expectations and values about how women should live. Similarly, Theophano observes in *Eat My Words*, "For women of varied cultural and religious backgrounds, the genre of cookery literature—and the terms of kitchen practice—have provided a vehicle for constructing, defending, and transgressing social and cultural borders. . . . Women of diverse experiences and backgrounds have chosen the genre as a suitable place to probe issues of social and cultural identity" (227). She continues, "[Cookbooks] . . . encoded messages of vigilance and transgression" (228). In other words, cookbooks suggested ways in which cultural borders could not only be defended but also how they could be crossed. Despite their conservative social role of teaching how to cook—traditionally one of society's most "feminized" gender roles—cookbooks address different concerns, speaking against society's prescriptions about "proper" gender roles for women.

Historically in the United States, women were the gender that commonly used cookbooks and other cooking literature as a venue for writing about social and political change. Traditionally, men have had other outlets for writing and speaking politically. Our culture has encouraged upper- and middle-class white males to be active members in the world outside the domestic realm, so for them there has rarely been a lack of communicative possibilities, although poor white males and non-caucasian men from different races and ethnic groups have more limited opportunities. This situation has been very different for women. Throughout the eighteenth and nineteenth centuries, upper- and middle-class women were supposed to allow men to speak in the public sphere, leaving females to take a more active role in the domestic sphere. Outside the home, women were expected to suppress their views about politics and social change. They were generally also not expected to write about such issues. Of course, some still spoke against social wrongs, but many members of mainstream society perceived them as "unnatural" figures, individuals to be dismissed or laughed at rather than listened to.

Although in earlier centuries women were seldom encouraged to pen overtly political treatises, they were encouraged to publish cookbooks. Society assumed that women should write them because cooking was a topic about which they were assumed to be experts. Writing cookbooks was a "natural" extension from women's domestic and household responsibilities, so it is not surprising that many women wrote cookbooks. But they generally were more than a place to record recipes; they were also sites to discuss political issues. Hidden among the recipes for cornbread or corned beef hash were lessons for social change.

In the eighteenth and nineteenth centuries, American women used cooking literature to explore a wide range of topics beyond merely passing on recipes. Even earlier in history, women and cooking literature have been linked. In her book, *America's Collectible Cookbooks: The History, the Politics, the Recipes* (1994), Mary Anna DuSablon observes, "Our national cuisine was conceived, developed, penned, and conserved almost entirely by women" (61).[10] Cookbooks fit into a larger tradition of feminine genres, including diaries, letters, and household manuals, that women have used to share their thoughts and shape American society.[11] As women did not always have access to ways of expressing themselves in a more public fashion, such as nonfiction polemics, they used other genres, including cookbooks. Neuhaus observes: "Cookbooks contain more than directions for food preparation. Authors often infuse their pages with instructions on the best way to live one's life—how to shop, lose weight, feed children, combat depression, protect the environment, expand one's horizons, and make a house a home" (1). Similarly, Theophano explains in *Eat My Words* that cookbooks are about "subtle ways of marking insider and outsider status in social and cultural life. . . . They are about the ways women write a place into being: to defy, delimit, manipulate, and infiltrate social, cultural, and geographical boundaries" (268). As Neuhaus and Theophano suggest, cookbooks in our country's earlier centuries helped guide women's lives both in and out of the kitchen, offering advice that covered a wide range of topics beyond the purely culinary. In addition, such books helped women to define, describe, shape, and enrich their lives and other women's in ways that did not necessarily agree with the dominant society's ideas.

In the first half of the twentieth century, women gained additional venues for political expression, but they were still marginalized in many ways. They often lacked the money or education to produce other forms of writing, but cookbooks were something that they could publish with little money and education. Cookbooks offered women from different social classes, races, ethnicities, religious backgrounds, and geographical regions a place to formulate social change. This included women from disenfranchised backgrounds who used cooking literature to question upper- and middle-class white norms. During the twentieth century, cooking literature conveyed many messages to women about their roles, sometimes lessons that subverted or undermined the mainstream's assumptions. Cooking literature offered women a site to articulate and oppose dominant social mores. Thus, studying this genre elucidates the ways in which women have used it to change society.

For anyone interested in understanding modern society and women's lives, the second half of the twentieth century is especially crucial. These fifty years have had a profound impact on American culture in numerous areas, including food and cooking. Our cultural expectations about who was supposed to perform the cooking shifted. In the 1950s, Mom was often in charge of cooking; by the 1990s, this changed to a degree as more women labored in the paid workforce and so were unable (or unwilling) to prepare all family meals. This shift stemmed from a larger cultural change that occurred in women's gender roles due to second-wave feminism. In the 1950s, women were expected to take care of their families, and their domestic duties were of foremost importance. During this time, many people disparaged women, especially married ones, who sought employment outside of the home. Second-wave feminism, however, allowed millions of women to recognize that they wanted more in life than housework. Our attitudes toward food altered tremendously. In the 1950s, America assumed it was the best-fed nation in the world; by the 1970s, it worried that it was the worst-fed, as natural foods proponents questioned the American diet. Whether shaping America's diet or questioning stereotypical gender roles, cooking literature in this half century has helped women challenge the American status quo.

Moving from the 1950s to the present, *Secret Ingredients* examines how cooking literature offers women from different racial, class, ethnic, and social backgrounds a way to debate many social issues. Whether writing against racism in the 1950s or arguing in favor of the 1970s natural foods movement, cookbooks have addressed a wide range of concerns, challenging norms and questioning assumptions about "correct" gender roles. Exploring this fifty-year span, the book demonstrates how cooking literature has played, and continues to play, a part in challenging assumptions about women's lives and socially defined roles. But cooking literature has questioned more than gender issues; it has also addressed how class, race, and ethnicity are constructed in the United States. Cooking literature has served as a vehicle for critically scrutinizing how American society is constituted.

The book's exploration of how cooking literature has allowed women to voice their dissent begins in the 1950s, a decade in which upper- and middle-class women were supposed to follow rigid stereotypes about what it meant to be female. For instance, they were supposed to enjoy domestic chores, especially cooking. They were expected to wish for little more than to spend all their time taking care of their families. Despite the persistence and vitality of such stereotypes, not all women were content as housewives; many wanted something more from their lives. One place where they expressed this dissatisfaction with cultural 1950s ideals was in cooking literature. Ironically, this presumably conservative genre became a site to question and undermine society's assumptions about how women should lead their lives. Rebelling against such stereotypes, cooking authors created a different image of what it meant to be female.

To understand how cooking literature challenged stereotypes of "desirable" female behavior, chapter 1 focuses on convenience food literature. Today, such instant foods are omnipresent in American society, so we rarely stop to consider their cultural significance. But they have altered the nature of cooking for millions, a change that has been especially significant for women. To understand changing gender roles in the kitchen, one must examine how convenience foods have altered females' relationship to food and cooking. Why did women welcome such foods? Convenience food literature helped spread these time-savers by suggesting that they should replace as many from-scratch foods as possible. Chapter 1 explores how convenience food literature conveyed a radical message that women should rethink how they cooked. Some culinary scholars have suggested that the 1950s occasioned a dramatic loss of control in the kitchen as more women used the convenience foods sold by giant corporations. According to this argument, women rushed out to buy boxes of instant macaroni and cheese and cake mix, so they could not experience the same creativity as when cooking from scratch. I understand the situation differently, however. Cooking literature that portrayed convenience foods played a positive part in freeing women from countless hours of kitchen work. Women were given a potentially liberating message: it was acceptable to take kitchen shortcuts and not cook "just like grandmother did." As well, cookbooks informed housewives that it was acceptable and even desirable to have a personal life aside from familial obligations and household chores. For millions, this message changed their relationship to cooking. Such a radical shift stemmed, at least partially, from popular cooking literature that lauded convenience foods as something every modern woman should adopt.

Turning from convenience food to Chinese food, chapter 2 focuses on how Chinese-American women used cooking literature in the 1950s as a podium to speak against racism. This chapter demonstrates that not all of the decade's culinary voices were white, despite a Caucasian dominance in the popular media. Other women also spoke up, including Chinese and Chinese-American women who wrote cookbooks to pass on lessons about Chinese cooking to an audience of Asians and whites. This cooking literature brought such food to a wider audience, encouraging a diverse group to try both "authentic" Chinese and Chinese-American recipes. In addition, Chinese cooking literature accomplished more than passing on culinary lessons; it promulgated the idea that the Chinese were not as alien as many white Americans assumed. Cooking literature helped to make Chinese people, as well as Chinese food, more culturally intelligible to a predominantly white society. Thus, Chinese cookbooks taught lessons about acceptance, which was vital in the decade after World War II, when a dominant discourse pigeonholed Asians as barbaric and alien, and the Red scare only intensified such xenophobia.

Like chapter 1, which questions the stereotype that women should prepare all meals from scratch, chapter 3 discusses another cooking stereotype: women should love to cook. This chapter focuses on Peg Bracken's best-selling cookbook, *The I Hate to Cook Book* (1960) and its sequel, *Peg Bracken's Appendix to The I Hate to Cook Book* (1966), two volumes that sold millions of copies and became staples on countless kitchen shelves across the United States (along with her popular housekeeping book, *The I Hate to Housekeep Book* [1958]). Bracken's message struck a common nerve for her readers. She articulated what many housewives knew: cooking, cleaning, and other domestic chores were dull and laborious. Although the popular media portrayed 1950s housekeepers as constantly cheerful, making yet another dinner for their families or tackling another load of laundry for their families, many women felt confined, stifled, and trapped by the expectations that they should perform the bulk of domestic work. This chapter explores the connections between Bracken's work and Betty Friedan's *The Feminine Mystique* (1963), showing how each indicated women's general sense of restlessness and dissatisfaction. Both authors revealed that the media's depiction of domestic labor as blissful was a lie, promoted to keep women in the household.

Moving from the 1950s and 1960s to the 1970s, the next chapter also studies how women used cooking literature to express their dissatisfaction with dominant social values. Chapter 4 focuses on natural foods cooking literature, which spread the ideology of natural foods for a simpler and healthier lifestyle. Hundreds of cookbooks and articles—the majority written by women—discussed natural foods, helping to promote one of the twentieth century's most significant food movements. This cooking literature helped to mainstream natural foods, showing that they were not only for faddists but also for anyone interested in a healthy diet. Along with passing down recipes for lentil loaf and tofu casserole, natural food cooking literature shared a political agenda about the necessity of changing mainstream Americans' consumer-driven mind-set and making them think about how their actions impacted people around the world environmentally and otherwise. Natural cooking literature sustained a movement that made a lasting impact on not just the American diet but also on the American cultural fabric. Natural foods cookbooks showed how marginalized groups, such as women and natural foods activists, could use cooking literature to instigate and influence broad societal change.

The next two chapters turn to the question of how different racial and ethnic groups use cooking literature to agitate for social change, providing a venue for questioning and subverting the dominant social order's value system. Cooking literature has been a space for nondominant voices that might be silenced in other genres to be heard. Chapter 5 analyzes African-American women's cookbooks from the 1980s and 1990s. Like the 1950s Chinese cookbooks, these works shared with their readers cultural and historical traditions that the white mainstream rarely addressed. Black cookbooks rebelled against a white society that wished to forget about the past, especially slavery. Along with discussing black history and culture, cookbooks shared and expanded on the long-standing tradition of women's cooking as central to African-American communities. At the same time, these cookbooks challenged white stereotypes of black women as being the "perfect" cooks, who wished for nothing more than to serve whites. This Aunt Jemima image has disturbing racist implications, helping to justify a white cultural fantasy where blacks enjoy their subordinate roles. Black cookbooks refuted the fantasy, demonstrating that blacks were forced by their low socioeconomic position to work for whites. In many ways, authors used their books to rewrite mainstream stereotypes about African Americans and their traditional foods.

Analyzing white trash cooking literature, chapter 6 also explores issues of race, ethnicity, gender, and social class. A number of white trash cookbooks, including Ernest Matthew Mickler's *White Trash Cooking* (1986) and Ruby Ann Boxcar's *Ruby Ann's Down Home Trailer Park Cookbook* (2002), have been published in recent decades, when an interest in everything about white trash lives filled the popular media; such cookbooks use humor to convey lessons about social class differences in the United States, including the social inequity that is an integral part of many American lives, especially those labeled "white trash." Mickler and Boxcar, as well as other self-identified white trash writers, use their works to give a voice to America's underclass. During the two decades when many upper- and middle-class whites rode the stock market and the technology boom to great wealth, white trash cooking literature reminded people that not all whites were wealthy, that some lived in poverty. Moreover, white trash writers also show that poor whites have always existed in the United States, shattering the illusion that all whites "naturally" are able to share in the American dream.

Like chapters 5 and 6, which focus on African Americans and poor whites, chapter 7 focuses on another disenfranchised group: vegans. In recent decades, vegan foods have not always had the most flattering press. They have commonly been depicted as appealing only to zealots who do not care if what they eat is unpalatable or nearly inedible; vegan foods have been associated with a radical fringe more concerned about animal rights than culinary pleasure. Many Americans do not even know what vegan foods and philosophies are, since the media has not popularized veganism as much as vegetarianism. Contemporary vegans are thus faced with a dual dilemma of addressing the popular media's negative images and making vegan ideas more visible to the mainstream. To address these issues, vegans have turned to cooking literature. In earlier years, vegan cookbooks were more utilitarian than anything, but this has changed in the last few decades as a number of women (and some men) have published cookbooks that depict vegan cooking as "sexy" and chic, making their audience rethink its ideas about veganism. These books include Jeani-Rose Atchison's *Everyday Vegan: 300 Recipes for Healthful Eating* (2002), Myra Kornfeld's *The Voluptuous Vegan: More than 200 Sinfully Delicious Recipes for Meatless, Eggless and Dairy-Free Meals* (2000), Robin Robertson's *Vegan Planet: 400 Irresistible Recipes with Fantastic Flavors from Home and around the World* (2003), and others. By showing vegan cooking to be hip and trendy, and as exciting as nonvegan cooking, these books are attracting a large audience that might never even have heard about veganism. Ultimately, contemporary vegan cookbooks, as did 1970s natural foods cookbooks, are affecting the way their readers view the world. Vegan cookbooks wish to influence people to adopt a more ethically involved stance toward not just cooking but how they impact the globe in other ways.

The final chapter turns from cookbooks to cooking shows. Increasingly, if one wishes to understand the changing nature of cooking literature and cooking culture in general, it is necessary to focus on television, where the Food Network's popularity has created a new venue for the culinary arts. Although popular televised cooking shows, including Julia Child's *The French Chef*, existed in previous decades, they never had the societal influence of a television network that features nothing but food shows twenty-four hours a day. Now, numerous programs and celebrities from around the world have been made famous or more famous through the Food Network.[12] Some of these celebrities and their shows seem well known primarily for their sleek, sophisticated gloss, but not all are equally glossy. This chapter analyzes *Two Fat Ladies*, the successful British import that appeared on the Food Network in the 1990s. Featuring the heavyset Jennifer Paterson and Clarissa Dickson, the show glorified the traditional dishes of British home cooking, and it was a surprise hit around the globe, including in the United States. Although lacking the slender, stunning stars featured in other cooking shows, *Two Fat Ladies* appealed to many women because it rebelled against a society in which being slim, young, and beautiful are considered essential attributes for "successful" females. This idea is so omnipresent in American culture that it is taken for granted. *Two Fat Ladies* challenged this notion, showing that a woman could be fat, old, and not attractive by any contemporary cultural standard and still be successful; in a world dominated by media images of an endless stream of barely clad beautiful female forms, *Two Fat Ladies* issued a subversive message.

Whether focusing on Chinese-American, African-American, or vegan cookbooks, *Secret Ingredients* examines how women from many backgrounds have used cooking literature to question society's expectations about gender roles and other issues. As the diverse topics of each chapter demonstrate, cooking literature is not monolithic, passing on a single message about issues related to gender, race, and class; rather, it conveys a wide range of views. To understand the complexity of cooking literature and cooking culture, one needs to analyze these different messages and the way they influence and shape society.

Secret Ingredients wishes to help its readers shift their thinking about cooking literature. Many people assume that it is innately conservative, especially with lessons about gender, since generations of cookbooks have focused on passing down traditional lessons about gender roles, including the lesson that Mom is supposed to be in the kitchen. All texts are complex, however, and convey a multitude of different meanings. Cooking literature is no exception; it passes on conservative messages about gender roles, but it also carries radical messages. Women have used cooking literature to voice their protests against a society where they are not always heard. Because cooking literature is an "acceptable" female genre, it has, since its beginnings, allowed women to write about their concerns. In recent decades, women have gained greater social freedom and are able to express themselves in a broader variety of genres, but cooking literature still provides a significant arena for their issues. Since domestic cooking continues to be gendered as a female task (although this is changing), it is not surprising that the bulk of cooking literature continues to be written by women and read primarily by women. This modern literature not only provides a place for discussing contemporary food issues, but it also creates a place for women to debate other social issues.

Cooking literature is a genre where nonwhite and working-class voices can be heard. It is vital to hear these voices because cooking culture's celebrities tend to share elite backgrounds. Many of our recent culinary stars are white and privileged, from Julia Child to Martha Stewart. Although, they and their counterparts have played and continue to play significant roles in cooking culture, it is equally important to hear voices from other classes and races. *Secret Ingredients* focuses on books written by middle-class white women and works written by women from different class and race backgrounds, who demonstrate that cooking culture is more varied and complex than revealed solely by Child, Stewart, and their ilk. Voices other than those of mainstream white authors deserve to be heard so that we can understand how women from various races, ethnicities, and economic backgrounds construct different narratives about their lives.[13]

This book also encourages readers to pay more critical attention to cooking culture in general, whether it be books, television shows, Internet sites, or magazine articles. Although our society is replete with culinary information, we rarely stop to analyze what messages are being distributed along with how to prepare a casserole. Culinary culture not only *conveys* recipes, but it is also equally intent on passing on implicit and explicit messages to people, confirming or challenging our roles in society. If we wish to understand our American lives, one useful place to turn is the vast culinary universe and its varied messages.

Finally, I hope this book will help readers better understand the role of food and food culture in their lives. This culture is an omnipresent part of our individual lives. Food and its messages are everywhere, from a trip to the grocery store to a visit to a restaurant. We are inundated by culinary lessons in everything from a copy of the *Gourmet* magazine that we flip through at a bookstore to a cookbook that we browse to find a recipe for lentil soup. This cooking universe informs us about food, but it does much more, as *Secret Ingredients* demonstrates. It shapes our perceptions of American society and the world and not only as those perceptions relate to food; studying culinary culture offers insight into our individual lives, including the gender roles that we adopt.

Chapter 1

"34,000,000,000 Work-Hours"[1] Saved: Convenience Foods and Mom's Home Cooking

Writing for the magazine *House Beautiful* in the 1950s, Jean Harris gloried in the new abundance of convenience foods, pointing out a grocery store shelf stocked with "165 choices of different types and brands" of canned meats (77).[2] In 1965, an article in *U.S. News & World Report* described the typical kitchen shelf as including "quick cake mixes, instant coffee, canned and powdered soups, dessert toppings, instant puddings, dry salad mixes, and many other quick-fix items" ("Better Days" 119).[3] Of course, one might wonder whether being able to purchase 165 types of Spam and other similar instant-meat products necessarily represented an improvement, but it did suggest the tremendous variety of convenience foods that had become available to women. The 1950s and 1960s were a boom period for convenience foods, and much mainstream cooking literature raved about their magic.[4] One article in *Parents* magazine proclaimed, "I'm eternally grateful for the wonderful assortment of commercial enriched breads, packaged ice cream and ices, preserves, and pickles. I would never find time to make these goodies at home. Convenience foods, I love 'em!" (Morgan 66).[5] Another article from *Better Homes and Gardens* declared, "With today's abundance of convenience foods and ingenious appliances at your command . . . the whole world is your oyster" (Eby and Kowtaluk 68). Such adulation was hardly unique; scores of other articles and cookbooks proclaimed the wonders of convenience foods, even suggesting that they were superior to their made-from-scratch equivalents.[6] The mass media depicted convenience foods as possessing the potential to alter American women's cooking duties, making them easier, quicker, and simpler. Convenience foods also helped to increase the selection of products that were available. No longer did cooks have to depend solely on what was in season; now, a vast variety of frozen, freeze-dried, and canned convenience foods were affordable for modest budgets in any season. "Simply put, processed foods presented women with a choice," observes food historian Erika Endrijonas (158). The plethora of convenience foods was described in especially positive terms by many female writers of cookbooks, perhaps because they knew firsthand how much work cooking demanded every day and how dull that routine could become. These authors rhapsodized about how convenience foods lightened women's workload, while also making cooking more enjoyable.

From the vantage point of today, it is difficult to imagine such positive responses to convenience foods in those earlier years; many view foods of the 1950s as frivolous and more than a little ridiculous, one of the most visible signs of an era known for its tastelessness. For example, Paul Levy, writing for the *New York Times Book Review* in 2004, observed, "Everybody who lived through the 1950s will recall how awful the food was. . . . Home cooks made sauces by adding a can of condensed mushroom soup to chicken—or incorporated the same cylinder of sludge, plus crushed cornflakes, into meatloaf that tasted just as nasty" (16). Sometimes the food even reached comical extremes, with towering Jell-O salads layered with everything but the kitchen sink. It is important, however, not to view convenience foods as only a joke. Despite the extremes to which some women might have taken convenience foods, they had a more important role than just providing comic relief. We need to try to understand them, as many women of the period did, as something that offered to cut cooking time drastically and promised new venues for culinary experimentation. Numerous women greeted the burgeoning growth of convenience foods with enthusiasm, as something that promised to alter how America cooked. This chapter demonstrates how cooking literature encouraged women to adopt the new convenience foods for three major reasons. First, women who used instant foods appeared more modern, since they did not have to stick with their grandmothers' labor-intensive, old-fashioned cooking methods. At a time when modernity was thought to be everything that was new and exciting, connecting women to modernity helped distance them from more traditional ideas about women's behavior. Second, it was important for women to tend to their own creative desires, both in the kitchen and the world. Women were supposed to be creative with convenience foods, but it did not end there. They were also encouraged to pursue their own interests outside of the home, a shift in cultural expectations about what women needed to be satisfied. Family was no longer enough. Third, convenience food literature conveyed the radical notion that cooks should speed up their work as much as possible, and it was acceptable not to cook from scratch. No longer did women have to spend long hours cooking to demonstrate their love for their families. Now, a frozen apple pie purchased from the grocery store could show as much love as one made from scratch. For many, those messages were alluring.

The promise of fewer hours in the kitchen must have been particularly appealing for millions of women in charge of the daily cooking for family members. Who wouldn't find such a task sometimes dreary, tedious, or repugnant? Who wouldn't wish to do anything possible to cut down those endless hours of toiling over a hot stove, especially when such cooking is rarely appreciated? Convenience food cooking literature promised to reduce time spent on cooking, suggesting that a woman had other more enjoyable pursuits. The literature stated that she could spend additional time with friends or devote more time to pleasurable activities, such as learning how to play tennis, finding employment outside the home, or donating her spare time to charity work. Convenience food literature made it clear that women should develop their own interests; this was a small step toward second-wave feminism in the 1960s and 1970s, which emphasized that women had to cultivate themselves as individuals who possessed concerns other than purely domestic ones. Instant foods played a part in giving women more time to think about and organize for rebellion and change.

Even today, convenience foods have a link to women's changing roles. Millions of women from all class, race, and ethnic backgrounds would find it difficult or impossible to pursue careers without the aid of convenience foods. Although critics lament the blandness and tastelessness of such foods, women (and men) rely on them, and, in actuality, they have sped up the cooking process. Now, it is common for a meal to be prepared in minutes, not hours, because many homes depend partially or entirely on convenience foods. For the first time in U.S. history, countless women have a choice about whether or not they will cook meals from scratch, pop fully prepared meals into the microwave, or go out for dinner. Never before have women, except for the wealthy, had this choice. Cooking from scratch has increasingly become merely one option among many, and the ramifications of this change are still being felt. Equally important, convenience foods have made it easier for even the most reluctant men and children to shoulder cooking burdens. No longer can a man or a child claim to be incapable of cooking, since almost anyone can learn how to heat up a frozen dinner in a microwave. No longer does Mom need to supervise. (A caveat: Sometimes men or children prove so inept at heating up a frozen pizza or a TV dinner that Mom is forced to stay in charge to prevent the house from burning down.) However, it is not unusual for mothers to be in charge of the bulk of the cooking in many families—even if only popping frozen dinners into the microwave—which is one reason that the connection between women and food preparation is slow to change. (This is because some males and children are content and prefer to glory in the ineptitude that keeps them out of the kitchen.)

It is too simple to suggest that convenience foods literature only encouraged social change by persuading women to leave the kitchen and pursue different pursuits. The literature also supported the status quo, failing to question that women should be the ones who did the majority of domestic cooking. Convenience foods literature encouraged women to pursue other activities, but only after all the cooking and other domestic chores were done. Such literature failed to argue that men should help with the chores, unless it was a rare treat to celebrate a special occasion or if the woman of the house were ill. Although convenience foods were simple enough for anyone to prepare, the cooking literature rarely suggested this—except if Mother were on her deathbed—perhaps because that would mean radically challenging established gender roles. Instead, women were expected to perform the meal planning, shopping, cooking, cleaning, and countless other domestic tasks inside the home; only after all of their work was finished were they allowed to sneak to their own pursuits during the time saved by using instant foods. Convenience foods literature was ready to support some changes for women, such as fewer hours in the kitchen, but stopped short of suggesting that the whole social system based on females doing the cooking should change dramatically. Ultimately, however, convenience foods did lead to a dramatic change.

Despite the ways that instant foods lightened countless women's cooking responsibilities, when scholars study frozen and other convenience foods, they frequently regard them negatively, rarely accounting for the freedom that they offered women.[7] For example, in his essay "Freeze Frames: Frozen Foods and Memories of the Postwar American Family" (2001), Christopher Holmes Smith holds a predominantly negative view of frozen foods and how they were advertised to a female audience in the 1950s:

> The frozen foods industry elicit[ed], and often solicit[ed], large amounts of coverage in the business, general interest, and women's press as a fundamental aspect of postwar life. Much like the arrival of television, the advent of the new market for frozen foods required that families, especially housewives, learn a diffuse corpus of rules to facilitate the incorporation of these products into the home. Toward this end, a panoply of articles and handbooks emerged to disseminate this range of expectations and conventions to the curious public. (180)

He continued, "The object for frozen foods proponents . . . revolved around teaching women how to use the new products to convince them that they were gaining ground in American society, even as they appeared to be losing it" (177). Smith perceived the rapid spread of frozen foods as yet another example of the efficiency of the marketing industry, which sprang into high gear to sell convenience foods to women. Frozen foods and their marketing, according to him, were among many signs that big business distracted women from the reality that in the 1950s they were losing ground in a variety of areas, including the workplace. By focusing attention on buying new products, companies made women forget about the ways that society was experiencing a backlash against them. If they worried about purchasing the new frozen TV dinner and other instant products, they would have less time to worry about the new restrictions imposed after World War II ended.

Smith is not unique in perceiving frozen foods and other convenience foods negatively. This attitude shows an upper- and middle-class bias that many researchers bring to the study of such food. Today, people from such classes commonly look askance at convenience foods, since they have the resources, education, and time required to purchase other foods. Such writers are apt to view scratch foods as desirable, while instant foods are portrayed in an opposite light. When studying convenience foods—or any topic for that matter—scholars inevitably bring in their own biases, which, in turn, influence their work.

Researchers should recognize that not all women from different socio-economic backgrounds considered convenience foods to be negative. Certainly, for many working-class women with little time to spare, they were sometimes a boon. Scholars should also acknowledge how different women, whether in the 1950s or today, regard convenience foods. One of the reasons for their great success is that they have met the needs of millions of women (and men) who have little time or desire to cook. Despite the long-standing upper- and middle-class tendency to disparage such foods, it cannot be denied that convenience foods have given many busy women, often straddling two jobs of managing a career and running a household, more time in their hectic schedules. When studying convenience foods researchers need to acknowledge their place in countless American homes, in the 1950s as in the present. Researchers must also consider how race, ethnicity, gender, socioeconomic class, geographical location, and a host of other factors influence what people think about these speedy foods; their rapid spread was not solely due to their marketing. Women reacted to these foods and perceived them as potential time-savers. Women were not dupes, led astray by big business; instead, frozen foods and other convenience foods were able to save several hours in the schedule of typical housewives, a tempting possibility for countless women tired of long daily hours in the kitchen.

In the 1950s, numerous women reacted positively to the new products that filled the shelves of stores. Authors of cooking literature discussed convenience foods in glowing terms.[8] Television cook show hostess Josephine McCarthy wrote in her book, *Josie McCarthy's Favorite TV Recipes* (1958): "The variety of convenience foods on the market today is a miracle of the era. . . . The convenience foods make it possible for inexperienced cooks, career women, and busy mothers to serve their families treats such as perfect fluffy cakes, luscious desserts, hot breads, [and] vegetables. . . . Yes, the convenience foods with their built-in maid services are one of the bright spots on a modern woman's horizon" (3). *House Beautiful* writer Poppy Cannon was even more ebullient about convenience foods, writing a love letter to the food industry:[9]

> I don't think I've ever told you how much I admire you, how big and fine and bold, imaginative and exciting you are. You might have thought I didn't really appreciate all your care and thought of me. Long before now I should have made it clear. Like any woman happy in her love, you've made me feel like a

queen. A queen in the kitchen eating Brown 'N' Serve crumpets or frozen butter biscuits with thyme-scented honey from Mount Hymettus by way of a Madison Avenue shop. ("Dear" 74)

She claimed that instant foods changed her cooking life, commenting, "Because of you, I have a new confidence in myself. I can do things I never dreamed possible before. Now I am no longer afraid to attempt an angel cake. . . . My popovers never plop. My piecrusts are never tough. The cream puff and éclair, even *beignets* and *pets de nonnes* are not beyond me, armed with that small package of pie-crust mix." (102). A busy career woman herself and a graduate of Vassar College, Cannon had the radical notion that it was acceptable for a woman to both work and also prepare meals that did not require countless tedious hours of labor (Shapiro, *Something* 89). The enthusiasm of McCarthy and Cannon stemmed from the potential of convenience foods to change the way women cooked. No longer did they have to worry that they did not have sufficient time or adequate culinary skills; convenience foods made it possible for every woman to prepare interesting meals. Of course, this was not entirely true; despite convenience foods, women were still going to make tough piecrusts, flat popovers, and inedible cakes. Instant foods helped, but they were not fail-safe. What they did offer, though, was a fantasy about how effortless cooking could be, and the media sold this fantasy to millions of women. This fantasy, however, was not entirely make-believe. Women's meals were not perfect, but convenience foods did make them easier to prepare.

Along with the popular media, many other groups, including home economics educators, praised convenience foods. For example, Edith Harwood Keck, supervisor in the San Diego City schools in the 1950s, wrote in *Practical Home Economics* about preparing students for their future lives. "Should we use commercial mixes and packaged goods in the teaching of meal preparation?" she questioned. Her answer was a resounding "yes": "A conscientious teacher can't be satisfied if she isn't improving the food-buying habits of today's homemakers and if she isn't helping the students become acquainted with the amazing new products on the grocer's shelves" (46). Not all home economics teachers were thrilled about the new products. Some thought they were too expensive and lacked flavor. For example, Bernice J. Gross and Kay Young Mackley, teachers of home economics at Hood College, wrote in 1950 that their students studied whether ready-made mixes were superior to baking from scratch. The students "concluded that the mixes have a place on the emergency shelf of modern homemakers but that they should be used only in case time is limited." The students decided that mixes did not belong "on the budget-wise grocery list" (451).[10] Different opinions existed in the home economics classroom about the place of convenience foods, but, ultimately, these foods would win the battle in countless classrooms; for many teachers, convenience foods were a way to make cooking more enjoyable, so why not introduce students to them? In this way, instant foods received the mark of approval of schools and were introduced to millions of students, who learned that it was acceptable, even desirable, to use instant foods. The message was subversive: abandon cooking full-scale from-scratch meals and, instead, turn to convenience foods—a shift that would alter mealtime for countless Americans.

Streamlined Cars and Convenience Foods: The Allure of Modernity

Why did many women, ranging from cookbook authors to teachers of home economics, respond positively to the new foods? One reason was their association with being modern, while from-scratch foods were aligned with being old-fashioned. Cooking literature declared that women should be modern and connected instant foods with such a notion. Modernity promised to change women's places in the kitchen, a move away from old-fashioned gender roles and toward more modern ones. Mary Drake McFeely describes how women felt about the new foods: "Modern women didn't expect to slave in the kitchen all day as they imagined their grandmothers had done" (94). Modern women wanted to lead lives different from those of grandmothers and mothers, and one way was to adopt convenience foods aligned with a distinctly modern sensibility.

American society was fascinated by modernity in the 1950s. After World War II ended, the United States was swept into an era that seemed to be modern and new. It was one when science and technology promised to cure the world's ills. It was one of streamlined cars and futuristic-looking furniture—designs that represented a distinct break with everything traditional. Although many were fascinated by modernity, others were wary or even strongly against the movement, viewing it as threatening to rip apart America's traditional fabric. Some people were disenchanted with the "sleekness" and "newness" of modernism.[11] For example, Elizabeth Gordon, writing for *House Beautiful* in 1953, observed, "something is rotten in the state of design" (127). She continued, "You may discover why you strongly dislike some of the so-called modern things you see. You may suddenly understand why you instinctively reject designs that are called 'modernistic' " (126). She went so far as to suggest that Mies van der Rohe and Le Corbusier's spare, uncluttered designs might be associated with communism. Although some viewed modernism as something that promised to revolutionize their lives, others, including Gordon, viewed it in more sinister terms, as something that could destroy America and American beliefs.

Nevertheless, many people were attracted to modernism in architecture and other arenas. This fascination with modernity, in everything from cars to buildings, also influenced how men and women wanted to lead their lives. They wished to be associated with modernity because it represented progress and change, which was especially important for women since, in the past, they had been stereotyped as antimodern. A long-standing American stereotype exists of women being aligned with tradition, while men are aligned with modernity. Thus, when women associated convenience foods with modernity, they also implicitly aligned themselves with it, too. Processed foods were not only a quick way to feed a family; they also served as a powerful sign that humanity had transformed food products into exciting new forms that had little or no resemblance to their earlier incarnations. Purchasing and consuming convenience foods demonstrated that a woman (and her family) was up-to-date. In addition, such foods showed that she was concerned with speed—one of the key attributes of the modern new age: "A 'modern' housewife—by definition—could not spend exorbitant quantities of time on her household duties, so if it could not be made quickly, it was not made" (Gitelson 76). Whether expressed as a Corvette or a TV dinner, the modern age was about speed and efficiency.

Literature on cooking presented convenience foods as modern and jet age. In her *The No Time to Cook Book* (1969), Roslyn Beilly described the local supermarket as "a treasure trove of jet-age convenience foods" (9). Lois Stilwill wrote in a 1963 *Ladies' Home Journal* article, "The pleasures of modern cooking can be instantly yours with the aid of today's convenience foods" (133). Similarly, women who used such convenience foods were also depicted as modern. For example, in a 1968 article in *American Home* magazine, Rita DuBois was enthusiastic about the possibilities that awaited the cook who added convenience foods to her larder: "The modern homemaker takes pride in finding shortcuts in the kitchen while maintaining her reputation as a good cook. . . . Packages labeled quick, easy, instant, minute, and ready abound and are growing constantly. And, rather than curbing creativity, these wonderful new products have actually enabled women to prepare dishes they once feared to attempt" (114). The Campbell Soup Company's *Easy Ways to Delicious Meals: 465 Quick-to-Fix Recipes Using Campbell's Convenience Foods* (1968) was dedicated to "all the modern, young-thinking cooks who enjoy using convenience foods in quick, easy recipes . . . to make family meals more tempting, party meals more exciting, and their own lives more satisfying" (Campbell 4). In these works and others, women who cooked using such foods were depicted as revealing their contemporary attitudes, which was appealing at a time when being modern meant being as jet age as the futuristic lines of a Cadillac's fins.

The media depicted women who failed to cook with convenience foods as old-fashioned. For example, in an article entitled "You Have 1001 Servants in Your Kitchen," in *House Beautiful* (1951), Jean Harris wrote, "Are you letting prejudices of twenty to fifty years ago hamstring you? Are outmoded ideas standing in the way of your benefiting from the thousands of servants working for you in freezing plants, canneries, dairies, bakeries?" (74). She was disturbed that many women were allowing old-fashioned notions about cooking from scratch keep them from trying convenience foods: "Prejudice about processed foods is keeping millions of women chained to old-fashioned, unnecessary drudgery" (74). In addition, she observed, "Tradition has hampered cooking. Attitudes handed down from mother to daughter have needlessly retarded our acceptance of food progress. We need to sweep from our minds the misconceptions inherited from former generations of housewives. We need to open our eyes to the fact that cooking possibilities are different from what they have ever been before in history" (76). Many convenience food proponents shared Harris's ideas. She wanted to free women from traditional cooking methods that demanded too much time. In this way, Harris and other food writers suggested that change in the kitchen was positive. More broadly, she advocated that such change was also important for women in general, who had to alter their alignment to past stereotyped gender roles and seek modern new ones.

Glamor Torte and Pink Perfection Peppermint Cake: Creativity and Convenience Foods

Along with their association with modernity, convenience foods were portrayed positively in cooking literature because they could be used creatively. When contemporary scholars study these new foods, they tend to perceive them as reducing or eliminating a woman's creativity, leaving her at the mercy of large food conglomerates. For example, McFeely writes that cake and pie recipes were "transformed into formula-made mixes by food manufacturers. The people behind the imaginary Betty Crocker had largely appropriated inventiveness. . . . All the cook had to do was add water—and sometimes eggs—and mix. . . . Her creativity was hardly her own" (92–93). What McFeely does not acknowledge is that even the cook preparing a cake from a mix possessed creativity. Like McFeely, Christopher Holmes Smith holds a negative perception of convenience foods as limiting creativity, noting, "Women's magazines, rather than bemoaning frozen foods as the end of the amateur chef's ability to infuse her culinary creations with individuality, instead advised their readers to consider the relatively bland seasonings of most frozen foods as their opportunity to express their unique sense of taste" (188). He overlooks that many women lack the time, energy, skill, or desire to make meals from scratch. Scholars tend to understand women as unwitting pawns of the food industry and media; this idea, however, suggests more about modern sensibilities than those of this earlier time. Today, it is easy for McFeely, Smith, and other writers to assume that such foods limited creativity for everyone. But was this true? One of the appeals of convenience foods was that they could be used creatively, even if a cook had only a short amount of time. Not all women had a whole afternoon to bake a birthday cake from scratch, but they might have an hour to make one from a box.

Convenience food cooking literature encouraged women to be creative with instant foods. At the simplest, cooking with convenience foods was no more complex than combining a few cans. If a woman wished to be more elaborate, she could add a simple topping of crushed potato chips or chopped olives. Soups were easy to liven up, Mary Elizabeth Wiley and Alexandra Field Meyer suggested in a 1951 *House Beautiful* article, if the "up-to-date" cook added "egg, parmesan croutons, or a dash of curry powder, or a spoonful of sherry" (105). The cookbook *Meals in Minutes* (1963) reminded readers, "When time's a-flying and the family is 'starving,' a can opener is your best friend!" (Better Homes 13). The book included a recipe for tuna jackstraw casserole, composed of a can of shoestring potatoes, a can of condensed cream of mushroom soup, a can of tuna, a can of evaporated milk, a can of sliced mushrooms, and chopped pimientos (13). This book also contained a recipe for soup-kettle supper, composed of a can of cream of vegetable soup, a can of chicken soup, a can of condensed onion soup, a can of cream-style corn, a can of Vienna sausage, and two cups of milk (11). A 1965 *Redbook* magazine article included a similar easy recipe for baked luncheon meat casserole (two cans of luncheon meat, a can of asparagus, and two cups of instant mashed potatoes) ("*Redbook*'s Timesaver" 99). Simple convenience foods, like the lowly frozen French fry, could be made more appealing with a few additions. Poppy Cannon provided recipes for French fries with walnuts (fries sprinkled with black walnuts), French-fried potatoes diablo (fries topped with chopped pickles and Worcestershire sauce), and French fries au jambon (fries topped with chopped cooked ham and prepared mustard) (105, 104, 107). Instant potatoes could be made more interesting by adding instant onions, herbs and spices, Velveeta, or artificial bacon bits.[12] Convenience food cookbooks offered endless possibilities to decorate French fries, instant mashed potatoes, and a variety of other plain foods. Such simple variations of convenience foods, whether by tossing together a few cans or sprinkling a topping on a dish of instant mashed potatoes, streamlined cooking and must have appealed to many busy women who lacked time (or desire) to cook more elaborate meals. Today, cooking shortcuts continue to be alluring for similar reasons. Creativity exists in such approaches to food, although in a more simplified form than an elaborate meal prepared by Martha Stewart (when she was still the Culinary Queen), but many people do not possess the same resources.

Convenience food cooking literature showed women that creativity could be more elaborate than simply throwing together two different cans of soup and topping the concoction with instant bacon bits, crushed potato chips, or fried onions. With the right touches, one could make a cake from a mix as creative as a made-from-scratch delicacy. In a 1950s *Good Housekeeping* article entitled "Mix in a Little Magic," a plain cake mix was transformed into cherry cordial cake, princess cake, jubilee cake, spicy white cake, butter-nut crunch cake, sky-high chocolate cream cake, and double marble cake ("Mix" 92). The most exotic cake in this article was the calorie-laden glamor torte—a white cake fancied up with a can of crushed pineapple, a cup of shredded coconut, chopped walnuts, candied cherries, and a cup of heavy cream (92). Similarly, the 1950s cookbook author Marion W. Flexner discussed how store-bought cakes or pies could be made more glamorous. Some of her "miracles with sponge cake" included turning a sponge cake into a Boston cream cake, Spanish almond cake, French mocha-praline cake, or Italian rum-and-macaroon cake (242). An angel food cake could be transformed into a strawberry dream cake or pink perfection peppermint cake; a cook was limited only by her imagination (244, 245). The introduction to Betty Crocker's *How to Have the Most Fun with Cake Mixes* (1950) observed, "Here's a whole book of new ideas for cake baking—every idea quick, easy, and fun. . . . And our mixes make even the fanciest 'company's coming cakes' practically no trouble at all" (Crocker, n.p.). Convenience foods could be as original and unique as foods made from scratch, but cooks needed to personalize them. A cake could be prepared in countless new and fanciful ways. In this fashion, even a simple cooking experience, such as baking a cake from a box, could be fancied up, encouraging greater creativity and innovation among women. Today, we tend to belittle such artistry and judge it, as does McFeely, as less ingenious than preparing a cake from scratch, but we need to remember that not all women have the time or desire to cook from scratch. For women without the time to bake from scratch, making a cake from a box and decorating it also might occasion a sense of creative satisfaction.

Cooks used their creativity to make many foods other than cakes more glamorous and exotic.[13] Jean Harris observed in *House Beautiful* magazine in the early 1950s, "The real secret in making ready-made foods acceptable is knowing how to glamorize them in their preparation" (150). One *Better Homes and Gardens* writer noted in the early 1960s, "Canned, frozen, and packaged foods are the major ingredients—they fairly jump off the shelf to partner each other in new and exciting dishes. For instance, the Chicken 'n Biscuit Pie . . . is a glamorous can-can combo of chicken and vegetables plus a topper of refrigerated biscuits" (Johnston 64). In a 1963 *Ladies' Home Journal* article, food editor Nancy Crawford Wood raved about instant foods and how they simplified cooking. Beef cottage pie could be made more easily when its ingredients included an envelope of hearty beef-soup mix, an envelope of spring-vegetable-soup mix, a box of instant mashed potatoes, and an envelope of sour-cream sauce mix (104); tuna-mushroom popovers were streamlined when composed of a box of popover mix, an envelope of à la king sauce mix, a can of tuna, a can of mushrooms, a package of frozen peas, and milk (111). How much simpler chocolate velvet mousse was when its ingredients included a convenient package of chocolate-fudge flavored frosting mix in addition to two cups of heavy cream, margarine, and coffee liqueur (113). Poppy Cannon's *The Frozen-Foods Cookbook* (1964) included exotic recipes, such as broiled perch with cucumber sauce (made with frozen perch and frozen cream of potato soup) and quenelles Seranne (made with frozen filet of pike), that were prepared more easily with instant foods (43, 32). She observed, "What a blessing to enjoy breast of chicken supreme or chicken cacciatore—whenever you have a mind!" (83). No doubt many women found that cooking tuna-mushroom popovers, chocolate velvet mousse, and other similar complex recipes was more satisfying than throwing together two or three cans. Women could be creative with more complex recipes, but they did not have to spend the same time that they would have spent preparing them from scratch, although making such complex recipes was more time consuming than opening a can of tomato soup and topping it with a can of Vienna sausages.

Another way that convenience foods literature encouraged women to be creative was by using international foods to jazz up their recipes. Lois Stilwill wrote in a 1960s *Ladies' Home Journal* article: "Go international with your speedy meals. Convenience foods, when they travel in imaginative company, know no boundaries. For instance, a favorite French casserole, *Riz au Thon*, can be yours in minutes when made from packaged pre-cooked rice, canned tuna fish, and spaghetti sauce" ("Instant Cook" 132).[14] Cannon's *The Frozen-Foods Cookbook* included numerous "foreign" recipes, although the foreignness was apt to be toned down. Chicken India contained one garlic clove and a quarter teaspoon of powdered ginger added to two pounds of frozen chicken (91). Mexican meat pies were seasoned with only salt and pepper (78). Indonesian drumsticks were flavored with "one clove garlic or a small piece of green ginger root" but not both (95). Shrimp bisque Senegal was composed of frozen condensed cream of shrimp soup flavored with a teaspoon of curry powder (12). Such recipes encouraged women to experiment not only with foreign flavors in creative ways but also in areas other than foods.

Aside from encouraging women to experiment, cooking literature also declared that creative cooking with convenience foods actually improved women's cooking abilities. A 1968 article from *Better Homes and Gardens* by Doris Eby and Helen Kowtaluk proclaimed: "[Women] use their ingenuity to cook up more distinctive meals than ever before. And they have fun doing it. They make the most of modern helpers, but use them in individual ways. Then they take the time they've saved and lavish it on more challenging recipes—on adding their personal signature with a special sauce or a garnish or a sprinkling of herbs" (68). The language is revealing. Eby, Kowtaluk, and other writers needed to defend convenience foods because of an underlying societal fear that such foods would lead to redesigned gender roles, since women would not have the same domestic demands as when they cooked from scratch. Thus, the authors had to make clear that any time saved would be spent on more elaborate cooking for families, not pursuing the cooks own desires. In reality, however, it was up to the women how they used their time, and many chose to work outside of the home or experiment with pursuits outside of the kitchen.

In the 1950s, convenience foods literature stressed that women should be creative. This emphasis was going to have a lasting influence because millions of women were learning that their creative concerns mattered. This marked a shift from earlier decades, when women were typically informed by cooking literature that they should cook something that appealed to their family members and not worry about their own innovative inclinations. Creativity might have started out in the kitchen, at least in convenience cooking literature, but it did not end there; readers were encouraged to try other imaginative pursuits and think about their own wants and aspirations. This emphasis on women's personal gratification would lead, ultimately, far beyond the kitchen.

"A Miracle of the Era"[15]: Convenience Foods and Speed

Along with suggesting that women should think about their own creative inclinations, some convenience food literature conveyed another subversive message: It was desirable for women to spend less time in the kitchen and more time pursuing other activities, even though "Grandma would be startled by some of [their] time-saving ways" (Wiley and Meyer 104). Convenience foods played a part in making this possible by speeding up the entire cooking process, which affected how millions cooked and ate home meals.[16] Mom's position in the kitchen underwent a change: No longer did she have to devote her entire day to cooking. Now, she could prepare a meal of convenience foods that could be ready to serve in minutes, freeing time for other activities. This was a radical shift, as Endrijonas notes: "Convenience or processed foods, which promised to save women tremendous amounts of time in the kitchen, . . . meant more opportunities for women's personal development. Such a development was tempered, however, by powerful messages that women should not neglect their domestic obligations to the family" (157). In other words, Mother had more time for her pursuits, as long as she did not shirk any of her home responsibilities. Her children and husband still were her first priority. Endrijonas points out that processed foods "meant shorter hours in the kitchen. . . . Unfortunately, the food itself only sped up one part of the process of producing a meal" (159). Although convenience foods made the cooking process quicker, they could not speed up all tasks, such as shopping for groceries and cleaning up. Many tasks continued to be laborious, but instant foods did speed up some, making cooking easier.

For women who worked outside the home, convenience foods were particularly helpful. Although a drop occurred in women's employment right after the war when soldiers returned to the jobs that they had left, this trend reversed as more women decided to work; by the end of the 1950s, 40 percent of women who were sixteen and older were employed outside of the home (Coontz 160). More married women were also in the workforce than in previous generations (May 167). Between 1940 and 1950, the number of working mothers increased by 400 percent (McFeely 105). Society had ambivalent feelings about the participation of married women in the paid workforce: "On the one hand, it was unfortunate if a wife had to hold a job; on the other hand, it was considered far worse if the family were unable to purchase what were believed to be necessities for the home" (May 167). Despite society's uneasiness, many married women had to or wanted to work. The stereotype of mothers in the 1950s being cheerfully homebound, similar to the Beaver's mother, did not apply to all women. Some upper- and middle-class women were able to afford that lifestyle, but for others, especially ones from the lower socioeconomic groups or different races or ethnicities than white, it was fiscally impossible not to work for pay. And many married women who had worked outside of their homes during the war continued to labor after it ended. They had experienced paid employment and did not wish to return to the monotony of being full-time stay-at-home mothers. Single women's employment also increased

(Coontz 160). Convenience foods proved a boon for women who worked outside the home: Millions of women wanted to speed up the cooking process, since they preferred freedom to pursue careers and interests outside the home to long hours spent cooking over hot stoves. Convenience foods offered the possibility of cutting down the hours spent on domestic labor.

Women no longer felt compelled to conceal their distaste for long hours spent preparing food. In a 1953 article from *Fortune* magazine, the author described "the loathing with which American women seem to regard prolonged labor in the kitchen." This led to the boom in convenience foods, which he regarded as the "most dramatic change in the food market" ("Fabulous" 271). Although this article did not describe all women, it did single out some who would prefer to do almost anything to spending long hours cooking; hence, many were willing to embrace convenience foods. This was a major change. For generations, women had felt compelled to be good cooks, ones who could prepare from-scratch meals; if they could not, they would not "get their men," the popular rhetoric claimed. They would end up single and alone. Now, convenience food literature made the bold claim that a woman did not need to cook anything more complex than a can of soup or a cake from a box. Using instant foods no longer signaled a woman's ineptitude; instead, it meant that she knew how to use her time efficiently.

Convenience food literature gave little attention to the importance of nurturing men by producing meals from scratch. Instead, it was filled with comments about all the time that women would save to pursue their own desires. *Meals in Minutes* rhapsodized about the wonders of short-cut cooking: "Dinner in 45 minutes? It's possible! The family will think you're a wonder—and you are, with the help of skip-a-step mixes and canned foods. . . . Still delicious? Of course!" (Better Homes 7).[17] A 1968 *Redbook* magazine article was equally enthusiastic about the time a woman could save: "Not so long ago, a typical housewife averaged about five and a half hours in the kitchen each day cooking three meals for a family of four. Today she can feed the family well with only eleven hours a week spent in the kitchen. This cutback in time is due largely to the advent of convenience foods" ("Convenience" 74). The article suggested a number of time-saving recipes that utilized convenience foods. For instance, strawberry meringue torte was composed of a package of white frosting mix, ladyfingers, three cups of instant whipped topping, frozen strawberries, and sherry—a dessert that could be prepared in a short time (75). Paella was much quicker for the busy cook to make when it included brown-and-serve sausage links, canned clams, canned chicken, and precooked instant rice (82). A *Ladies' Home Journal* article stated, "Every mix is a bagful of tricks. Each 'instant,' canned and frozen food, too. Open a box, and presto!— puddings, pies, potatoes, pastas . . . even whole meals in minutes" (Wood 90). The magic was that cooking meals no longer required hours but just minutes using instant foods. Writers raved about how such foods saved housewives' time. In the 1950s, June Owen wrote in the *New York Times*, "The housewife who taps keys by day could get home at 6 o'clock, grab individually packed frozen dinners from her refrigerator, 'cook' them in the oven, and have them on the table in jig time" (26). Similarly, another 1950s *New York Times* article discussed the time that canned foods saved:

> American housewives have helped free themselves from 34,000,000,000 work-hours annually in meal preparation time, the home economics department of the American Can Company reported yesterday. . . . A far cry from the barbaric eras when the man of the house took it for granted that he was entitled to a heavy dinner of fresh foods in consideration for his role in putting bacon and eggs on the table seven days a week. ("No Relief" 43)

This writer made clear that a battle was being fought in many kitchens over which gender roles were appropriate for women and men. Did a woman owe it to her husband and family members to spend countless hours preparing meals entirely from scratch because that was what was expected of her grandmother and great-grandmother? The answer was a resounding "no." The shock of this "no" was going to be felt throughout the United States and influence all races, ethnicities, and socioeconomic groups. Instead of staying in the kitchen from dawn until dusk as generations before her had done, a women owed it to herself to streamline cooking as much as possible, including using canned goods, frozen meals, and other instant foods. This radical notion would later blossom as part of second-wave feminism. For generations, women had devoted themselves to the kitchen and taking care of others, but this was not enough to satisfy them. Women needed more time for their own pursuits. Convenience food literature played a part in helping females to recognize that they should demand more.

Even home economists acknowledged the many hours convenience foods could save any busy woman. For instance, Dr. Gertrude S. Weiss, a staff member of the Bureau of Human Nutrition and Home Economics in Washington, D.C., described a study she performed that compared convenience foods to their made-from-scratch equivalents. She discovered, "the saving in time from using prepared foods is large compared with the added cost. The meals using ready-to-serve foods cost over a third more but took only about a quarter as much of the homemaker's time as did meals for which more preparation was done in the home kitchen" (98). She observed, "It is well known that pre-preparation adds to the cost of food" and "releases the homemaker's time for other activities" (98). Not all food writers assumed that convenience foods were necessarily more costly, however. One cookbook proclaimed, "A meal can be long on flavor and short on cost, if you take best advantage of convenience foods" (Campbell 144). Similarly, a cooking article from *Better Homes and Gardens* declared, "When you open a package of mix, you save yourself hours in the kitchen. When you pair them with leftovers, you save yourself money" ("They're All" 54). Convenience foods were not only time-savers, they were also money-savers. In this fashion, cooking literature encouraged women to use convenience foods because they could save time and money. What man could complain?

Some did. Not all men were happy about how convenience foods sped up women's cooking time. After attending the newspaper food editors' conference in New York City, one male lamented in the *New York Times* in 1952, "Even mother is using pre-mixed pie crust preparations, powdered soups and most of the other shortcuts from grocery store to dinner table . . ." ("Speed" 30). He called upon men to rebel: "if possessed of sufficient strength after years of consuming what are called 'easy innovations in home cookery.' . . . The way to a man's heart is still through his stomach, and there are no wholly acceptable short cuts" ("Speed" 30). This writer represented the thinking of a number of men who were concerned that convenience foods were making home cooking less palatable. They worried about what it meant and what it would lead to when women spent less time tending to family needs and more on their own. Men were uneasy that women did not seem content spending the same long hours on housework and cooking that they had in the past. At the root of this uneasiness was the change in women's roles in the 1950s, an aftereffect of how World War II permanently altered their place in society. Many had worked outside of the home and found that paid jobs were rewarding and fulfilling; they also discovered that they did not have to depend on a husband's paycheck and could even thrive on their own. After millions of women learned to survive without male assistance throughout the war years, it must have felt strange for them to relinquish that freedom, autonomy, and control, especially to men who assumed that women would graciously accept their role as docile helpmates. Although some women were satisfied with such responsibilities, others were not. Restless stirrings indicated that all was not well with women. They needed to be more than home decorators and chauffeurs for their children. Women's roles had changed dramatically with the war, and those changes would burst into flame during the fire known as second-wave feminism.

Cake from a Box: Mom's Home-Cooking?

One of the most radical messages of convenience food cooking literature was that a woman could be a good cook—or a great one—even if she did not make anything from scratch but relied entirely on convenience foods. In actuality, her cooking might be better if she depended on instant foods because she could be more creative and experiment with interesting new dishes. This notion challenged centuries of social assumptions that "Mom's cooking" was best, that it must always be from scratch or her children and, more importantly, husband would be upset. This ideology about home cooking has kept millions of women in the kitchen. It was a tremendous shift to suggest that Mother's culinary work could now entail assembling a meal based solely on convenience foods, and, more radically, that such a meal should not be condemned but praised by everyone, even her husband. And, with her saved time, Mother would be encouraged to pursue other interests and hobbies. The American kitchen was never going to be the same.

Convenience food literature also strongly supported being a modern cook. Cooking literature made it clear that any woman who cooked with instant foods was showing herself to be modern when modernity was viewed as jet age as a Cadillac's fins or a Frank Lloyd Wright home's smooth lines. This connection between modernity and convenience foods helped to encourage their acceptance at a time when modernity was associated with being up-to-date. Cookbook literature assured women that cooking should change, that Grandmother's recipes were not always the best, even if they were from scratch. This was a major shift from earlier times when Grandmother's or Mother's cooking was supposed to be superior to any packaged or convenience foods. Now that it was no longer assumed that cooking from scratch was best, women's relationship to food and cooking would be altered permanently. By aligning modernity with cooking, cookbooks and cooking articles also suggested that women should abandon other traditional roles for widespread innovation.

Another change that convenience food literature supported was that women should speed up the whole cooking process by using convenience products. No longer did cooks need to spend countless hours laboring over hot stoves to display their love for their families. They could find the quickest, easiest methods to prepare instant meals, spending as little time in the kitchen as required to heat up some frozen dinners and a frozen pie in the stove. This was revolutionary, suggesting that women might not be content with their work as cooks and wish rather to pursue other activities, a notion that rebelled against centuries of belief that a woman should "naturally" wish to spend as much time as possible cooking and doing other chores. Implicit in the idea that cooking should be sped up was the notion that *all* housework also should be sped up because women found it dull and tedious. Thus, when convenience food literature discussed speeding up cooking, it implied that women deserved more time for their own pursuits.

Convenience food literature also suggested the radical notion that women could decide if they wanted to cook from scratch or rely on convenience foods. For the first time in U.S. history, this was a possibility. Convenience foods had existed in previous decades and it had been common for women to use an occasional can of soup or box of Jell-O; what changed in the 1950s was that the selection of convenience foods expanded greatly and they became less costly, making them choices more accessible to a greater number of families from different classes. In this period, it became easier for women to rely entirely on convenience foods, a dramatic shift in women's relationship to cooking, one that has reverberated through American culture. Today, it has become acceptable for women to depend entirely on such foods, and it is considered unusual if they cook solely from scratch. Although this shift has many disturbing aspects, it has given women (and men) millions of hours to pursue other endeavors, including careers. The frozen fish stick, the TV dinner, macaroni and cheese in a box, and other convenience foods are the women's movement's unlikely helpers.

Chapter 2

"Unnatural, Unclean, and Filthy"[1]: Chinese-American Cooking Literature Confronting Racism in the 1950s

"The Chinese do the most wonderful . . . things with food. Completely different from American cookery but so delicious and refreshing that even dyed-in-the-wool, steak-and-apple-pie Americans fall straight in love," wrote Helen McCully in a *McCall's* article, "Let's Cook Chinese Tonight" (1954). Even the staid *Farm Journal* included an article in 1957 for a company supper based on chow mein. The author, Louise Stiers, wrote, "We've an easy, exciting recipe for a sing-a-song-of-spring supper party we know you'll like. The main event: a big bowl of steaming chow mein" (115). *McCall's* and the *Farm Journal* were a part of a larger interest in Chinese food that appeared in 1950s cookbooks and articles.[2] Although they never threatened the dominance of more Europeanized recipes, Chinese recipes did appear, if not frequently, at least regularly.[3] Some were Americanized versions that had little resemblance to authentic Chinese foods, but others were surprisingly authentic, perhaps because much of the literature—but not all, as represented by the articles of McCully and Stiers—was written by Chinese or Chinese-American women, a bold move in an era of McCarthyism and the Red scare.[4] During a time known for extreme xenophobia, Chinese cooking literature served as a bridge between cultures.[5] Further, cooking literature did more than pass on recipes; it conveyed lessons about Chinese culture and history. The literature also taught that Chinese and other Asian people, despite their varied food and cultural traditions, were not very different from Caucasians. This lesson was especially important after World War II, when many white Americans still held strongly racist views about all Asian people.

Mainstream cooking literature of the 1950s was filled with white faces, which was a small element of a much larger culture of whiteness that appeared everywhere in the media. Whether television, films, magazines, or advertisements, U.S. popular culture was predominantly white. Movies featured white stars from Doris Day to James Dean.[6] Television shows, including everything from *Lassie* to *Leave It to Beaver*, portrayed all-white universes.[7] If blacks, Chinese-Americans, Hispanics, or other races made an appearance, they were commonly depicted as servants, villains, and buffoons.[8] These white faces worked to establish whiteness as the norm. Although mass culture did not reflect America's true demographics, it created an illusion that the "normal" American was white, an ideology that had disturbing racist implications and one that pervaded the decade. Cooking literature was a part of this larger trend. Flipping through any mainstream cookbook or article, one would see countless pictures of white women, beaming blissfully as they whipped together chiffon layer cakes or mixed together tuna-fish casseroles. White cooks, with Betty Crocker being the most famous, were celebrated. Accordingly, cooking literature rarely depicted nonwhite faces, so works that did focus on Chinese food and cooks challenged this emphasis on whiteness.[9] The predominantly female authors asserted the importance of hearing non-European or white American voices. The writers also helped share historical and cultural facts about China, diminishing Asian exoticism. In addition, cooking literature showed that Chinese food, although unusual, was more palatable than many assumed—an idea that rebelled against the traditional white assumption that Chinese food was scarcely edible.

In the 1950s, or any other era for that matter, Chinese cookbooks and other ethnic cooking literature allowed alternate voices and cultures to be heard in the United States. Cookbooks are, as Doris Witt observes, relatively democratic works (214). A variety of races, ethnicities, and socio-economic groups can afford to publish them, which makes them more open to different voices than other genres. As well, almost everyone, including people from different classes, ethnicities, and races, purchases and uses cookbooks. They are also democratic because numerous ways exist to publish them, from an inexpensive community cookbook printed by a church or school to a slick, expensive hardback produced by a major publishing house. Due to its democratic nature, the cookbook serves as an excellent outlet for diverse voices, including ones that question the dominant white American ethos.

In the 1950s, Chinese and Chinese Americans used the democratic venue of cooking literature to speak against anti-Asian racism and share Chinese foods with whites. It was important that whites ate Chinese food, but it was even more crucial that Chinese people be accepted as Americans. The acceptance of a racial or ethnic group often goes hand in hand with the acceptance of their native foods. For example, when Italians and other southern Europeans moved to America in the early decades of the twentieth century, many white Americans who had immigrated earlier perceived the newcomers as barbaric, so their Italian cultural and social habits had to change through Americanization courses, which stressed the significance of discarding native Italian foods in favor of presumably more nutritious meat and potatoes. One observer before World War I described an Italian family eating a dinner of spaghetti as "not assimilated" (qtd. in Gabaccia 123). Such an attitude was not unusual, as many reformers thought that pasta and other Italian foods were regrettable holdovers from the old country. This attitude changed rapidly early in the twentieth century as Italians and their foods became accepted as part of America's mass diet. By the 1930s, spaghetti was so sufficiently mainstreamed that Betty Crocker published a recipe for it (Levenstein 30), and canned spaghetti appeared commonly on the shelves of grocery stores (Gabaccia 122). A major shift occurred in how white Americans perceived Italian foods, which went along with a general acceptance of Italians.[10] For mainstream Americans, accepting a culture is closely connected with eating its foods, so much was at stake when Chinese-American women wrote cookbooks.[11] These books served as conduits to bring two cultures together, leading to a greater tolerance and acceptance of Chinese people and their foods.

"A Booby Nation"[12]: History of Anti-Chinese Attitudes

To understand the significance of Chinese food literature as a bridge between cultures, one must recognize the tremendous social pressures faced by Chinese Americans in the 1950s, when being of Chinese descent could mean possible prison time or deportation. It was an era of intense ethnocentrism. Almost anyone could be labeled a "Red," including many who had no affiliation with the Communist Party; government authorities used the fear of communism to harass a broad spectrum of people. The threat was intensified for the Chinese, who struggled to blend into the white mainstream, and they faced worse persecution than other racial or minority groups. In addition, the Chinese were persecuted because of their presumed connections to China and communism.

Before the 1950s, Chinese Americans had encountered white American xenophobia countless times. When Chinese men arrived in the Gold Rush years, they were excluded from many of the best jobs in mining camps and had to work as servants or in restaurants and laundries, at jobs that the white miners thought were beneath them. Outside of the camps, too, the Chinese found their employment opportunities severely limited. Thousands worked to construct the transcontinental railroad in the 1860s, a dangerous job that many whites rejected, leaving predominantly Chinese workers to labor on the section from the Pacific side, the most difficult part of the railroad to construct because it traveled through the Rockies (Zia 27). Since their only tools were shovels, drills, and explosives, the work proceeded at an arduous pace of seven inches on a typical day.[13] By the 1870s, Chinese immigrants worked making shoes, cigars, and shirts, all lowly paid jobs (Choy, Dong, and Hom 19). They discovered that racism was not limited to the gold rush camps but that it thrived across the whole of the United States. In the 1800s and early 1900s, white America discriminated against the Chinese in shocking ways; xenophobia was widespread at all social levels, including the highest. Even upper-class white intellectuals like Ralph Waldo Emerson and Horace Greeley viewed the Chinese as less than human. In the 1820s, Emerson called China a "booby nation" and its culture "a besotted perversity" (qtd. in Gyory 17). Decades later, Greeley described the Chinese as "uncivilized, unclean, and filthy" (qtd. in Gyory 17).[14] Similarly, speaking in 1879, the Rev. Charles Hodge, president of Princeton University, observed that the Chinese influx was "an evil so great [that] something surely ought to be done" (qtd. in Gyory 102). In the same year, Cornell University president Andrew White commented, "I confess to a very deep-seated dread of this influx of Asiatics" (qtd. in Gyory 102). One of the first politicians to support limits on Chinese immigrants, James G. Blaine, wrote, "You cannot work a man who must have beef and bread, and would prefer beer, alongside of a man who can live on rice" (qtd. in Gyory 3).[15] Blaine was one of the many whites who commented negatively on the Chinese diet and the vital role of rice. A popular stereotype existed that the Chinese could survive on a diet of "rice and rats" (E. Lee 26).[16] Such attitudes were common, and the popular press depicted the Chinese as "degraded, dangerous menaces" that had to be controlled before they took white jobs and, ultimately, white women (E. Lee 6).

This rampant racism led to the passing of strict laws that limited the number of Chinese who could immigrate to the United States. They held the dubious distinction of being the first group singled out to be excluded from immigration to America due solely to their race, although they were not the last. Japanese and Koreans were barred a few years later, and restrictions against all Asians were tightened in the twentieth century. In 1882, the Chinese Exclusion Act was passed, which barred laborers for ten years. In 1892, the Geary Act extended it for ten more years. In 1904, the act was extended indefinitely.[17] These restrictions caused the Chinese population in America to fall from 107,488 to 71,531 over the twenty years from 1890 to 1910 (Chen 12). This decline was the result of a white society that was deeply suspicious of the Chinese and worried that they could undercut the wages that working-class white males earned, since the Chinese would work for less than any "decent" white man. The stringent restrictions of these acts caused the number of Chinese immigrants to decrease sharply, but they did not stop entirely, as some found creative ways to join the merchant or professional classes, which never suffered the same restrictions (Yung 23). Whites did not think that middle- or upper-class Chinese posed the same threat to white dominance as the supposed "hordes of coolies" ready to take workingmen's jobs—an anti-Chinese bias that was classist as well as racist.

It took decades for anti-Chinese attitudes to shift. During World War II, feelings toward the Chinese did change, predominantly because China was an American wartime ally, so Chinese Americans were treated as "valiant allies and loyal sons and daughters of Uncle Sam" and not treated to the harassment and imprisonment that many Japanese faced (Yung 250). Americans knew that the Chinese had confronted the brutal Japanese invaders firsthand.[18] The Chinese had been fighting Japan's imperialist aspirations since 1931, the year of the invasion of northeastern China. In 1932, the Japanese invaded Shanghai, killing and bombing soldiers and civilians (Yung 225). In 1937, Japan invaded China, leaving a "bloody trail of rape, pillage, and plunder" (Yung 227). White Americans began to perceive

Chinese and Chinese Americans more positively during China's war nightmare, a sharp change from attitudes earlier in the century. Other factors influenced this shift. By showing the horrors of the Sino-Japanese conflict, Pearl Buck's best-selling book, *The Good Earth* (1931), and its hit 1937 MGM cinematic translation altered the predominant image of the Chinese. Madame Chiang Kai-Shek also helped to influence American beliefs, touring the United States and speaking about the war in cities across the United States, including New York, Boston, and Los Angeles. She was a Wellesley College graduate, and her "beauty, charisma, and elegance" influenced many Americans to rethink their stereotypes about China (Iris Chang 226). Her impact was immense; she even spoke in front of Congress, and her forceful words helped it to repeal the Exclusion Acts, after sixty-one years of existence (Yung 251). This positive image of the Chinese, however, was doomed to be short-lived.

In the 1950s, the image changed again, largely due to the Korean War, the institution of the People's Republic of China, and the onset of the Red scare. Together, these three events had a sharply negative impact on white Americans' views of China and the Chinese. When the Korean War broke out in 1950, the Chinese became America's enemies. The mass media showed white Americans how brutally the other side, North Korea and China, treated prisoners of war, fanning hatred of the Chinese. In his book *The Chinese Americans* (2003), Benson Tong notes that with the outbreak of the war, Chinese were depicted as inhuman, deceitful barbarians, a sharp shift from the positive press that they received during World War II (121). One *New York Times* article from 1953 described the "relentless . . . mental torture" to which Chinese Communists subjected captured American servicemen ("Tortured" 3). Another article from the *New York Times* in the same year described soldiers being subjected to Communist brainwashing, including "prolonged, unending questioning, brilliant lights pored on the subject's face, and repeated suggestion" ("Some" 3). Such stories helped to shift the xenophobia that the United States had directed at the Japanese to the Chinese and Chinese Americans, and the anti-Chinese feelings that had been submerged during World War II reemerged.

Along with the Korean War, the Cold War and Red scare also reignited anti-Chinese feelings. Suddenly, it seemed (at least to J. Edgar Hoover) that a subversive lurked everywhere. The head of the FBI, Hoover assumed that the Chinese-American community was filled with spies or potential spies for the Communists (Iris Chang 260). The Chinese were suspect because of their possible ties to the PRC, which led to a greater suspicion of not just Chinese with Communist links but all Chinese in the United States. Historian Xiojian Zhao observes, "The Cold War had a profound effect on the lives of Chinese Americans and their families. . . . In the name of investigating Communist subversive activities, the government went after those who had successfully gained permanent residence and citizenship in the United States. No leftist groups survived, and thousands of Chinese Americans lived in fear" (152). All Chinese worried that they would be identified as Communists. To escape the label, Chinese tried different methods to demonstrate their patriotism, including joining groups, such as the Anti-Communist Committee for Free China and the All-American Overseas Chinese Anti-Communist League (Monique Avakian 148). Others marched in Loyalty Day parades, which were started to compete with the Communists' May Day celebration. At one such New York City parade in 1956, the large Chinese-American contingent carried signs reading "Up with Freedom, Down with Communism," "Beware of the Soviet Smile," and "Loyalty Insures Freedom Forever" ("Two" 56). Despite such attempts to show their loyalty and patriotism, thousands of Chinese and Chinese Americans were questioned about their Communist affiliation, whether real or imaginary; in 1955, the Communist Control Act made the Communist Party illegal, so almost any left-leaning citizen could be questioned as a presumed Communist or subversive.

    Chinese worries about deportation were exacerbated because a number had entered the country illegally in earlier decades. Due to the stringent requirements for Chinese to enter the United States, some had pursued fraudulent schemes in order to immigrate or let other Chinese immigrate. One of the most common was the "paper son" scheme; when Chinese Americans visited China and returned to the United States, they claimed children who were not really their own, allowing illegal immigrants to slip in. The paper son scheme raised U.S. government suspicions that Chinese Communists had also slipped in. The fears were increased when Everett F. Drumwright, Hong Kong's U.S. consul, wrote a report that "almost all Chinese in America had entered the United States illegally, all the way back to those who mined for gold" (qtd. in Iris Chang 250–251). Despite the ludicrous nature of his claims, a backlash occurred, with the Immigration and Naturalization Service (INS) seeking out illegal Chinese immigrants; often the INS used illegal tactics, such as unlawful home searches and phone taps, to capture perceived Communist spies. In addition, to gain residency, Chinese Americans were urged to confess that they were illegal or turn in others whom they thought to be illegal. From 1957 to 1965, 11,336 Chinese Americans confessed to being illegal (Tong 126). Even if Chinese Americans were not illegal, many lived in fear of being deported because the Cold War had brought to the surface deep "suspicions of so-called un-American or alien behaviors and attitudes" (Tong 111). In such an environment, anyone could be guilty.

Even eating Chinese food could be suspect. In his book, *China to Chinatown: Chinese Food in the West* (2002), J. A. G. Roberts observes that some white Americans were ambivalent about Chinese restaurants because of the Korean War and the Communist threat (164). Eating Chinese food became a potential signifier of one's Communist leaning. Of course, not every person who ate a Chinese-American meal of chow mein was labeled a "Red." Since the 1800s, Chinese-American food had gradually become a part of American culture, and it was not going to be discarded suddenly. Writing about Chinese food, however, especially for Chinese or Chinese-American women, gained political significance. They had to reassure their readers that the Chinese were not the subversive elements depicted by the mass media. Food writers had to pass on Chinese recipes and negotiate the Cold War—a difficult balancing act for anyone. In an era of intolerance, cooking literature questioned racist attitudes and assumptions. It provided Chinese and Chinese-American women a forum to speak out against the dominance of a culture based on whiteness as the norm.

"Fascinating, Unusual, and Romantic"[19]: History of Chinese Food

Prior to the 1950s, Chinese food had already a long history in the United States. It was introduced by mid-nineteenth-century Chinese immigrants, who came to work in the California gold fields and on the Union Pacific Railroad. Homesick for familiar foods or simply out of a desire to make money, Chinese businessmen established restaurants that offered Chinese foods at modest prices. These places, many located in the flourishing Chinatowns found in large cities, including San Francisco, Chicago, Boston, and New York, proved popular with Chinese immigrants, predominantly men who had no women to cook for them.[20] Most Anglos did not dare venture into these restaurants with their different customs and foods, but a few diners did. To cater to white American tastes, restaurant owners developed Chinese-American dishes, such as chop suey and egg foo yong.[21] Although they might have not been authentic Chinese dishes, these new dishes proved popular with whites who wished for something different but not too unusual.

In the late nineteenth and early twentieth centuries, Chinese restaurants grew increasingly popular with some whites. Food historian Donna R. Gabaccia writes, "No enclave businessmen enjoyed greater success attracting culinary tourists in search of inexpensive exoticism than Chinese restaurateurs in the Chinatowns of New York and San Francisco. Even more than Italians, however, they had to modify their offerings to accommodate American tastes" (102). Chinese food took longer to catch on with "more sedate" diners. Gabaccia describes it as still being too unusual for many Anglos, who viewed it as unsanitary, in accord with what they thought of the Chinese (103). The popular press often depicted Chinese food negatively. Food historian J. A. G. Roberts writes, "In 1924 Chinese immigration to the United States was further restricted. . . . Popular magazines reiterated the widely held view that one reason why the Chinese could not be assimilated was because of their eating habits" (147). If Chinese were not willing to accept American foods, they would not be willing to accept American culture. Here, the Chinese and their culinary preferences were both rejected as too unusual for U.S. white society. As time passed, however, more Anglo-Americans tried Chinese food and found it palatable and appealing. Going out for a Chinese meal became an established part of big-city life—especially in cities with Chinatowns—for many whites by the 1920s and 1930s (Lee 28–29). "A whole range of eateries now beckoned from the city's Chinese district: simple rice shops, noodle shops, chop suey and chow mein shops, along with night clubs and finer restaurants, all competing for the tourist trade" (Gabaccia 104). It took longer for Chinese restaurants to gain the same popularity in smaller towns, which lacked the culinary sophistication of bigger cities. It also took longer for whites other than some urbane sophisticates to cook Chinese food at home.

After World War II, Chinese food became even more broadly available and accepted in the United States. Cookbook author Calvin Lee wrote in the 1950s: "Today, although Chinese food is still considered to be fascinating, unusual, and romantic, it has become a habit and a regular diet for many

Americans. They no longer eat just chop suey and chow mein but have expanded their diets to Niw goo yok, . . . Wor shew opp, . . . Char shu ding, . . . and many others. . . . We have finally reached the day when Chinese food is a part of American everyday life" (29). Despite his words, Chinese food was not a part of every American's life, but it did gain in popularity, a change that was the result of different factors. The increasing prevalence of Chinese restaurants in cities and towns across the United States made it possible for whites to become familiar with a wider range of Chinese foods and incited the desire to experiment with cooking them at home. Chinese food was also popularized by dozens of Chinese cookbooks and cooking articles published in the 1950s. As mentioned earlier, this cooking literature did more than present Chinese recipes; it spread Chinese culture, lessening the gap between the East and West. In many ways, these books and articles served as ambassadors of China and its people. If one wishes to understand the 1950s interest in Chinese food and cooking and how Chinese food gained popularity despite the Red scare and racism, Chinese cooking literature is an invaluable resource.

Bridging the East and West: Chinese Culture and History

Along with conveying recipes, 1950s Chinese cookbooks emphasized the need to build connections between the East and West. For instance, Mary Li Sia, who was in charge of a Chinese cooking school in Hawaii in the 1950s, wrote in the preface to *Mary Sia's Chinese Cookbook* (1956), "Being Chinese, I have sought the ultimate in cooking in the Chinese way. Enthusiast that I am, I have spent a lifetime in opening a new culinary world to thousands of people, both in the East and in the West" (ix).[22] She expressed a common attitude found in Chinese cooking literature. It was not only about conveying recipes; it was also about conveying historical and cultural lessons, and, in doing so, reducing the gap between the East and West.

One of the reasons that it was vital to bridge this gap between cultures was that the division shaped and influenced how the Western world viewed the Eastern world. The West represented all that was advanced and modern. The West was affiliated to technology and science; the East was allied with mysticism and superstition. The West represented progress; the East represented cultural stasis. The world was divided into two halves, with the West depicted as all that was good, up-to-date, and desirable, and the East as all that was undesirable, antiquated, even negative or evil. Accordingly, many Westerners did not perceive the East and its inhabitants as fully human. This mindset was used in both World War II and the Korean War to justify the killing of Japanese, Chinese, and Koreans. This division between East and West has been used for centuries to perpetuate racist ideas.

Trying to bridge the gap between the East and West, Chinese women asserted their humanity and that of other Asian people. Chinese women used cookbooks as a venue where they could describe China's history and culture, showing that China was not inferior to the United States. Thus, Chinese and Chinese-American women filled their works with observations about China's rich culture and history. This was essential at a time when the white mainstream discriminated against Chinese and Chinese Americans, and they did not always have access to other ways to describe their experiences in different forms of writing, such as more traditional history books. In her book, *Unbound Feet: A Social History of Chinese Women in San Francisco* (1995), Judy Yung observes that the 1950s public school curriculum did not include Chinese-American history or that of any other minority in America (187). Chinese women's history was doubly negated as minority and female, so these Chinese women writers had to find different mediums to discuss their experiences and cultural background.

One medium to discuss Chinese culture was the cookbook, and in the 1950s, Chinese and Chinese-American cookbook authors frequently focused on the importance of their readers learning about Chinese culture and history as well as its cuisine. Chinese women adopted a similar strategy earlier in the twentieth century. For example, food historian Janet Theophano describes how a Chinese woman from the 1940s, Buwei Yang Chao, used her cookbook, *How to Cook and Eat in Chinese* (1945), to convey messages about Chinese culture along with culinary lessons. Theophano writes, "Chao's book is more than a memoir. It is also an anatomy of culinary, cultural, and linguistic patterns" (150). In a similar fashion, 1950s cookbooks included cultural messages. In this decade, however, when mainstream America held a more negative view of Chinese people, it became even more vital for cookbook authors to convey cultural and historical facts, which many did. Doreen Yen Hung Feng wrote about her book *The Joy of Chinese Cookery* (1954) that it would "bring . . . a little bit of China into your kitchen, home, and life" (12). The book contained cultural and historical facts about China, including detailed descriptions of a number of Chinese festivals: the Festival of the Flowers, the Dragon Boat Festival, the Kite Flying Festival, the Festival of the Moon, and the Festival of the Winter Solstice (Feng 8). In *Mary Sia's Chinese Cookbook* (1956), Sia included a section on the history of tea (5), customs about rice (119), and the history of the Chinese feast (3). These sections were sprinkled with facts about food and also explored aspects of Chinese culture. Isabelle C. Chang's *What's Cooking at Chang's* (1954) began, "While the maple spareribs broil and the grapefruit bakes, let the charming legends of Old China and the fascinating bits of history set the mood. For this is more than 'just another cookbook'—it is an informative and enthralling guide to another way of life" (n.p.). The book depicted Chinese history and culture as well as recipes. Many recipes were accompanied by brief descriptions of Chinese holidays, among them the Chinese New Year, Harvest Moon Festival, and Lantern Festival. The book also included lessons about the Chinese calendar, the Kitchen God, and Chinese pottery (13, 15, 19).[23] Feng, Sia, and Chang used one of the few genres available to them to teach others about Chinese culture and society; people reading these books received cultural as well as cooking lessons. In addition, these books allowed the Chinese and Chinese Americans to undercut racist images in the white mainstream press, which was especially crucial when many white Americans received their knowledge of Asian Americans solely through such accounts.

When Chinese authors described China's history, they questioned white American stereotypes that depicted the Chinese as barbarians. For example, the writers discussed the longevity of China's cultural history, including its culinary aspects. Shen Mei Lon and Ruth Chier Rosen wrote in their cookbook, *Ancestral Recipes of Shen Mei Lon* (1954), "Chinese cookery is an art that takes a page out of ancient history. Chinese civilization was highly developed at a very early period. One aspect of this great culture was and is the knowledge of skillful food preparation" (3). During an era when countless white Americans thought of Chinese culture as nonexistent, this book and others suggested that China had a long history with a highly cultured society that had existed for centuries. In fact, the book subtly pointed out that China's cultural history dates back earlier than America's, and that China had a highly developed cuisine even before the United States was founded. This book demonstrated that China and its people possessed a rich history, but that the white mainstream media, which focused solely on the country as a threat, ignored China's history before the Communist revolution. Be it a Chinese or any other ethnic cookbook, such literature discusses history and culture in order to counter white stereotypes that depict people from different races and ethnicities as lacking a culture or having one that is inferior to white mainstream America's, so people judged to be "different" or "barbaric" have to be assimilated, their ways changed. These assumptions function as a kind of cultural genocide.

When ethnic cookbooks describe history, limitations exist as to what can be discussed. For example, Chinese and Chinese-American women did not write about China's communism or the Korean War but, instead, focused on benign, "safe" historical and cultural facts. However, one should recognize the historical limitations that these women confronted. In the 1950s, Chinese and Chinese-American women were not able to publish anything too volatile, since writing about communism could have resulted in deportation. As women living in a patriarchal society, they were also not allowed to speak out too openly or boldly, so they had to sneak historical and cultural details into their writing, which was still a radical move. Such women needed to articulate their ideas within a framework of larger societal impositions. (In a similar way, Thai-American and Vietnamese-American women today face different constraints than do white women when writing cooking literature.) To understand how ethnic cooking literature gives women from different cultures a voice, one should consider the varied cultural and historical constraints that they must address.

Escape From a "Culinary Straitjacket"?[24] Tame Food

Along with spreading lessons about Chinese history and culture, Chinese cooking literature sought to make Chinese foods more acceptable to mainstream American society. When discussing Chinese food in the United States, it is easy to disparage what I refer to as "tame"—commonly known as Chinese American—recipes specifically made to appeal to Anglo-American tastes and that might not even have originated in China. In his book *The World on a Plate: A Tour Through the History of America's Ethnic Cuisines* (2003), Joel Denker describes Chinese-American food as "quickly assembled, easily assimilated dishes," including egg foo yong, sweet and sour pork, shrimp fried rice, and other inexpensive recipes (98). Food scholars and a range of others interested in food culture belittle such dishes as lacking culinary authenticity. Scholars shy away from studying ethnic foods that have been Americanized for acceptance by a mass audience, but analyzing such tame foods in their myriad forms reveals a great deal about how different ethnic foods gain acceptance.

When discussing Chinese food, or any ethnic food, however, one must be careful when identifying what is "authentic." What does it mean that Chinese people created many of the tame Chinese dishes, although sometimes to appeal to Anglo-American preferences? We should remember that Chinese cooks and others from different races and ethnicities "employ all manner of techniques to influence the ways in which their cuisine is taken up by the Euroamerican consumerist machinery" (Heldke 21). Thus, resistance can be found everywhere, including the bowl of chow mein or chop suey. This was certainly true in the 1950s, when Chinese food authors wrote about tame foods to gain a larger acceptance for *all* Chinese food and, ultimately, Chinese people. Writing about relatively tame recipes, authors attracted white readers who might have been frightened away by more authentic dishes. In addition, tame recipes reassured whites that Chinese foods were not that unusual, countering the long-standing stereotype that they were too different to be eaten, so the Chinese could not be assimilated into American society. Such tame recipes were subversive, suggesting that Chinese foods (and Chinese people) should be accepted as contributions to U.S. culture.

Among the best-known tame American-Chinese foods are chop suey and chow mein. Countless 1950s Chinese-American restaurants from coast to coast served them, and almost every Chinese or Chinese-American cookbook included recipes for these dishes.[25] Instead of downplaying chow mein and chop suey, food historian J. A. G. Roberts suggests, "For Americans to eat and like home-made chow mein . . . [was] a distinct step toward breaking out of a culinary straitjacket" (147). This is an interesting notion because it is easy to interpret chow mein and chop suey as nothing more than the worst examples of the excesses of Chinese-American cooking, possessing little or no connection to authentic Chinese recipes. Issues of authenticity are not limited to Chinese food. Similarly, Indian cookbook author Madhur Jaffrey views curry as disrespectful in the same way that the term "chop suey" degrades the cuisines of China. By comparing curry to chop suey, Jaffrey underscores the un-Indianness of curry. "Chop suey is a dish invented by American Chinese restaurants" (Heldke 38). Jaffrey, however, shows a class bias. Not everyone is able to afford the time or money necessary to make authentic foods. And what does it mean to say that Indians or Chinese—often lower-class ones—frequently sell and market curry, chop suey, and similar dishes? As Roberts suggests, such recipes might have had a more subversive role, helping to spread these foods to whites. Chow mein and chop suey were early attempts by white Americans to experiment with different ethnic foods—faltering steps that would lead the way to others, ultimately moving toward a greater tolerance of more authentic recipes by the white mainstream.

Although it is important to recognize the impact that chow mein, chop suey, and other tame foods had on broadening the food preferences of whites, one should also remember that such foods were not Chinese. In *Ancestral Recipes of Shen Mei Lon,* Lon and Rosen warned that chop suey and chow mein were not "authentic Chinese dishes" but included them because they were "Chinese-American dishes and that is why they are here, because you want them" (6).[26] There is tension here; the authors include such recipes to appeal to popular white taste preferences, but they did not necessarily value these recipes. Tension exists in any ethnic cuisine when recipes are given to outsiders; different people will hold different ideas about what should be passed on and how authentic those recipes should be. It is important to acknowledge that tension and to recognize that not all Chinese authors held the same beliefs about how "authentic" their recipes should be.

But not every 1950s Chinese and Chinese-American cookbook authors resisted the inclusion of Americanized versions of Chinese recipes. Many writers did include them, most likely to attract a broader audience of readers, including non-Chinese.[27] Cooking literature reassured nervous Westerners that Chinese tastes were not as unusual as they originally assumed. Feng commented in *The Joy of Chinese Cookery* that "There is no mystery involved in Chinese cooking" (12). As mentioned earlier, the American stereotype was widespread that Chinese cooking (and Chinese people) was too unusual for assimilation, so Chinese authors worked to show that this was not true.[28] Some Chinese cookbooks sought to present Chinese cooking as simple and straightforward, something any Anglo-American housewife could tackle if she overcame her fear of the unknown and embraced some new ingredients. For example, Myrtle Lum Young's cookbook *Fun with*

Chinese Recipes (1958) simplified Chinese recipes for American tastes. "There is nothing fantastic here—no startling ingredients," the book's dust jacket observed. "From rice to Chinese ravioli, from *yong doong goo* (stuffed mushrooms) to *long ha jop wui* (lobster chop suey), and on to 'Mother's Chinese pretzels,' everything is inviting to the Western palate." The book contained recipes that "any housewife with a flair for cooking should be able to master . . . and to become what the Chinese call *fo loo see fu*, an artist of the kitchen. . . ." This cookbook was typical of most 1950s Chinese cooking literature, which sought to change the white perception of Chinese food as inedible and unusual. For Young and other authors, the trick was to present Chinese food in a manner that would be a culinary adventure but would not scare away wary Anglos. *Wut ngnau yuk* (Chinese pot roast) was a pot roast flavored with soy sauce and one slice of crushed ginger (30); *kum chin gai* (chicken with ham) was composed of chicken breasts with sliced ham and a green onion garnish (31); and *bark jarm gai* (chicken with ginger garnish) called for dressing a chicken with ginger and one green onion (3). Such mild dishes were suitable for mainstream white Americans' tame tastes. The recipes had a touch of Chinese flavor—a teaspoon of soy sauce, a piece of ginger, or a scallion—but were not too unusual.

Male Chinese and Chinese-American authors, as well as female ones, included tame recipes. For example, Fred Wing and Mabel Stegner's cookbook, *New Chinese Recipes, Using Only Ingredients Easily Obtainable in Neighborhood Stores* (1951), combined "the successful teamwork of Mabel Stegner, an experienced American home economist, and Fred Wing, an educated Chinese gourmet and amateur chef" (n.p.). Presumably wary American women would feel reassured that a white home economist translated Wing's recipes. The book stated, "Of course you are glad to know that these recipes made with American ingredients by the Chinese method of cooking are good for you. . . . Best of all, these Chinese recipes made with American ingredients are flavorful, appetizing, and delicious" (n.p.). The repeat of the word "American" is noticeable here. No unusual ingredients appear in these recipes because everything can be purchased at an "American" grocery store. Although this book's recipes were Americanized, often containing little that appeared even vaguely Chinese except for soy sauce, the book did contain a brief section of recipes with Chinese ingredients, "simplified and tested" by Stegner (101). Wing and Stegner used tame and simplified Chinese recipes to reassure white readers that nothing was going to be too mysterious.

Some women authors went to great lengths to include recipes that would appeal to Westerners. For example, Mei-Mei Ling's book *Chop Suey: A Collection of Simple Chinese Recipes Adapted for the American Home* (1953) contained reasonably authentic recipes, but others were more questionable. Chinese chili beans called for one pound of ground round, kidney beans, ketchup, and soy sauce (18). Cabbage with corned beef included cabbage, canned corn beef, an onion, and soy sauce (23). Gail Wong's *Authentic Chinese Recipes* (1953) included not only recipes that would have seemed unusual to many white Americans but also recipes for Swiss steak (Chinese style), corned beef and cabbage, ground beef stew, pot roast beef, ground beef with macaroni, ground beef with cabbage, and broiled steak (114, 115, 112, 112, 111, 110, 105). How can we explain the addition of such distinctly non-Chinese recipes? Of course, some of these "Chinese" recipes could reflect a lack of authentic Chinese ingredients available in the United States, especially outside the large urban centers, so substitutions in recipes were common. For example, one 1957 article in *Sunset* magazine suggested that a can of chicken and rice soup should be added to the recipe, for Chinese noodles with chicken ("The Secrets" 158). But Ling and Wong's recipes were not merely the result of a lack of ingredients. These authors did something subversive, pushing for the acceptance of other more authentic Chinese recipes. If Anglo-Americans could be persuaded to eat Chinese chili beans seasoned with a teaspoon of soy sauce, they might be persuaded to try something slightly more authentic, even if only chow mein or chop suey, and then, perhaps, venture further to more adventuresome dishes. Ling and Wong assured readers that Chinese recipes were no more unusual than, for instance, cabbage with corned beef or broiled steak. The authors recognized that making whites accept Chinese foods was a challenging task, so their books included acceptable, familiar recipes, demonstrating that turnips braised with beef was the next step after cabbage with corned beef.

Fighting Assimilation: Authentic Food

Not all Chinese cookbooks provided only tame recipes. Some 1950s cooking literature ventured far beyond the tame realms of egg rolls and egg foo yong to include more authentic fare, even during a period in which authentic Chinese recipes were apt to meet resistance, at least from Anglo-American readers.[29] The women who published such recipes sought another avenue for questioning and subverting white mainstream norms. While some authors tried to gain acceptance and tolerance for Chinese food and people by publishing tame recipes, women who published more adventuresome recipes sought to preserve their cultural heritage. Due to the pressure to downplay authentic Chinese recipes, their inclusion was a way to uphold Chinese values, a dangerous business in the 1950s. By conveying such recipes, the writers hoped to share them with white Americans, demonstrating that the most authentic Chinese foods were more interesting and palatable than whites assumed. Similarly, the Chinese people were also rendered more acceptable through the positive depiction of their traditional foods.

"Authentic" should be defined more closely because it is a complex word with many nuances.[30] It is troubling because it implies that something can be non-authentic. Is chow mein less authentic than turnips braised with beef? They both show different paths that Chinese and Chinese-American foods have traveled. "Authentic" also can be defined in several ways. As Lisa Heldke asks, "Which kind of authenticity is authentic?" (118). Different cooks prepare the same dish in countless ways. A cook preparing a Chinese dish in the United States might not have access to the same ingredients or methods of preparation that she would in China, no matter how authentic she tries to make it. Despite the troubling nature of "authentic," I use it because no other term is applicable. I define authentic Chinese dishes as similar to those originally created in China and not changed greatly to appeal to white tastes. Due to the nature of food and cooking, however, authentic recipes can have variations, since cooks vary in their preparation of dishes.

The Chinese authors who included authentic recipes rebelled against the idea that the Chinese should try to be as American as possible to avoid ideological stigmatization. At a time when there was broad scrutiny of Chinese people as being potential Communists, one way to avoid such unwanted attention was to blend in as much as possible, moving out of Chinatowns across the United States or changing names; in the bland world of America's white suburbia, Chinese immigrants tried to blend in so that they would fit and not face possible deportation.[31] Even some Chinese-American leaders and social commentators argued that the best plan for racial acceptance was assimilation. For example, at the 1949 Chinese Young People's Conference in California, leaders told youth that they should leave Chinatowns and forget about Chinese traditions to advance racial understanding (Iris Chang 246). Thus, Chinese and Chinese-American authors who included authentic recipes rebelled against a society in which they were expected to become as American and as "white" as possible, including modifying the foods that they ate. By using authentic recipes, writers emphasized that they were Chinese and were not going to conceal their values and traditions. Including authentic recipes in these or other ethnic cookbooks is a means by which minority groups affirm their cultural values. Such recipes suggest that a racial or ethnic group does not wish to be assimilated by the dominant Anglo-European society and desires to uphold its unique culture.

The Chinese and Chinese-American women writers who included authentic recipes wanted to cross cultural boundaries and share their society with people who were unfamiliar with it. This is something these writers did earlier in the twentieth century as well. Before World War II, Chinese-American women also published cookbooks with authentic recipes.[32] After the war, Chao in *How to Cook and Eat in Chinese* (1945) included authentic recipes. "By bringing an 'authentic' version of Chinese food and Chinese ways of eating into American homes, Chao [was] . . . crossing a cultural boundary" (Theophano 145). In a similar fashion, 1950s writers also crossed a cultural boundary when they shared authentic recipes with their white readers, demonstrating that such cross-cultural contact benefited both sides—a vital message when many Chinese and Chinese Americans felt wary of contact with whites who, time after time, had shown their racist tendencies.

Numerous 1950s cookbooks contained authentic recipes for Chinese dishes. Feng's *The Joy of Chinese Cookery* included recipes for *pay daahn* (ancient eggs), *law baak chow ngow yook* (turnips braised with beef), *yeung gwaah* (stuffed braised squash), *yeung fooh gwaah* (bitter melon stuffed with meat), and *chow yook soong* (fried tasty meat mince [sic]) (Feng 93, 153, 102, 158, 154). *Mary Sia's Chinese Cookbook* included recipes such as jellyfish and cucumbers, pork hash and preserved black beans, pork hash and dried squid, squid with bean sprouts, and salted taro balls (Sia 28, 101, 100, 60, 115). Gail Wong's *Authentic Chinese Recipes* (1953) included pork with *chien gee* (fungus), spareribs with red bean curd, stuffed fish bladder, and stuffed bitter melon with pork hash, that would have seemed unusual to many white Americans (53, 71, 75, 65). Mei-Mei Ling also conveyed authentic recipes in her book *Chop Suey*. The introduction stated, "Appreciating the growing interest in Chinese cookery, Miss Mei-Mei Ling has produced [this book] to introduce Chinese cooking methods and ingredients to the modern American kitchen. . . . Though a few of the ingredients are substitutes, Miss Ling is careful that every dish retains its true Chinese characteristic" (Ling v). She included recipes for authentic dishes such as pickled cabbage with pork, cabbage with dried shrimp, and siu mai (19, 21, 29). Authentic recipes affirmed that the authors, although including Americanized versions of some Chinese recipes, thought that it was essential to convey authentic Chinese recipes, despite the risk of criticism from whites. Also, such recipes sometimes contained ingredients that would not have been palatable to Westerners, such as fish bladder, jellyfish, and dried squid. The ingredients affirmed the significant role of Chinese and Chinese-American readers, since the authentic recipes were aimed at them, as well as any white who might wish to experiment with something more authentic than chow mein or chop suey. These cookbook writers were not willing to ignore their Asian readers, making them simply disappear into the culture of whiteness. Instead, the authors and others affirmed the significance of acknowledging Chinese and Chinese-American readers and recognizing their tastes and food preferences.

But were white Americans ready for fish bladders or dried squid? There was some question about whether they would actually use authentic Chinese cookbooks, filled with unusual and unfamiliar ingredients. A *New York Times* article in 1952 observed about Wallace Yee Hong and Charlotte Adams's *The Chinese Cookbook* that there was "no question" that it "more nearly approaches the real cooking of China, and more specifically of Canton, than any other such volume written for Americans. Whether Americans will actually use his genuine recipes is another matter. Will they go to the trouble of procuring red cheese, Chinese turnips, etc.?" (Nickerson 163). In this book and others, the emphasis was on trying to teach people, including Anglo-Americans, about authentic Chinese foods. The question persisted, however, whether whites would actually try the recipes, especially if they demanded ingredients not available at many mainstream grocery stores. Still, just reading about such recipes must have provided some whites with a broader perspective of the world's peoples and food cultures. Equally important, the books preserved Chinese recipes and passed them down to new generations of Chinese and Chinese Americans, affirming their cultural and culinary values even during the Red scare.

Rewriting Their Lives

Whether in the 1950s or in any other decade, cookbooks have shared the concerns of women from different races and ethnicities. Although women might not have access to other literary genres, as Witt argues, the cookbook is a democratic genre that gives women a voice. Thus, it is important to understand how various races use cookbooks in ways that might or might not agree with dominant white values. For example, Chinese and Chinese-American women used cooking literature to convey a picture of Chinese people and Chinese foods that rebelled against dominant white stereotypes. Literally, these authors rescripted their lives, rejecting the script that whites had assigned to them. In a similar fashion, other ethnic groups have used cooking literature to rewrite their own lives.

Chinese-American women used both authentic and "tame" recipes to appeal to the widest audience, including whites. Some authors described only the tamest versions of Chinese dishes, ones with a scant teaspoon of ginger or soy sauce, hoping that these would appeal to white Americans. Others included authentic recipes, asserting the significance of the Chinese background of such dishes; this was a way for the writers to affirm their ethnic identity, despite outside social pressures to be quiet about their cultural backgrounds. Whether using tame recipes, more authentic ones, or a combination, Chinese-American authors sought ways to spread Chinese cuisine. In addition, they conveyed lessons about Chinese history and culture, working to change Western stereotypes of the Chinese as barbarians.

If one examines how Chinese-American women used authentic and tame recipes, the significance of not privileging authentic recipes as "superior" to tame ones is clear. To understand the spread of ethnic foods in the United States or any other country, one must recognize that they are not diffused singularly or unilaterally. For instance, Chinese and Chinese Americans promoted Chinese-American recipes, although they were not authentic, in restaurants and cookbooks. Should food scholars today condemn or criticize such foods because they lack the "authenticity" of other foods? We need a flexible approach to such foods, because we should recognize, as Heldke does, that cuisines "grow in healthy ways as a result of outside influences" (xx). Having a flexible attitude helps one to recognize that both authentic Chinese and tame Chinese-American foods have had and continue to have a part in changing the American diet and influencing how mainstream society preceives Chinese people.

Finally, this chapter has shown the significance of exploring the changing place of Chinese and Chinese-American foods in different eras. One cannot understand how white Americans reacted to Chinese food in the 1950s or today without recognizing how they rejected it as alien and unusual in the nineteenth century. This history needs to be remembered when considering how today some white Americans still react with uneasiness and distrust if asked to eat Chinese food, a reaction that they are less likely to express if asked to eat Irish, Italian, or German cuisine. Such behavior carries weight far beyond the dinner table in the way Americans treat Chinese, Italians, Irish, Germans, and other ethnic groups. White Americans are still more apt to discriminate against Chinese because of long-standing racist attitudes. In a similar fashion, whites are less likely to consume Vietnamese or Korean foods due to racist attitudes. How different foods are accepted in the United States is intimately intertwined with how people have or have not been accepted.

Chapter 3

"All Those Leftovers Are Hard on the Family's Morale"[1]: Rebellion in Peg Bracken's *The I Hate to Cook Book*

Reflecting on domestic life in the 1950s and early 1960s, one is likely to conjure up an image that is more than a little colored by *Leave It to Beaver, Father Knows Best, The Adventures of Ozzie and Harriet*, and similar family-oriented shows. One imagines a time when the whole family would gather around the dinner table every evening, savoring Mom's newest creation—Spam meatloaf or Velveeta Surprise—and engage in a lively discussion about the day's events. But this era was not as domestically blissful as television depicted it. Peg Bracken reveals a different image of home life in her cookbook, *Appendix to The I Hate to Cook Book* (1966): "Cooking in real life is much different than in cooking literature: The fact is, the family's evening meal isn't always the lightsome, stimulating occasion it is in the picture books. With Dick and Jane happily describing their school field trip through the glass factory, and Mother and Father acting motherly and fatherly. Families are sometimes cross, as a result of too much togetherness . . ." (170). Bracken shattered an icon: the family dinner. American society has had an enduring stereotype of the family dinner as a joyful occasion of togetherness, a meal shared by everyone. More than any other meal, the family dinner has been depicted in U.S. culture as crucial to forming and building family ties.[2] Bracken suggested that was a myth, one that shared little in common with "real" families' lives. In this book and its best-selling precursor, *The I Hate to Cook Book* (1960), Bracken created a more realistic account of domestic life than that found in the Beaver's home.[3] Her comical books were popular because they broke the stereotype that housewives were content with and thrived on their domestic responsibilities, paving the way for women in the late 1960s and 1970s to break away from traditional gender roles.

Subversively, Bracken suggested that women did not just tolerate cooking but hated it, a revolutionary observation because generations of Americans have assumed that women enjoy cooking or at least find it tolerable as one of their "natural" gender roles, just as mowing the grass was a "natural" chore for men. The assumption that females had an innate love of cooking and other domestic tasks that are labeled "feminine" has kept women inside the home. After all, if Mom loved cooking, why not keep her happy? Bracken said that this whole setup was a lie. Mom had never enjoyed cooking; she had done it only because she was forced to do this odious, time-consuming chore that no one else, certainly not Father or the children, would volunteer to perform. Bracken also suggested that the media had lied to generations of women. All those pictures of smiling housewives producing marvelous meals and loving it? This was media hype, and the women who did enjoy cooking meals needed, at least in her opinion, a trip to the psychologist. Bracken demonstrated that the entire media project of glorifying cooking was in stark contrast to the tedious work of "real" cooking. The media had created a pipe dream. In addition, they had glorified all housework, when, in reality, it was typically dreary, difficult, and demanding work that no one, including Mother, really enjoyed doing.[4] This message was, ultimately, going to change American society.

"A Baked Potato Is Not as Big as the World"[5]: Betty Friedan and *The Feminine Mystique*

To understand the influence of *The I Hate to Cook Book*, it helps to turn to another successful book of the same period: Betty Friedan's *The Feminine Mystique* (1963). It argued that women were not as cheerful and content with their lives as the popular media portrayed. Rather, the press created an image of femininity and of "correct" behavior for middle- and upper-class women that was impossible for many to achieve. Friedan demonstrated that millions of women tried to become the happy homemakers of American fantasy but frequently ended up feeling stifled and miserable. She urged women to fight against the mass media message that being a happy homemaker was the best role for a woman. *The Feminine Mystique* suggested that something was wrong in suburbia. There were restless stirrings that they wanted more than just suburban ranch houses to clean from top to bottom, kitchens to fill with shiny new appliances, children to feed and nurture, and station wagons to drive their husbands to and from the train. American women gazed around their new homes filled with new acquisitions and felt a growing apprehension that their lifestyles were stifling them. Friedan's book was a sign of women's discontent, their desire to be something other than domestic drudges.

Friedan wrote *The Feminine Mystique* because of a creeping sense that all was not well in her life or the lives of countless other women. "Gradually, without seeing it clearly for quite a while, I came to realize that something [was] very wrong with the way American women [were] trying to live their lives today," she wrote (20). To ferret out why many women seemed depressed and miserable, she turned to her former Smith College classmates, asking two hundred of them to fill out a detailed survey in 1957, fifteen years after their graduation. She discovered that these women and others suffered from what she termed "the problem that has no name," a general feeling of malaise that women suffered, a feeling of being empty, incomplete. This problem "lay buried, unspoken, for many years in the minds of American women. . . . Each suburban wife struggled with it alone. As she made the beds, shopped for groceries, matched slipcover material, ate peanut-butter sandwiches with her children, chauffeured Cub Scouts and Brownies, lay beside her husband at night—she was afraid to ask even of herself the silent question—'Is that all?' " (15). Millions of women, Friedan argued, suffered from this feeling of discontent and sense of dissatisfaction. She sought the reasons for this epidemic that seemed to strike countless women but not men.

She turned to women's daily domestic rituals to find the causes for the disease. "Can the problem that has no name be somehow related to the domestic routine of the housewife?" she asked. "When a woman tries to put the problem into words, she often merely describes the daily life she leads. What is there in this recital of comfortable domestic detail that could possibly cause such a feeling of desperation? Is she trapped by her role as a modern housewife?" (25). Friedan found that many women were dissatisfied with their daily work rituals. Home life was supposed to fulfill women's desires, but she discovered that it was not true. No matter how much the media made domestic work appear alluring, it was still, in reality, not fulfilling.[6] Friedan noted, "A baked potato is not as big as the world, and vacuuming the living-room floor—with or without makeup—is not work that takes enough thought or energy to challenge any woman's full capacity" (60). But even though housework was not as "big as the world," Friedan discovered that the popular media promoted this image, selling women the idea that domestic work should be sufficient to meet all their needs for personal achievement. For "normal" women, domestic labor was supposed to be enough to satisfy their desire for creative expression. After all, they could make housework as creative as they desired by preparing gourmet meals, sewing their family's clothing, decorating their homes, and a host of other tasks. If a woman approached housework with the right mind-set, it could be as creative as she wished it to be, according to the media. And, of course, for some women this was sufficient, and they found pleasure and creative fulfillment in the home, but many did not. No matter how hard these women tried to make domestic work more satisfying by sewing their own clothes, learning to wallpaper, baking their own bread, or refinishing old furniture, they still felt something was lacking in their lives.

When women turned to the media for advice, they found little support for their feelings of malaise. The media were filled with housewives who gloried in their dull tasks. Friedan was skeptical of what she termed the "happy housewife" image, a stereotype that filled women's magazines, newspaper advertisements, and television shows. A well-dressed and carefully groomed woman with a broad smile plastered on her face beamed at readers or viewers. She delighted in the simple joy of housework. She was *always* happy; she never seemed to complain about her husband or children, even when they tracked mud all over her newly scrubbed floor or scorned the tuna casserole that she prepared for dinner. She was omnipresent: "Millions of women lived their lives in the image of those pretty pictures of the American suburban housewife, kissing their husbands goodbye in front of the picture window, depositing their stationwagonsful of children at school, and smiling as they ran the new electric waxer over the spotless kitchen floor" (14). *The Feminine Mystique* pointed out that this happy housewife fantasy had little in common with real American women, whose lives were not always content and happy, but it was an image that was tremendously influential.

Friedan claimed women could escape from being trapped as happy housewives if they understood "housework for what it is—not a career, but something that must be done as quickly and efficiently as possible. . . . Then, [they] can use the vacuum cleaner and the dishwasher and all the automatic appliances, and even the instant mashed potatoes for what they are truly worth—to save time that can be used in more creative ways" (330). Women had been sold a false image of housework as a fulfilling "career" that was equally as rewarding as work outside the home; Friedan showed that this was a myth. Housework, however, could be done in an efficient manner, leaving women more room for development and personal growth in arenas other than the home.

Accompanying Friedan's feminine mystique is what I refer to as the cooking mystique, which, similarly, has had a lasting impact on women's lives.[7] Like the feminine mystique, the cooking mystique has been held up to women as "fact" when it is actually only a socially constructed group of beliefs about food and gender.[8] The cooking mystique is composed of four major ideas: (1) cooking is "naturally" women's duty; (2) cooking is a duty that women ought cheerfully to accept; (3) cooking is creative for women; and (4) cooking is the best way for women to show their love for family members and friends. Throughout America's past, these beliefs have held sway. This ideology has been so powerful in U.S. society that in innumerable households women still perform the bulk of the cooking.

The connection between women and the cooking mystique is an enduring one, but the period when it was preached most strongly was the 1950s. After millions of men returned from the war, women, at least according to the popular press, owed them home-cooked meals—although women were apt to include dishes made with convenience foods—that they had longed for while gone. No longer did women have to work in factories; now they could stay at home and make meals for their families to enjoy, and many women, although not all, left wartime employment to return to full-time domestic duties.

One reason that women returned to cooking for their families—if they had ever left this responsibility during the war—was that they believed the cooking mystique's tenets. Women were told that cooking was "naturally" their responsibility, so they had to accept it with as little fuss as possible. If a woman complained, voiced any resentment, or suggested that someone else should be responsible for these tasks (such as her husband), she could be considered not feminine enough, perhaps requiring psychological counseling for such "abnormal" gender behavior. If she complained, it also suggested that she was not approaching food with the right attitude. She had to think of it as creative and enjoyable, striving to make it more exciting if her interests flagged. If lime Jell-O was a bit ho-hum just topped with Cool Whip, a good cook could transform it into a five-flavor Jell-O mold filled with marshmallows, coconut flakes, canned fruit, maraschino cherries, and mandarin orange slices. If a plain meatloaf was boring, she could transform it into an entrée fit for company by mixing the meat with Lipton's onion soup mix, covering the loaf with a crust of instant mashed potatoes piped from a pastry bag, and then decorating it with green olives cut into festive shapes. If simple canned tomato soup was mundane, she could jazz it up by adding a can of cream of potato soup and topping the new bisque with a decorative squiggle of Easy Cheese from an aerosol can. Through such creative cooking, women ostensibly showed their love for the people close to them. If women did not display an interest in creative cooking, this might indicate that they did not love their families as much as they should. Although a woman might use convenience foods, she was still expected to do the cooking to show her love for her family.

With the dominance of the feminine mystique and the cooking mystique in this period, we can better understand the impact of Bracken's cookbook. She challenged both by suggesting that cooking was not a joyous pursuit and that she and countless other women abhorred it. In the 1950s and early 1960s, this idea clashed with the stereotype that cooking was "naturally" women's responsibility, a duty that they embraced with pleasure because it was an element of their feminine genetic makeup, one of the features that distinguished the boys from the girls. If this was not true, it raised the disturbing specter that other traditional gender roles were also not innate. Bracken's book sold well because many women agreed with its premises; she gave a voice to American women who did not find satisfaction in cooking or other household chores.

I Hate to Cook—Rebellion in the Kitchen

Some women, it is said, like to cook. This book is not for them. This book is for those of us who hate to, who have learned, through hard experience, that some activities become no less painful through repetition: childbearing, paying taxes, cooking. This book is for those of us who want to fold our big dishwater hands around a dry martini instead of a wet flounder, come the end of a long day. (Bracken, I Hate to Cook *vii*)

Bracken's opening words to her classic book describe the hatred that some women felt toward household chores, including cooking. For these women, household chores were something that was endured and not loved. And many actively hated the tedious, repetitive tasks, including cooking, that filled their lives so completely that finding time for a martini was a challenge, if not an impossibility. As food historian Jessamyn Neuhaus observes, "Cooking requires constant planning, shopping, and cleanup" (3). Unlike other tasks that can be done occasionally, for the majority of women, cooking consists of an endless series of tasks that never let up and receive little encouragement or praise, although Dad's cooking skill is likely to be praised like the Second Coming if he steps into the kitchen on the weekend to make pancakes from a box of Bisquick. No wonder women rebelled against cooking. Bracken revealed and criticized this tedious, unappreciated, and undervalued labor.

As did *The Feminine Mystique, The I Hate to Cook Book* showed women's smoldering discontent. Like Friedan, Bracken brought to light women's displeasure with their daily lives and the drudgery that composed much of domestic life. She showed that the media had created an unrealistic portrait of women's household tasks as something that any "normal" woman would be blissfully happy to perform. What woman wouldn't wish to prepare a five-course meal when her husband called unexpectedly at 5 P.M. to say that he had invited his boss home for dinner? What woman wouldn't be delighted to bake, frost, and decorate four dozen cupcakes when her daughter announced that she needed something for the next day's bake sale at school? What woman wouldn't want to cook completely different meals for all her family members because she knew they were fussy eaters, and little Jimmy refused to eat anything except macaroni and cheese, while teen Sally only ate grapefruit? What woman wouldn't want to cook her family's every meal for days, weeks, months, years, and decades to show her devotion? The popular media suggested that women loved to perform such tasks since they all enjoyed cooking and could not wait to whip together another elaborate meal. Bracken held a different opinion and thought that such chores, and other domestic ones, were tedious, and unappreciated. As did Friedan, Bracken demonstrated that a difference existed between how the media

portrayed women's roles and the reality of their lives. Bracken's book was a
sign that women were not content with their lives and society's expectations
about the gender roles that they should perform.

Because it accurately described women's feelings of dissatisfaction, the
book was a success with readers and critics when it was first published.
A slender work that doled out equal shares of humor and culinary knowledge in chapters with amusing titles—"Potluck Suppers: Or How to Bring
the Water for the Lemonade," "Desserts: Or People Are Too Fat Anyway,"
and "Last-Minute Suppers: Or This Is the Story of Your Life"—Bracken's
book provided pithy, humorous commentary about women's lives and
kitchen responsibilities. It was a best-seller when originally published and
has sold steadily over the years; by 1998, it had sold over three million
copies and made the author into a "culinary icon" (Florio E1). The critical
reception of Bracken's *The I Hate to Cook Book* was also positive.[9] A critic
writing in 1960 for the *Bulletin from Virginia Kirkus' Service* stated, "If you
can bring yourself to admit it, and if you are not a purist, or a masochist,
this collection of recipes to 'swear by instead of at'—cheap, easy, quick,
classic, and of 'misty' origins—is for you. . . . Peg Bracken's custodial
instructions throughout are unashamed and amusing" (Review 603). A
critic for *Booklist* wrote that the work was "a breezy, amusing, but highly
useful aid for anyone responsible for meal preparation who dislikes to
cook. . . . There is no claim to creativeness; the recipes are those that have
been proven economical of time and effort, yet are tasty and generally
popular" (Review 78). Another critic for *Library Journal* observed that it
was a "gently facetious cookbook for the woman who really hates to cook,
wants to spend as little time as possible on it, but wants good results"
(Saunders 3444). The reason for Bracken's success with readers and critics
was that she was ahead of her time, recognizing the difficulties facing
women in the kitchen and at home. As a writer for the *Washington Post*
observed in the 1990s, "Bracken was a working mother who clearly sensed
the end of the little wifey era. Julia Child had recently ignited a competi-
tive cooking frenzy among overeducated married couples, but Bracken
knew that, on a daily basis, women needed quick and easy recipes that
turned out right every time" (Florio E1). Women did not want cookbooks
filled with gourmet recipes that they could rarely prepare; they needed
ones that could be made everyday. Women did not desire to spend the
countless hours that Julia Child devoted to a meal.[10] They wanted something quickly prepared so they would still have sufficient time to collapse

in a favorite recliner for a few minutes. Women also needed recipes that even the pickiest husbands and children would eat—a difficult, if not impossible, challenge in any era.

Bracken's cookbook was not the first to express an ambivalent attitude toward cooking, but it was the most successful. A similar one was Ethelind Fearon's *The Reluctant Cook* (1953), but the British work viewed cooking more positively. "This book is not to teach you how to dodge cooking," she wrote. "It's only to show you how to dodge the obstacles, and so simplify the job that you will like doing it and not want to dodge it" (9). Fearon's attitude toward cooking was basically positive: "It isn't so much cooking that gets you down. After all, cooking, when properly approached, is a kind of consoling therapy. . . . And the rewards are immediate and very great. . . . It's the drudgery, not the cooking, that we want to eliminate. If I can show you how to cook like an angel and only have one saucepan to wash up, that would be different, wouldn't it?" (11). Fearon's premise was that cooking was enjoyable, but it had become more complex than it should be because women had not tried to make it as simple and streamlined as possible. She thought that cooking could be made enjoyable given the right equipment and recipes, and her book set out to do exactly that. The difference between Fearon's work and Bracken's was that the latter did not believe that cooking could be "consoling therapy" for anyone but those who were mentally ill. Bracken would also have some serious questions about cooking's "great" rewards for anyone.

One of the primary reasons for Bracken's success was that she went beyond Fearon and others who expressed a mild dislike of cooking; Bracken admitted to hating it, an emotion that many other women shared. She disclosed that the book's "genesis was a luncheon with several good friends, all of whom hate to cook but have to. At that time, we were all unusually bored with what we had been cooking and, therefore, eating. For variety's sake, we decided to pool our ignorance, tell each other our shabby little secrets, and toss into the pot the recipes we swear by instead of at" (viii). This was a shift in focus since most cookbooks were designed to share culinary knowledge rather than a lack of it. Bracken made the bold assertion that one did not have to love cooking or even to know much about it. She also made clear that a big chasm existed between cooks who enjoyed cooking and those who did not: "We who hate to cook have a respect bordering on awe for the Good Cooks Who Like to Cook—those brave, energetic, imaginative people who can, and do, cook a prime rib and a

Yorkshire pudding in a one-oven stove, for instance, and who are not frightened by rotisseries" (*I Hate to Cook* ix). Women who hated to cook had a different relationship to rotisseries as well as newfangled technology: "New kitchen equipment poses a problem for people who hate to cook. We're either reluctant to spend a cent on that end of the house or we're subject to short-lived but expensive spasms of buying a new gadget in the wistful hope that it will solve everything. But we've learned that nothing ever does" (*Appendix* 56).[11] Bracken was not alone in hating cooking and trying to ease its tedium by whatever means possible. Millions of women did not enjoy it. She reassured them that it was fine to feel that way; moreover, it was also acceptable to be dismayed at perfect cooks who knew everything and owned every kitchen gadget known to humankind.

When Bracken stated that many women hated cooking, she questioned society's assumption that Mom's cooking was, in some way or another, an indication of love. It is an enduring stereotype that women's domestic cooking is a primary way to show love for their family members and friends.[12] This stereotype has roots in America's early past.[13] In colonial times, a woman was responsible for a range of cooking tasks: baking bread, milking cows, churning butter, and cooking over an open hearth, to name a few. These tasks were considered a woman's responsibility and cooking was one of the ways that she indicated affection for family members (M. Margolis 114–115). In the nineteenth century, the link between mother's cooking and love was reaffirmed; here she played a vital role in bringing up America's citizens. One way that she assured their health was by monitoring their food consumption and serving them healthy, hearty homemade dishes (M. Margolis 121). For generations, American society has assumed that a woman's love for her family was best demonstrated by a dinner table heaped with home-cooked food. For a holiday meal, in particular, a woman had to cook copious amounts of food to show her love; a man did not have that same pressure. Even today, the stereotype of Mom's cooking as a sign of her love is ubiquitous. As feminist scholar Dolores Hayden observes, "In American life, it is hard to separate the ideal of home from the ideals of mom and apple pie, of mother's love and home cooking" (53).[14] Visit the grocery store to buy some cookies, and one is deluged with brands that feature the word "mother," including the national brand Mother's Cookies. Visit countless restaurants across the United States, and do they feature Dad's cooking? No, almost all star Mom's. When a college student is homesick, what is sent from home? Mom's cookies or brownies. Think about the

American symbol, apple pie. Who bakes it? Mom does. Mother's cooking, which serves as a powerful sign of domesticity and the home, represents love and nurturing.

Bracken scoffed at the idea that good cooking meant love: "I believe that the Irritation Quotient, or I.Q., of the reluctant cook is higher than most people's, and this can lead to unnecessary trouble. For instance . . . she can get sicker quicker than most people do hearing a little jingle like 'Nothing says lovin' like something from the oven' " (*Appendix* 51). The connection between Mom's cooking and love was a gender role that kept her trapped in the kitchen, preparing a batch of cookies or a five-course meal to prove her affection. Moreover, she could never escape that role because she always had to prepare another meal or batch of cookies. Bracken made her readers rethink this assumption, showing that many women hated cooking and that this did not suggest anything negative about their maternal talents.

Bracken revealed some of the reasons why millions of women hated to cook. One was because it was monotonous and repetitive, a never-ending cycle that was rarely appreciated by those who partook of Mother's meals. "All days lead but to the kitchen, or so it often seems at 5:00 P.M. And there is an astonishing number of days in the average lifetime," Bracken observed (*Appendix* 19). "Never doubt it, there's a long, long trail a-winding, when you hate to cook. And never compute the number of meals you have cooked and set before the shining little faces of your loved ones in the course of a lifetime. This only staggers the imagination and raises the blood pressure," she wrote (*I Hate to Cook* 11). For these monotonous meals, the first chapter of *The I Hate to Cook Book* included thirty "everyday main dishes" (11). The recipes include Stayabed Stew—designed "for those days when you're en negligee, en bed, with murder story and a box of bonbons, or possibly a good case of flu"(13)—Hurry Curry, Bisque Quick, and Old Faithful. Most women needed quick and easy recipes; Bracken recognized that for the average cook, life was composed of the meals that she had to prepare regularly, not the special meals for guests or meals out. There was a large divide between the monotonous daily cooking of most women's lives and the glamorous media image of cooking. Family members rarely appreciated Mother's cooking, although at least she received more praise for cooking than any of her other tasks. Bracken observed wryly, "Cooking is better than dusting the basement water pipes when it comes to getting appreciated" (*I Didn't* 6). Cooking is seldom appreciated, then or today. Frequently, family members either assume it is a task that women enjoy or

do not notice it, as part of a household's invisible daily rituals. Cooking and
other domestic responsibilities, many of which are women's, are taken for
granted. Today, men typically do not perform as much work inside the
home as women, although this varies dramatically from household to
household. Scott Coltrane observes, "Men's average contributions to the
so-called feminine chores of preparing meals, washing dishes, cleaning
house, and laundry/ironing have roughly doubled since the 1970s. . . . By
the late 1980s, men had more than doubled their contributions so that they
were doing over 20 percent of the inside chores" (53). Even so, this meant
women were doing 80 percent of the work still. Another study showed
that today's married women perform 70 percent of the meal preparation
and dishwashing (Steil 50). Women do most of the laborious food-related
chores of planning meals, shopping, cleaning, and putting food away,
and yet these chores and other similar ones continue to go unappreciated
(Coltrane 64). Bracken made women recognize that they were not alone in
feeling frustrated and malcontent with the drudgery of daily cooking and
housework.

According to Bracken, another reason why women hated to cook was
because it was always they who spent long hours preparing everything from
dull family meals to festive dinners and parties. Everyone assumed that
Mom would perform all the cooking, except cooking something on the
grill—a task handed to Dad after Mom had done all the preparation work
of purchasing the food, preparing a salad, cleaning and cutting up vegetables, making garlic bread, and marinating the steak. No one questioned that
women were "naturally" the ones to prepare all meals from the simplest to
the most complex. For a party, cooking had to be more elaborate than
meals for family members when a bag of hotdogs could be boiled and
slapped into buns. Bracken gave women who hated to cook some sugges-
tions for eliminating entertaining: "Never accept an invitation to dinner.
The reason is plain: Sooner or later, unless you have luckily disgraced yourself at their home, or unless they get transferred to Weehawken, you will
have to return the invitation" (*Appendix* 64). Entertaining trapped women
into cooking more elaborate and fantastic meals. Bracken noted,
"Unfortunately, you entertain to pay people back or to honor them, or
both . . . and you cannot honor people satisfactorily with a pride of hot
dogs. Some work is expected of you and perhaps something a little unusual"
(69). Bracken pointed out that entertaining was a competition in which

women had to cook elaborate meals to celebrate an occasion properly. She suggested not throwing celebrations that featured cooking since, ultimately, women would be responsible for food preparation, and no one would think of Mom, laboring away folding 200 pigs into biscuit blankets or wrapping bacon around chicken livers and water chestnuts for rumaki. "When the sun is over the yardarm and the party starts to bounce," Bracken lamented, "you want to be in there bouncing, too, not stuck all by yourself out in the kitchen, deep-fat frying small objects or wrapping oysters in bacon strips" (*I Hate to Cook* 79). The only reason for a woman to give a party was if she desired a respite from cooking herself: "Too well you remember the golden tranquility that bathes you, all day, when you know that *somebody else* is going to be doing that fast samba from pantry to sink" (64). That pleasure, however, was fleeting, as the guest would soon have to return the favor. Although parties could remove the woman from her kitchen responsibilities, she still had to return to her daily cooking chores.

Bracken's critique moved beyond the kitchen. She also criticized *all* women's domestic work, observing there was "one inescapable fact which every girl must sooner or later come to grips with: housekeeping and cooking are miserably intertwined" (*Housekeep* 49). Bracken made clear that cooking was just one part of the domestic duties labeled "women's work," composed of "scutwork . . . chores that any boob can do" (4). Unlike the Happy Housewife who thought housework was a vital career and was blissful as she mopped her kitchen floor until it was spick-and-span clean, Bracken's miserable housewife understood that housework was drudgery that offered little satisfaction to any woman. It could even drive her insane:

> Sometimes you stumble over a day of doing nothing—or a series of them—which you can ill afford. For if you continue to stand immobile among deeds undone and resolutions vain, you'll find that you can't even do the things you want to do, and presently you may lose your mind. . . . The reason for these occasional periods of standing and staring while the work piles up is usually malaise of the spirit. (98)

Bracken showed what happened to women whose domestic responsibilities became insurmountable. Like Friedan, she revealed what occurred to intelligent women who were not challenged intellectually by their home chores: they could go insane because they did not find the pleasure in household work that mainstream society suggested they should, and, tragically, it perceived such women as "abnormal."[15] Both authors demonstrated that this was not true, and the societal system that kept women in such positions needed to change.

For the woman who hated to cook, no respite existed. Cooking was a part of her chores that she could do little to avoid. It had to be done every day, unlike other chores that could be done weekly, monthly, or yearly, or avoided entirely, such as dusting the basement pipes. Few ways existed to escape cooking. Every time a woman rolled out of bed, she was faced with the necessity of having to cook. It was enough to make her want to climb back into bed for the day. But the woman who hated to cook had a few rewards. Bracken noted, "Though the reluctant cook will never really enjoy her kitchen work, punctuality, kind words, and clean plates are the carrots that will keep the little donkey plugging along" (*Appendix* 171). Nothing could be done to eliminate cooking entirely, but it could be made easier if women received assistance. One of the reasons that many hated to cook was that their work was seldom appreciated by family members, who seemed to feel that mother's role in life was to set heaping plates of food in front of them, which they could poke at, give her a look as though she were attempting to poison them, and comment, "What's this? Is it edible? Is it food?"

"No Lumps or Knobbly Places"[16]: A Media Fantasy

Women who hated to cook did not find reassurance in the popular media that other women hated cooking and domestic tasks. The media created a fantasy of the housewife that had little to do with reality. Bracken wrote that she was "tired of the word Homemaker, and the way we housewives were being eternally chucked under the chin. We were versatile experts—or so we were daily assured in the public print—every one of us a skilled business manager, practical nurse, house cleaner, child psychologist, home decorator, chauffeur, laundress, cook, hostess, gay companion . . ." (*I Didn't* 12). Bracken had a more realistic vision of homemakers as endlessly juggling a dozen different projects, which threatened, at any moment, to crash down on their heads. Housewives generally "just mouse along, putting one tennis shoe in front of the other, which is generally in the flypaper, bending over to pick up the floor mop and dropping the baby" (12–13). One reason that the author was perturbed by the media's fantasy was that society used it to perpetuate the gender status quo. Housewives were praised and such platitudes attempted to reassure women that being a housewife was valued. In reality, she was elevated to a pedestal to keep her performing her domestic tasks. In a similar fashion, Friedan's Happy Housewife was an image used to conceal many women's real dissatisfaction. Friedan and Bracken revealed the chasm that existed between the media's image of the housewife and reality.

In particular, Bracken questioned the media images of women who enjoyed cooking:

> When you hate to cook, life is full of jolts: for instance, those ubiquitous full-color double-page spreads picturing what to serve on those little evenings when you want to take it easy. You're flabbergasted. You wouldn't cook that much food for a combination Thanksgiving and Irish wake. (Equally discouraging is the way the china always matches the food. You wonder what you're doing wrong because whether you're serving fried oysters or baked beans, your plates always have the same old blue rims.) (*I Hate to Cook* vii)

Bracken questioned the media culture that created an unrealistic, unattainable vision of cooking. In addition, she pointed out that she (as well as many other women) only owned one set of plates to serve all meals, no matter how plain or fancy, suggesting that the media fabricated an image of cooking that was not within the reach of most. She broke with the cooking mystique's tenet that women should strive endlessly to improve their cooking and its presentation because that was the "natural" way for them to show love for their families. She demonstrated that women had more pressing concerns than just preparing elaborate meals or worrying about their china patterns.

Bracken pointed out that magazines and cookbooks created a fantasy about how food should appear. She warned, "Don't expect your company meals to look precisely like the company meals you see in the full-color food spreads everywhere. . . . Food photographs do not play fair and square" (*I Hate to Cook* 67). "In gourmet-cookbook life, there are no lumps or knobbly places," she wrote. "But in real life, the clarion call to dinner is often the signal for the man of the house to start taking apart his outboard motor in the basement while the daughter of the house disappears in a panic search for hair curlers" (*Appendix* 106). A major difference existed between reality and how the media glorified food. Even refrigerators appeared differently: "All those leftovers are hard on the family's morale when they open the refrigerator door. Wondering what's for dinner, they begin to get a pretty grim idea, and presently they begin to wonder what's with Mother. The inside of her icebox doesn't look like the insides of the iceboxes they see in the magazine pictures, and Mother loses face" (*I Hate to Cook* 32). Again Bracken revealed how the media created an unrealistic vision of cooking—no one could have a refrigerator that looked like the one on television cooking shows or in popular magazines—but it was an image that shaped many people's perceptions, including how family members viewed Mom's cooking.

Another media stereotype Bracken questioned was the one that linked a woman's sexual appeal to her cooking skills. Today, the idea endures that a woman needs to be a good cook to attract a mate, although he does not have the same worry. It is not sufficient for her to pop a frozen meal into a microwave or order out for Chinese food; more effort is demanded to attract a man. Popular women's magazines and books are still filled with recipes that are designed to appeal to a man, acting as "date bait."[17] Bracken questioned this stereotype: "I've noticed that some misconceptions are being disseminated by new or newish cookbooks. To take only one, consider those odd little books that keep pairing cooking with sex. For instance, how to cook him a Sunday morning breakfast that will make him propose. . . . Now we who hate to cook wouldn't dream of cooking Sunday morning breakfast for a man until he *has* proposed" (*Appendix* xviii). She continued, "This whole tie-up of food and sex has been overdone. . . . Through the years, we who hate to cook find that there's usually a nice man around somewhere whether we are in one of our non-cooking periods or in one of our totally non-cooking periods" (viii). Bracken subverted the cooking culture in which women's desirability was connected to their cooking prowess. She undermined the cultural assumption that their cooking was essential to their sexual appeal. This old-fashioned stereotype, according to the author, had kept women at the stove for too long. Instead, she suggested that even a noncook could find a mate, which went against the generations-old stereotype that the way to a man's heart was through his stomach. If she listened to Bracken, a woman did not have to worry about cooking at all, and she could still be attractive as a potential partner.

"An Awe-Inspiring Experience"[18]: Convenience Foods

Bracken also questioned whether women had to make everything (or anything) from scratch. For women who hated to cook, the best tactic was to use as many convenience foods as possible; moreover, such items could make them better cooks, not worse ones. Like the authors of many convenience food cookbooks, Bracken showed that instant foods were a blessing to anyone who wanted to streamline her kitchen time. Bracken suggested that convenience foods could be the main elements in a woman's cooking, writing, "It is truly an awe-inspiring experience to gaze down the opulent ready-mix aisle of the supermarket, its shelves brilliant and bulging with nearly everything you ever heard of, from Lady Baltimore Cake to Hush Puppies, all ready for you to add water to, mix, and bake" (*I Hate to Cook* 90). She noted that when preparing appetizers, "rely heavily on store-bought items. . . . There are some excellent frozen and refrigerated dips available . . . not to mention tubs of delicious cocktail cheeses and boxes of exotic crackers to spread them on, and prepared pizzas you can buy from the pizza man . . ." (80). For women who hated to cook, the grocery store supplied a plethora of instant foods that could be prepared with ease, and they should not feel guilty using such foods since they could actually be superior to anything that a woman who hated to cook prepared at home from scratch.

Bracken did not suggest that a meal could *sometimes* be composed of instant foods; she wanted convenience foods to replace all from-scratch cooking, including desserts. "In the ordinary course of human events, there is no reason why you should ever have to cook a dessert," she wrote. "With ready-mixes, fresh fruit, frozen fruit, canned fruit, and ice cream in thirty-seven fascinating flavors, your family should certainly be able to make out" (*I Hate to Cook* 91). Bracken assured women that they should use convenience foods whenever possible, and this did not necessarily mean that they were failures as wives or mothers. This was an important shift, one that, ultimately, helped lead to America's contemporary cooking culture in which many women rely entirely on instant foods, a practice that is widely accepted by our society today.

Another subversive idea about convenience foods in Bracken's work was that they did not need to be personalized or customized by something even as simple as adding an egg. She observed, "We don't get our creative kicks from adding an egg, we get them from painting pictures or bathrooms, . . . or writing stories or amendments, or, possibly, engaging in some kind of interesting type of psycho-neuro-chemical research" (*I Hate to Cook* 103). She was against garnishes, observing they were "those mad gay touches that are yours alone. These are the things you see in cookbooks and magazines that have you thinking, 'Now that's a cute idea; I ought to do that,' but you never remember to" (130). Including no special touches went against what much convenience food literature suggested. She wrote, "Recipe books are always telling you to get a can of a ready-prepared dish and spike it with something. . . . But my own feeling is that you should give the prepared thing the benefit of the doubt and taste it before you start spiking. . . . Furthermore, if you add seven different herbs and grated cheese to everything that is supposed to be all ready, you might as well have started from scratch in the first place" (117). Bracken's ideas were radical because she suggested that women did not have to do the minimum cooking involved with adding an egg to a cake mix or decorating convenience foods, a major step toward suggesting that women did not have to cook anything more complicated than a frozen dinner, pursuing creativity in other endeavors. But she did let some personal touches slip into her cooking with convenience foods, as one modern commentator observes: "Bracken's readers still had to chop the garlic and a couple of onions, but the recipes allowed them to dump in convenience foods—canned soups, seafood, vegetables, and sauces. And, despite their often plebeian nature, dishes included some surprisingly sophisticated touches, like curry powder and chopped apple in Sunday Chicken or Sauternes in Melon Wine Compote" (Florio E1). With their combination of convenience ingredients and from-scratch ones, such dishes showed how difficult it was for Bracken and other women to forget entirely about personalizing their cooking in a culture where love was still associated with women's cooking for their families.

Bracken warned women not to perform more cooking work than necessary because using instant foods lightened their labor. "Never could one cook so little and eat so well, thanks to the ready-mixed people and the frozen people. . . . Of course, there are a few minor problems left. Something we must fight is the dissemination of the idea that just because some things are easier to do, one should do more of them," she cautioned (*I Didn't* 16). Again, she made a radical assertion, suggesting that women could resist society's assumption that any time saved by instant foods should be devoted to more elaborate cooking. She argued that the opposite was true; any time women saved should be devoted to their own pursuits.

Bracken also acknowledged, however, that all people were not going to be enthusiastic about instant foods and how they sped up women's cooking. Men could complain because they wanted more home-cooked meals. They expected women to cater to their desires and needs, and that did not mean ordering out for pizza:

> When you hate to cook, you buy frozen things and ready-mix things, as well as pizza from the pizza man and chicken pies from the chicken-pie lady.
>
> But let us amend that statement. Let us say, instead, that you buy these things as often as you dare, for right here you usually run into a problem with the basic male. The average man doesn't care much for the frozen-food department, nor for the pizza man, nor for the chicken-pie lady. He wants to see you knead that bread and tote that bale, before you go down cellar to make the soap. This is known as Women's Burden. (*I Hate to Cook* 24)

Although her words were sarcastic, they were truthful. Many men were ambivalent about convenience foods because such food meant that women spent less time in the kitchen. This attitude stemmed from what such a shift could mean to established gender roles. Both convenience foods cookbooks and Bracken's books were part of a major cultural shift toward accepting instant foods, one that was going to have a significant impact on women's lives, changing the meaning of Mom's cooking forever.

Peg Bracken Meets Martha Stewart

The I Hate to Cook Book challenged society's belief that cooks and house-wives always enjoyed their work. The stereotype of a woman who beamed while she worked and who "naturally" enjoyed cooking has had a long-lasting influence on U.S. society and has kept women performing much of the cooking. Bracken challenged the stereotype by writing that she, and other women, hated cooking. It was a thankless task, which, she argued, should be sped up any way possible, including using as many convenience foods as the grocery store stocked and as could be packed in the home freezer. She also declared that the only reason that countless women cooked was because no one else would take responsibility for the thankless task. Mom was stuck with it. Again, Bracken's view was radical because it was not Mom's love that kept her cooking but her lack of other options. A prefeminist voice, Bracken made it clear that millions of women were not content with their kitchen or other domestic responsibilities.

Friedan and Bracken both showed that housework and cooking were repetitive and tedious. In addition, the authors demonstrated that the media had created an exalted image of homemaking that had little relevance to reality, a fantasy that seduced many women into thinking that domestic chores should be pleasurable. When they discovered that such work was not always as fulfilling or enjoyable as the media had proclaimed, they were left with Friedan's sense of malaise, of something not being right because they could not make their housekeeping experiences as rewarding as the Happy Housewife did. Likewise, Bracken explicitly stated that housework was not as glamorous as popular culture depicted it and that women were not insane because they found it dreary. It was a dull task, and, in real life, nothing could change that. The only way to make it slightly more tolerable was to finish it quickly and move on to other more rewarding activities.

Bracken's critique of the media fantasy of cooking remains germane today. There is still a great divide between how the media depicts cooking and its reality. Flip through a magazine or watch a television cooking show, and one encounters not a portrayal of the realities of cooking, with all its mistakes and surprises, but a fantasy with all the rough sports removed. For example, witness Martha Stewart's elaborate recipes and fanciful menus before her prison sentence. Her meals existed only because a veritable army of assistants help her to prepare them. In addition, she also had food stylists, food photographers, and a host of others who made it possible to create and photograph her elaborate meals and their fancy table settings. The typical cook, with a limited budget and time, could never create these meals in a regular kitchen. The media create a fantasy about cooking that has little connection to reality. Some women, however, still feel pressured by Stewart and other similar cooking shows or books to experiment with impossible meals, or they feel as though they ought to prepare them. Bracken is needed today to reassure women that such media-based cooking is pure fiction, and it is acceptable to reject that fantasy and pull out a frozen pizza for dinner so that one can have a minute or two to enjoy a martini.

Chapter 4

"Boredom Is Quite Out of the Picture"[1]: Women's Natural Foods Cookbooks and Social Change

One does not usually think about cookbooks when reflecting on social change and women in the 1970s. Instead, other images spring to mind, including women burning their bras, picketing outside of Playboy Clubs, protesting at beauty pageants, or speaking out in consciousness-raising groups. Cookbooks fail to make an appearance among these images of activism. One does not imagine second-wave feminists coming home, exhausted after a long day of picketing or protesting, putting on their aprons, and pulling out *The Betty Crocker Cookbook* to peruse before preparing the evening meal. If anything, one imagines them being more interested in throwing such a book in the trashcan, since such works have been dismissed as playing a part in keeping women in the kitchen. Despite this stereotype, cookbooks played a significant role in women's activism, especially in the natural foods movement. Natural foods cookbooks written by women did more than provide recipes to bake a loaf of bread; they provided recipes to change society. Focusing on these books, this chapter examines how women used them to promote social change. In particular, the chapter focuses on two of the most influential—Frances Moore Lappé's *Diet for a Small Planet* (1971) and Laurel Robertson, Carol Flinders, and Bronwyn Godfrey's *Laurel's Kitchen: A Handbook for Vegetarian Cookery & Nutrition* (1976)—which were tremendously popular in the 1970s, showing up on bookshelves across the United States. Both the books suggested that a dietary revolution was necessary to save the world and women should play important roles in it. Analyzing these books and others, this chapter reveals how they used a stereotypically feminine realm, the kitchen, to promote radical notions. The works sought to change not only American food habits but also consumption patterns in general. In addition, these writers used the science of nutrition to give the natural foods movement new validity, showing that science supported the belief that natural foods were healthier. Moreover, using science gave home cooking an entirely new significance.

These authors were not the first Americans to show an interest in how diet shapes society and individual character. We have had a long-standing "concern for diet as one manifestation of the search for perfection, purity, and long life" (McFeely 130). We have often sought ways to redesign our lives, pursuing longevity and moral purity through many paths, including the one that leads to the dinner table. In this same vein, the concern about diet created a fertile ground for dietary reform movements in earlier centuries. For example, nineteenth-century food reformers were fairly well known—at least if they were men. In the early nineteenth century, Dr. Sylvester Graham attracted a large following.[2] Believing in a vegetarian diet, with no alcohol, coffee, tea, or excessive stimulants in other forms, he encouraged people to eat vegetables, fruits, and cereals. His dietary plan was successful enough to become the official dietary regime at Oberlin College (130–131). Another nineteenth-century reformer interested in changing the American diet, Horace Fletcher, was committed to the thorough mastication of one's food, believing that adopting his dietary practices would cure a wide range of human ills, from gout to excessive weight. His regimen attracted many followers, including prominent physicians, educators, and physical education teachers; in the 1910s, he claimed that more than 200,000 families were living according to his principles (Whorton 198). Like Fletcher, John Harvey Kellogg was another health reformer interested in dietary reform. He believed in a vegetarian diet and promoted it at his Battle Creek Michigan Sanitarium, where he developed and sold many food products, including meat replacements, such as Battle Creek Steaks and Battle Creek Skallops [sic] (early equivalents to the modern veggie burger) (206). His theories proved so popular that over 300,000 people, including famous politicians, physicians, and educators, visited the sanitarium during his tenure (204). In the early twentieth century, Bernarr MacFadden, a popular health reformer and physical health expert, was also interested in dietary reforms. No doubt, his ideas were made more appealing to the masses because he was a muscular man with a superb physique, which he enjoyed modeling to admiring crowds. In his *Physical Culture Cookbook* (1929) and other works, he advocated "natural foods in contrast to the artificial foods, obviously made to please the eye and palate" (vi). He suggested that people cook without white flour, reduce their consumption of fried foods, and cut back on sugar and salt. In many ways, he would have been right at home with the natural foods movement of the 1970s. Although possessing a different background from MacFadden, Jerome Irving Rodale in the 1940s was also concerned about healthy eating. He was introduced to organic farming early in life and, for the next thirty years, he focused on the importance of organic foods, writing about his beliefs and founding the Rodale Press. He advocated that all refined foods be eliminated from one's diet (Whorton 328). Graham, Fletcher, Kellogg, MacFadden, and Rodale were a few of the male food reformers who sought to change America's eating habits for the betterment of individual as well as social health.

Women, however, were just as involved in food reform, a logical relationship because they had always been primarily responsible for domestic cooking. Who better able to shape the nation's diet? Among the women reformers was Mary Sargent Gove Nichols, a Graham follower who gave lectures on physiology and operated a vegetarian boardinghouse (Engs 48). The mid-nineteenth-century reformer Catherine Beecher Stowe was also interested in changing women's diet and exercise. She particularly discouraged the use of condiments. Another nineteenth-century food reformer was Ellen White; the co-founder of the Seventh-Day Adventists, she promoted vegetarianism and temperance. In the 1890s, Sallie Rorer was the outspoken leader of the Philadelphia School of Cooking. She believed that everyone should eat salad regularly and encouraged people to consume their food more slowly (Fernandez-Armesto 45). In 1890, Ellen Swallow Richards founded the public New England Kitchen, which specialized in nourishing meals of pea soup, Indian pudding, and other New England foods (Whorton 142). Designed to provide nutritious food to the poor, the kitchen proved so popular that similar ones opened across the United States. In the mid-twentieth century, another influential food reformer was Adelle Davis. In the 1940s and 1950s, her books on nutrition, *Let's Cook It Right* (1947), *Let's Eat Right to Keep Fit* (1954), and other volumes proclaimed the merits of organic foods and vitamins, laying the way for the 1970s natural foods movement. Her works stressed that people could lead longer, healthier lives by changing their food habits. This message was widely accepted, and her books sold more than ten million copies (McFeely 133). These women reformers and others shared in common the desire to change the American diet.

The 1970s natural foods movement differed from earlier food reform movements in its motivation, as historian Mary Drake McFeely observes in her book, *Can She Bake a Cherry Pie? American Women and the Kitchen in the Twentieth Century* (2000): "The natural food movement of the seventies was based not solely on the benefit to the individual but also on ideas about living the simple life; not only on personal betterment but also on the good of the world" (136). This was a shift in attitude to food and its consumption. Instead of being primarily a private concern for the individual or a concern for only the social good of Americans, it was transformed into an ethical concern for the entire world. Food choice was moved to a larger arena, and natural foods cookbooks, including *Diet for a Small Planet* and *Laurel's Kitchen*, played a part in conveying this new global understanding. In addition, these books (and others) suggested that women would have important roles in the worldwide food system. This literature gave their cooking a new level of significance because what they cooked helped determine the survival of the entire human race. This was an especially pressing concern when many Americans were deeply anxious about whether the world could support its inhabitants due to the population explosion, a fear increased by the media's often-sensational accounts. For example, in *The Population Bomb* (1968), R. Ehrlich claimed that the world was "rapidly running out of food" (18). In *Too Many: A Study of Earth's Biological Limits* (1969), Georg Borgstrom suggested that humanity was "losing the race between food production and population growth and is thus undermining both health and prosperity" (322).[3] These books and others fueled fears that the world no longer had sufficient food. In this context, vegetarian and natural foods literature offered hope, providing ideas about how to consume fewer resources, feeding more people in an economic fashion.

"The Times, They Are A-Changin"[4]: Rebellion and Change

One reason that these books were successful was because they were a part of a much larger culture of change. The 1960s and early 1970s were a time of widespread social transformation in the United States, impacting people from all class, race, gender, ethnic, and age groups. The Civil Rights movement challenged how individuals thought of race. Millions demonstrated and protested for African-American rights. When in the 1950s Rosa Parks refused to relinquish her seat to a white man, an act that sparked the Montgomery Bus Boycott, she showed that individual actions could make a difference. Americans saw how an individual's protest could result in nationwide change. The youth movement made millions of young people aware that their actions mattered. Similarly, the women's movement caused women to recognize that they had the wherewithal to change society. The gay rights movement also demonstrated to people how vitally important it was to agitate for social change. The impact of these movements needs to be recognized to understand the roots from which the natural foods movement sprang. All of these movements demonstrated that social change was possible through individual accomplishments.[5] In addition, these movements made people aware that the government could not always be trusted; this idea was reinforced by the Vietnam War, Watergate, and other events. Many Americans no longer assumed that the government was working in their best interests. And hand in hand with government was big business; a majority of people no longer thought that business would do what was best for consumers. This questioning mind-set fueled the natural foods movement. If government and business could not be trusted about other issues, why would they tell the truth about food?

The natural foods movement was not isolated from other movements, but, in many ways, they were intertwined. People involved in the youth movement also were involved with the natural foods movement. Women engaged with the women's movement were involved, although not all feminists were equally enthusiastic. After all, they were fighting for freedom from the kitchen. For centuries, American women's stereotypical place had been in the kitchen, cooking meals. In the late 1960s and 1970s, feminists wanted to break this supposedly "natural" connection. Thus, some found the natural foods movement, with its emphasis on women and cooking, to be reactionary. But not all feminists were wary, and some embraced the movement, discovering that much of feminism shared similar concerns. Both movements believed that society needed to change. Feminism wanted patriarchy to crumble; the natural foods movement wanted large agribusiness to crumble. Feminism assumed that the government was uninterested in gender equality; the natural foods movement assumed that the government was uninterested in people's health. Feminism assumed that the personal was political and wished women to recognize the significance of gender issues in their individual lives; the natural foods movement assumed that personal food choices were political and wanted people to recognize that these decisions mattered. Whether the Civil Rights movement, youth movement, gay rights movement, or the women's movement, all wanted to change mainstream America's value system. Using different platforms, including natural foods, these activist groups questioned and undermined the status quo.

The natural foods movement threatened the status quo because it suggested that Americans had been lied to: we were not the best-fed people in the world but the worst. Of course, our dinner plates were heaped high with frozen Salisbury steak, instant mashed potatoes, and canned green beans, but these foods were not the best ones for us. Chock-full of chemicals, preservatives, and other additives, they did not even taste that good; a bowl of fluorescent orange Jell-O topped with Cool Whip tasted suspiciously as if it had been concocted in a chemical laboratory. (And don't even start thinking about Twinkies, Sno-Balls, Cheez Whiz, and other faux foods.) We were led to believe that such instant foods represented the epitome of modern American food, and countless Americans purchased them every week with little thought about their nutritional content. Millions assumed that the food industry was feeding America the best diet, one that represented progress and modernity. If food manufacturers declared Wonder Bread more nutritious than wheat bread, many people believed it. And numerous companies, earning huge profits from inexpensive products such as the air-filled loaf of white bread, did not want anyone to change the status quo. General Foods, for instance, threw a campaign that explained to consumers, "Foods could have the keeping qualities, convenience, flavor, and appearance they cherished only because of additives, processing, and dabs of artificial flavor and color" (Levenstein, *Paradox* 197–198).[6] This company was not alone; many others did not want to shake up a system based on artificial ingredients and colors, especially since such additions made products more profitable by increasing shelf life and making appearance come across as more attractive to consumers.

But not all Americans were content with what the food industry offered them. Some wanted change. Thus, a health rebellion resulted that radically altered the U.S. diet. A 1972 *Time* magazine article observed, "The American kitchen has become a battleground as people in growing numbers rebel against the American way of eating" ("The Perils" 68). Marjorie Miller noted in her book, *Introduction to Health Foods* (1971), "Young people are rebelling. Critical of the synthetics that have become a part of the American way of living, they are popularizing what has been a steadily growing movement by nutritionists to combat the harm done by the increasing deluge of processed, refined, empty foods" (14). In her *Natural Foods Cookbook* (1972), Maxine H. Atwater observed, "The revolution toward a better way of life has begun. Organically grown foods, foods that are unprocessed and as close to their natural state as possible, lead the way. Already beans are sprouting, home-made yogurt is incubating and whole-wheat flour is grinding in hearth-side hand mills while juicers chomp on home-grown vegetables" (n.p.).[7] Living in the San Francisco bay area, my family was one of many affected by the natural foods movement. My mother had both wheat germ and sprouts growing in her 1970s kitchen. One of my regular chores growing up was to water the sprouts, drain them, and find a sunny location for them on the windowsill. They were a dietary staple, as were homemade wheat bread and our own homemade yogurt. A change was happening, one felt, when a woman (or man) brought home a jar of wheat germ or grew her own sprouts in the kitchen window.[8]

Many people wanted to be a part of this food rebellion, and it sprang up in some surprising locations. Cookbook author Jeanne Voltz observed, "A return to simple foods is surfacing in unexpected places—the lunch bag of a businessman escaping the devastation of martini lunches, the fruit dessert instead of cake or pie at family dinner tables, the whole grain sandwich for teenagers' snacks in place of the gooey candy bar" (7). Even *Vogue* magazine in 1971 hired a New York caterer to prepare an organic buffet, including poached pike with yogurt sauce, zucchini with brown rice, soy bread, and Catawba grape juice, for the magazine's staff members ("Reality" 72). The article about the spread stated, "The newest—and most delicious—party foods are real ones—no sprays, chemicals, additives, preservatives, stiffeners, or laboratory dyes used or needed" (72). *Seventeen* magazine also supported natural foods; one of its articles declared, "Earth lovers this is for you—a whole new way of eating that grows straight out of the land. It's ecology served up with economy." The article suggested serving "low-cost rice and pasta products" to "extend the earth's resources" ("Earthologies" 152). "Earth lovers' party fare" included red bean salad and international pilaf, recipes designed to help readers "enjoy the new earthy way of eating" (153).[9] Never before had a natural foods movement spread so rapidly and widely, although this growth had certain geographical limits. People were more apt to be interested in natural foods if they lived in a large urban area. The coasts, especially the West Coast, accepted natural foods more rapidly and completely than other regions. Natural foods flourished in college and university towns, where students and professors were keenly interested in changing their diets. Natural foods were also consumed more by middle- and upper-class whites.

Across the United States, millions of individuals helped spread the natural foods movement. The people involved recognized that personal and group innovation was necessary to produce healthy foods. Microbusinesses and concerned individuals, it seemed, were the best resources for develop- ing and selling healthy foods, since big businesses seemed uninterested or were interested only in producing natural foods that were highly profitable, such as granola and yogurt, which could be made inexpensively and then marked up astronomically. A grassroots-level natural foods movement emerged that changed the American diet.

From coast to coast, women were involved in different roles, including owning natural foods restaurants, bakeries, and cafés. One of the most famous restaurants was the Chez Panisse Café, founded by Alice Waters, who wished to use organic ingredients from local farmers, recognizing the envi- ronmental significance of such an action. Another famous eatery was the Moosewood Restaurant, opened by Mollie Katzen and friends in Ithaca, New York, in 1972. In the same year, Jill Ward and Dolores Alexander estab- lished New York City's Mother Courage Restaurant, the first feminist restau- rant that featured healthy food (Belasco 94). In Ithaca, Julie Jordan opened the natural foods Cabbagetown Café in the late 1970s. Deborah Madison was one of the founders of the vegetarian Greens Restaurant in San Francisco in 1979, while Nora Pouillon began her natural foods restaurant Nora in Washington, D.C., in the same year ("America's" 1). In Madison, Wisconsin, Odessa Piper started L'Etoile in 1976, a restaurant that focused on organic foods and locally grown produce (Lappé and Lappé 361). Seeking to change not only the way foods were cooked but also the way they were grown and distributed, women formed and joined cooperative natural foods groceries and bakeries and owned or managed organic farms and dairies. Crescent Dragonwagon used the proceeds from the publication of a book to purchase an organic collective farm (Belasco 95). In 1975, Lee Armstrong, Anne Light, and Julia Lee founded the Women's Community Bakery in Washington, D.C., a cooperative devoted to baking bread with organic ingredients and teaching women how to operate a business (L. Miller 11). All of these forms of natural foods activism were particularly appealing to women because such work demanded limited supplies of capital at a time when many still earned considerably less than men. Also, since women had a long relationship with food and cooking, it was a logical step to turn this experience into running small natural foods businesses.[10]

Women were involved with other aspects of the natural foods movement. Apart from running businesses, they also wrote the literature that created, supported, and spread the movement. Hundreds of women-authored cookbooks and cooking articles appeared that discussed the nutritional and ethical importance of natural foods, described recipes, listed community contacts, and, more broadly, encouraged people to live environmentally aware lives, including everything from the foods that they ate to the goods they recycled.[11] Natural foods literature played an essential role in building and spreading a political ethos that would dramatically alter how many Americans thought about food and the environment.

Today, it might be difficult to understand the extent of the influence of this literature. After all, many people now have the Internet and are used to finding information on any subject, including culinary ones, within minutes. Want recipes for tofu? Need information about natural foods? Want information about living a more environmentally aware life? For any issue related to natural foods, hundreds of websites, if not thousands, are available. American society is inundated with information about natural foods and healthy living, so it is difficult for some to imagine how things were a few decades ago when the Internet was not available. Previously, to locate information about natural foods, people had to turn to natural foods books, magazines, pamphlets, and mimeographed copies. This literature was especially important because many traditional, older cookbooks—*The Joy of Cooking*, for example—did not include information about natural foods or offered only minimal facts. Because of this lack, food writers in the late 1960s and 1970s jumped at the opportunity to write new cookbooks for a new movement.

Writing about natural foods was a crucial step because some people, at first, viewed natural foods with suspicion, complaining about their high costs and dubious health benefits. In a *Better Homes and Gardens* article from 1972, health editor Gerald M. Knox wrote, "Too many people simply like the idea of adopting any fad that comes along. And many people are easily impressed by the words 'health,' 'organic,' or 'natural' " (30). He lamented the "fuzzy" thinking of people who promoted natural foods (30). In a 1972 edition of *Harper's Bazaar*, Natalie Gittelson was no more enthusiastic: "Health foods—our current, expensive quest for self-purification through pure food consumption—may constitute one of the costlier rip-offs of these times" (32). She noted that nutritionists, including Dr. Frederick J. Stare at Harvard University, thought that an organic diet provided nothing that could not be obtained from a nonorganic one (32).[12] Such criticism of health foods and their promoters was not unique to the 1970s. The United States has had a long history of doubting food faddists and their claims. Dr. Graham and his vegetarian diet, Fletcher and Fletcherism, and Kellogg and his cornflakes were met with harsh criticism. While some Americans embrace such movements immediately, others are just as quick to critique them; people have always had an uneasy relationship with food reform. Many seek to change their diets for better individual health—spiritual, emotional, and physical—yet tend to wrestle with fear of change versus the desire to stay with their traditional foods.

In the 1970s, the popular media criticized natural foods for different reasons, not just for high cost and uncertain health benefits. Some also found them unpalatable. A writer for *Harper's Bazaar* described one natural food, granola, as "about as chewy as leather" and "not quite so tasty" (Gittelson 32). Similarly, D. Keith Mano, writing for the *National Review* in 1978, described natural foods as "booby-trapped with ground-glass-hard lumps that crack and splat and hurt" and tasting of "Maalox tablets [that] have been left in someone's overcoat pocket since last winter" (291). John L. Hess observed in the *New York Times* in 1973, "The phenomenon of the publishing season has been the demand for 'natural food' books on how to cook 'organic foods,' how to bake bread, how to use edible weeds, how to sprout beans, how to shop to avoid additives and merchandisers' traps. . . . Nearly all of the dozens of 'organic' or 'wild' or 'consumerist' food books that I have seen this fall have some merit. Most of them, however, are stronger on the alleged health factor than they are on the joy of eating" (52).

Other people were unaware of all the foods that they could purchase and what recipes they could prepare with the new ingredients. But there was a noticeable shift, with more Americans accepting natural foods stores and their products. In earlier years, such stores had been considered oddities, filled with unidentified foods. In 1974, one cookbook author wrote, "When you enter a natural food store, you will see . . . crocks, barrels, sacks or bins of whole grains, stone-ground grains, germs of grains, cereals . . . and a variety of seeds and nuts. . . . Many of these may be strange to you" (Pritzker 82). Similarly, two other 1970s food writers noted, "Full-fledged 'health food' has a slightly mysterious and dubious aura about it, while health food stores are interesting, but somewhat strange with their shelves of . . . brewer's yeast, cayenne, bone meal, lentils, and kelp" (Goeltz and Lazenby 17). Such attitudes were common since natural foods stores had not yet been mainstreamed, but this situation began to change in the late 1960s and 1970s, as they opened in towns and cities across the United States. An article in *Time* from 1972 declared, "The current interest in organics is unprecedented. In 1965 there were only 500 stores in the U.S. specializing in health foods. Now there are more than 3,000. Virtually every major supermarket chain is either carrying or considering handling a line of health-food items" ("The Perils" 69). Another writer observed, "Health food stores, all claiming to sell natural foods, are springing up in the wildest competition to hit the food industry since franchise chicken" (Voltz 7).[13] This was a dramatic shift. Natural foods stores were all the rage, and natural foods were increasingly available at major grocery chains.

Grocery stores were filled with unfamiliar foods that many Americans had never tasted and did not know how to prepare and cook. People also worried, as mentioned previously, that such foods were as tasty as gnawing on one of grandfather's old slippers. Help was needed, and writers stepped in, recognizing that Americans wished to try natural foods but did not know how to use them. Eleanor Levitt wrote in her cookbook, *The Wonderful World of Natural-Food Cookery* (1971), "All those strange grains and seeds you find in the health-food stores labeled alfalfa, millet, bulgur and heaven-knows-what-else, can be cooked and used exactly as if they were the old familiar white rice, farina, or cream of wheat" (84). She urged readers to "have the heart of the true adventurer" and try new grains (84). Levitt was not alone. Other food writers helped people experiment with unusual foods found in health food stores, spreading the natural foods movement that was rippling through the United States.

Not everyone, however, was ready to embrace health food or its fans. To some Americans, it seemed as though proponents of natural foods were crackpots who shunned meat for tofu. In her *Natural Foods Primer: Help for the Bewildered Beginner* (1972), Beatrice Trum Hunter wrote, "Many mass media articles have ridiculed natural food partisans with epithets such as cultists, faddists, crackpots, and a few less kindly!" (16). A *Time* magazine article also was doubtful about natural foods fans: "It is fitting that one of the kinkiest divisions in the army of culinary skeptics, the health-food addicts, should operate with almost religious conviction. Believing that good health, not to mention beauty, longevity, and even sexual potency, depend on the proper foods, they spurn most pre-packaged products" ("The Perils" 68).[14] Many Americans assumed that such people should be ignored or not taken seriously, so natural foods fans needed to be careful about how they represented themselves to the mainstream. Not all were cautious; some made grand claims for natural foods, including that they could revitalize the body and strengthen the sex drive. In her book, *Natural Foods: Eat Better, Live Longer, Improve Your Sex Life* (1971), Wendy Pritzker stated that health food could build a healthy body, "a primary requisite for a fully expanded sexuality" (109). No wonder many were eager to adopt a natural foods diet. Others were more cautious in promoting natural foods. Hunter warned, "Don't be a zealot. If you have become enthusiastic about natural foods but meet with skeptical or even scornful responses from members of your family, go slowly. . . . Your ultimate aim will . . . be to convert your family, but try to do it gradually" (19). She suggested that women should introduce new foods in limited quantities, "sneak some brewer's yeast" into a soup or "add small amounts of whole-grain flour" to bread loaves (19). Since many people viewed natural foods proponents as fanatics, authors had to tread carefully. Both Lappé and Robertson found ways to convey their messages to a larger audience, which was essential because more was riding on changing America's diet than whether someone ate a hamburger or a veggie burger for dinner. The fate of the world, natural food adherents believed, depended on people making the right choices about the foods they consumed.

Making Natural Foods Scientific

One book that raised awareness of the global importance of food choices was Lappé's *Diet for a Small Planet*, which "merged the political and the personal by combining economics and autobiography, consumerism and therapy, sober biochemistry and tasty recipes" (Belasco 57). It proved tremendously appealing, becoming "*the* vegetarian text of the ecology movement," selling close to two million copies in a decade (56). What explains its success? As mentioned earlier, it did more than sell a recipe for soybean casserole; it also promoted a recipe for living that could influence the entire globe. Lappé wrote *Diet* to remind readers about how humans impact the planet. "Reestablishing a sense of our direct impact on the earth through food," she wrote, "may be the first step toward changing our cultural pattern of waste" (xiv). She wanted Americans to rethink the role of consumption and waste in their lives. She wanted them to adopt not just a different way of cooking but also a different way of thinking about their places in the world.

From its early years, reviewers praised *Diet*. Writing for *Library Journal* in 1972, Priscilla Wegars noted that Lappé's "useful and impressive compendium could win even more converts to meatless meals" (1938). Another reviewer in the same year remarked that Lappé's "special twist to the argument for natural foods coupled with her discriminating selection of recipes makes this book superior to many similar books currently flooding the market" (Margaret Porter 692).[15] Reviewers were not the only ones who appreciated this work; consumers did too, flocking to buy copies from coast to coast. One reason for its success was that it avoided "the usual mystical prose. There was no mention of karma, yin, or yang" (Belasco 58). At a time when many were unfamiliar with natural foods and connected it to a fringe element of the population, Lappé's straightforward writing made her work appeal to a broader audience. She demonstrated that a person did not need to run her dogma over with her karma to eat better food but simply needed to be interested in healthy eating.

In addition, Lappé attracted a larger audience due to her use of science, a notable change from earlier books that had been more concerned with the karma of natural food consumption than the science. Lappé challenged stereotypical notions about cookbooks lacking science. Today, mainstream society often perceives cookbooks as frivolous, insignificant texts; who needs another 101 new recipes for Jell-O salads? Lappé challenged the popular assumption that cookbooks were not serious works by using economics and science to support her claims, giving her book a gravity that other similar works did not possess. Specifically, it appeared more legitimate because it was carefully researched and documented, exactly as a science textbook would be. The cookbook also looked scientific, packaged with diagrams, pictures, charts, and appendixes about protein and human needs for it. This was crucial because many mainstream Americans were wary of vegetarian diets or ones low in meat, worried that such dietary fare would not provide necessary protein. *Diet* did much to lay those fears to rest. Lappé's use of science raised the dialogue about natural foods to a new level, showing that she, as well as other women, could back their arguments with documentation and evidence.

Much of *Diet* is an elaborate discussion of how the world's protein sources could be distributed in a more equitable fashion. The book is filled with charts and graphs that list the protein content of various culinary combinations. Lappé focused on protein because she believed that the world's supply was distributed in an unequal fashion, with some wealthy nations receiving more than they needed, while other nations received less. The United States was the worst culprit, wasting tremendous amounts of protein as animal feed. Also, Americans ate more protein than required to stay healthy. She wanted them to have a greater awareness of the protein they consumed, as well as a greater dependence on protein from plants (33). This emphasis is evident in her recipes, as they were arranged in a different format from most cookbooks divided into appetizers, soups, vegetables, salads, entrées, breads, and desserts. Lappé separated recipes based on different protein combinations, so the book contained recipe sections on rice and legumes, whole wheat and soy, cornmeal and beans, beans and milk, beans and sesame seeds, and potatoes and milk. Every recipe listed its percentage of a person's daily protein allowance. The recipes also included extra protein from different sources: nutritional yeast, dry milk powder, sesame meal, wheat germ, soy grits, soy flour, and other nutritious, protein-rich additions. By changing traditional protein sources, Lappé hoped to feed millions of malnourished people. Thus, food choices became political ones with profound global ramifications.

Food choices were also ethical. Lappé queried her readers:

> When your mother told you to eat everything on your plate because people were starving in India, you thought it was pretty silly. . . . Since then you've probably continued to think that making any sort of *ethical* issue about eating is absurd. You eat what your family always ate, altered only perhaps by prodding from the food industry. . . . The act of putting into your mouth what the earth has grown is perhaps your most direct interaction with the earth. But, depending on the eating habits of a culture, this interaction can have very different consequences—for mankind and for the earth. (3)

For Lappé and other natural foods writers, one's protein sources and, indeed, *all* food choices had an ethical dimension that too many ignored. But knowledgeable consumers could make the difference, as *Diet*'s back cover stated: "The world has come a long way toward recognizing some of its problems in the last few years. No final solutions have been found, but a trend that has been realized and acknowledged—at least on the part of young people—is the movement away from waste, away from heavily polluted foods.... Here, step by step, is how you, the individuals, can improve your own style-of-life—and at the same time help your very small planet." Recognizing the ethical issues that were involved with food choices was a step in making Americans more aware of their place in the larger global community. Lappé's book was one part of a larger cultural movement that emphasized the importance of global awareness for the United States. No longer could Americans act as though the rest of the world did not exist; they had to be cognizant of how their choices had ethical implications for the rest of the world. If an American wasted food or ate more protein than necessary, a less affluent person went without. An awareness of the complex web of relationships of gender, race, ethnicity, socioeconomic class, and geographical location that surrounded the world's distribution of food was a first step for Americans to become more ethical as individuals and, ultimately, as a society.

Although Lappé wanted people to account for the ethical dimension of consumption, she did not think that food should be insipid: "Many of you may well fear that my appeal for a more rational use of our earth will only take the pleasure out of eating and make of it a terribly complicated, even dull affair. Certainly not! Experiment a little and both your palate and your creative sense will likely tell you the opposite" (123). *Diet* included recipes for protein combinations in savory, interesting dishes. They were often international in flavor, including ones for Oriental fried rice, curry rice, sweet and pungent vegetable curry, and zesty Lebanese salad. Such recipes demonstrated that nutritious cooking was not essentially dull. Lappé thought that food should be more interesting, not less, because cooks necessarily were thinking about new issues. Even shopping could become an adventure: "As new types of food combinations [become] more attractive, shopping for food and cooking [is] no longer unconscious and boring, but real adventure" (xiv). Her book's success was not only its groundbreaking use of science, but also its presentation of natural foods as interesting, enjoyable, and tasty.[16] For her, searching for natural food ingredients was an exciting adventure, rather than a frightening one, a major shift from some mainstream popular literature of the period that presented natural foods and natural foods stores as alien, unfamiliar, and strange. Lappé encouraged her readers to reconsider their views about natural foods.

Lappé's beliefs about food went beyond the kitchen. Although her cookbook focused on protein complementarity, her goal was something much grander. She wanted her readers to rethink their relationship with an American society that was based on mass consumption. She wanted them to recognize that they did not have to be mindless consumers of whatever the media advertised as the next "new thing" that week. Instead, they could be thoughtful consumers who were aware that what they used and how much they used was a choice, one that had repercussions for the rest of the world, so it was important to analyze and think about every purchase. Lappé's notion of being a mindful consumer was a radical notion in a society where countless Americans did not give much thought to what they bought and how it was produced. *Diet* made them more conscious about the selections that they made in relationship to consumption. It made them aware that such choices affected not only the United States but also the rest of the world. Thus, consumption was not a purely private affair but a public one, as the world's fate rested on consumption decisions.

Lappé's theories about food consumption had a particularly radical meaning for women, who were the ones responsible for purchasing most home supplies and performing the bulk of food preparation in the domestic sphere. For generations, mainstream society had belittled such labor as insignificant, claiming it lacked the importance of men's responsibilities outside of the home. Lappé, however, argued that a woman's food-related work was essential not only to her family's health but to the world's. Shopping for groceries and cooking were politically charged activities; this idea reshaped women's domestic roles, giving them new weight both in and out of the home. In many ways, Lappé's ideas were aligned with the tenets of second-wave feminism. She believed that women's work mattered more than society had acknowledged in earlier decades and demonstrated that women's food work had a significant role outside the home. Her encouragement of women (and men) to cook was not a socially conservative function but quite the reverse.

Democratizing Health Food

Like *Diet*, *Laurel's Kitchen* was interested in making Americans rethink their consumption patterns, both in and out of the kitchen. It also was highly successful, selling over 80,000 hardbound copies in two years (Robertson et al. xx). Critics praised it. Writing for the *New York Times Book Review* in

1976, Mimi Sheraton wrote that it was "irresistible" and "original" (94).[17] McFeely describes it as "the Fannie Farmer of vegetarian cooking" (142). It was one of the most popular natural cookbooks of the 1970s and appeared in kitchens across the United States. Having a meal based on *Laurel's Kitchen*'s recipes was a common experience for countless Americans interested in a healthier diet. I remember my mother owned a copy, a standard book that she turned to for breakfast, lunch, and dinner menus. One of the reasons for the book's popularity was that it was decidedly less scientific than Lappé's work. Instead, Robertson presented natural food as something that any woman would want to cook because it was tastier and more interesting. Also, cooking such foods offered women new societal power because they determined their families' well-being; for Robertson, consuming a healthy diet was the foundation to all other activities. She helped spread natural foods to a wider audience by showing that they were essential to *any* person. This book, and other similar works, helped to bring the natural foods movement into the mainstream. As was Lappé's, Robertson's message too was revolutionary: change how Americans ate and what they thought about the world. "The way people eat is closely connected with the way they live," she observed (3). She wished to change how people ate so that they would also reconsider their entire lives and, ultimately, alter them, too.

A combination cookbook and nutritional guide, *Laurel's Kitchen* provides detailed instructions on how to follow a vegetarian lifestyle. The book emphasizes that adopting such a life would have broad-ranging effects. It would make a generation of Americans healthier. It would provide more food for the world's population, relieving famine. It would save the lives of millions of animals. In other words, a vegetarian lifestyle could change the world.

It was not sufficient just to eat vegetarian foods, but people also had to eat nutritionally sound meals, carefully balanced to obtain the correct nutrients and adequate protein. Like Lappé, Robertson paid conscientious attention to nutrition. Her book contains a detailed discussion, but it is not as scientific as the earlier work. Although both books were accessible to a wide readership, Robertson's was even more so, with little scientific jargon. Both included lengthy sections on nutrition since the authors had to justify their food choices because, as mentioned earlier, this was a period when many mainstream Americans assumed that a vegetarian diet was not healthy or could not offer the same benefits as a meat-based one. With their discussions of foods' nutritional values, Lappé and Robertson showed otherwise. They wanted to do more than provide just a list of nutrients; they wished to demonstrate that nutrition was interesting. Cooking could be exciting, if women thought about it: "In the old days, cooking dinner was just a matter of getting something onto the table that people would like. A certain listlessness pervaded the whole affair. Now, though, nutrition is as crucial as appetite appeal. I'm interested in what I'm doing—and boredom is quite out of the picture" (Robertson 45). Robertson tackled a problem confronted by generations of cooks. How does one make the daily chore of cooking into anything other than drudgery? After a while, any cook would grow weary of the day-in-day-out routine. Robertson promised to change this by adding nutrition. If cooks had to think about nutrients, their daily meal planning would gain new interest and possess an intellectual side that it had lacked previously.[18] In this fashion, she gave a fresh impetus to women's home cooking and demonstrated that it played a highly significant role outside the private realm.

Like Lappé, Robertson gave women a central place in redesigning the food system. "Women have a vital role to play in steering our small planet out of its present disaster course," she wrote (43–44). "As never before, the 'gift of life' is [American women's] to give or withhold" (38). They "need to become trustees, not just for our immediate families, but for the entire planet" (39). With famine threatening millions, women's roles as trustees of our food supplies were crucial to human survival. For Robertson, women had to recognize that their decisions about food consumption, and consumption in general, impacted the world. Also, they were responsible for teaching others, including their family members, about careful consumption habits. She was concerned about the culture of consumption that was destroying the United States and the rest of the world, but this lifestyle could change: "It can only take place if women like us will change our own habits and help family members to change theirs. I say 'women' . . . because we are still the ones who decide how most of the money is spent. More important, by example and instruction, we are the ones who influence coming generations most directly" (42). Both Lappé and Robertson raised women's household decisions to a new level of importance, showing they were not isolated in the private sphere but also had a profound impact in the public realm.

Along with recognizing that their domestic choices influenced the planet, women had to acknowledge that their food choices and consumption habits also impacted how their families lived. Women's responsibility was not only to purchase and use healthy foods but also to create a whole new environment of well-being in their homes. Robertson wrote, "Women can bring warmth, self-sufficiency, and interdependence to our homes . . . " (50). One of the key places to bring this warmth was the kitchen, which was described in glowing terms on the back cover of Robertson's book:

> Welcome to Laurel's Kitchen. . . . Sun splashing on wood and crockery, bright colors and green houseplants, the aroma of baking bread and bubbling soups. . . . Cupboards filled with jars of beans, seeds, dried fruits, and chopped nuts. Bins of wheat, rye, and soy flour ready for scooping. . . . Rediscover the joys of your own kitchen, where wholesome meals artfully prepared and lovingly served amid talk and laughter reunite the home.

This cookbook and others conveyed the idea that women did not only have to serve natural foods, but they also had to create the right ambience.[19] Of course, women have a long history of being responsible for the kitchen and home. For generations, they have been accountable for cultivating a nurturing environment for family and friends, so, in many ways, Robertson's words hark back to a long-lasting tradition. Nonetheless, cooking is given a new political significance because the domestic sphere is linked to the rest of the planet—a radical shift with a lasting influence on American culture.

Another way that Robertson and the natural foods movement reconfigured cooking was by suggesting that it could be an interesting, enjoyable occupation for women. She wrote, "The less than thrilling side of homemaking will always be there. But as soon as we take into our own hands some of the tasks we'd previously consigned to machines and manufacturers, our works becomes vastly more gratifying" (45). Her idea of taking charge of food production reverberated throughout the natural foods movement. Women (and sometimes men) took charge of food tasks from growing sprouts to making their own yogurt, discovering the creativity that lay in such activities.

For Robertson and others, the baking of bread was especially significant. Author Jeanne Voltz wrote in her the *Los Angeles Times Natural Foods Cookbook* (1973) about making bread: "In the '50s and '60s the housewife who made a fancy party dish with a conglomeration of . . . packaged foods was regarded with admiration. Since then, there has been a turnabout. The home cook who bakes good honest bread . . . is regarded as the culinary genius of the 70s" (7).[20] Food historian Warren Belasco describes bread's significance: "Baking brown bread nicely balanced the personal and the political—a craft and a statement, a first step toward self-balance. . . . Bread baking was a . . . ritualistic affirmation of membership in a subculture that viewed itself in direct opposition to the plastic death culture" (50). Making a loaf of whole-wheat bread was a powerful symbol of the natural foods movement and its rebellion against the established American food system. For Robertson, baking bread was a sign that a woman wished to control food production and was no longer content that Big Business would always include the healthiest ingredients in a loaf of bread or any other food item. Being in charge of production gave women's domestic responsibilities a new significance by suggesting that such activities were essential to people's health and well-being.

Robertson's ideas about creativity in the kitchen, however, had short-comings. Making a loaf of bread demanded more time than buying one at the grocery store. Thus, such cooking was sometimes limited to middle- and upper-class women. Also, creativity in the kitchen had a disturbing connection to the long-lasting stereotypes that women's place was in the kitchen. Belasco writes, "Feminists debated whether the priority of craft over convenience was sexist, for women did most of the cooking. . . . Cooking without packaged aids and appliances was more work, especially if you were not used to going primitive" (54). Despite the limits of Robertson's views on cooking, she did suggest a new outlet for creative expression in the kitchen and that creativity could impact the world. No longer was someone cooking just for a family but, instead, for the globe.

"Unhulled Rice and Curried Carrots"[21]: A Revolution in the Kitchen

People today might not understand the impact of the natural foods movement. Belasco writes, "It may be hard to see revolutionary significance in the eating of unhulled rice and curried carrots, or granola and yogurt" (27–28). These foods, however, were part of a larger revolution that changed the American diet. Lappé, Robertson, and other writers helped to formulate this culinary transformation, causing many Americans to adopt a new awareness about food that placed it in a larger arena. People had to think not only about how food impacted themselves, but they had to consider how it impacted the global community, a shift that changed Americans' perception about food and, more broadly, the world.

Along with helping to create a new global vision, these natural foods writers demonstrated the significance of women's voices in this international discourse. In previous decades, many considered women's concerns about food to be unimportant or important only within the home; natural foods writers showed that such awareness of food was essential to everyone. Thus, women's kitchen roles took on a new significance, although there was a potentially conservative aspect of situating women again in the kitchen, a place that has been associated with femininity for generations. But one revolutionary aspect of many natural foods cookbooks was their call for women to have a more important role in society while still remaining in the kitchen. It was not sufficient only to bake a good loaf of bread; one also had to adopt an active role in changing one's community and the world.

As well as calling for a change regarding how readers thought about food, natural foods literature wanted them to rethink their relationship with everything that they purchased. Food was part of a larger protest against "the consumer culture of the United States, the homogenization of everything, the promotional packaging, the corporate decisions about how we liked our soup, the assumptions about what a family was and how families lived" (McFeely 139). Lappé, Robertson, and others went beyond the kitchen in their critique; they criticized American society and its value system by suggesting that people needed to rethink their relationship to consumption. Natural foods writers brought into question the American dream based on high consumption and suggested that this dream was, in reality, a nightmare for millions around the world who lived in poverty in order to support the overconsumption of the United States and other industrialized nations.

The impact of the natural foods movement was felt in the United States long after the 1970s. It has changed our society in countless ways. Today even at mainstream grocery stores, one encounters dozens of soy products, from tofu to soymilk. And this is just the beginning. Many stores have organic foods sections, including everything from frozen dinners to fruits and vegetables. The cereal aisle bursts with different varieties of granola, and yogurt has become a staple of the American diet. Restaurants have also changed. Many feature natural foods, and even fast food franchises have jumped on the natural foods bandwagon, with Burger King offering a vegetarian burger. School cafeterias have joined the natural foods movement, too, with many offering vegetarian choices. Natural foods are very much a part of U.S. society.[22] The natural foods movement, however, has not impacted everyone. Many people still have diets that are high in meat and processed foods, changing little despite the recent emphasis on healthy eating. The natural foods movement has altered some diets, but race, ethnicity, class, gender, and geographical region have had an influence, as well. Not everyone can afford to purchase organic foods. Not everyone can have the luxury of sufficient time to prepare such foods. Not everyone will eat natural foods because they still consider them too unusual. Nevertheless, the natural foods movement has influenced and continues to influence millions of Americans.

Chapter 5

"More American than Apple Pie": Modern African-American Cookbooks Fighting White Stereotypes

"African-American cooking is possibly even more American than apple pie," writes Zanne Zakroof, editor at *Gourmet* magazine.[1] Compared to the French roots of the apple pie, African-American food has more "American" roots that reveal as much about U.S. culture as the "all-American" apple pie. To understand the significance of African-American cooking, one needs to turn to the black women who have passed down this culinary tradition.[2] Whether cooking or writing about food, they address a complex network of stereotypes about food, gender, women, and cooking. When black women write about food, they have to consider how their work fits into a long history of African-American culture and its relationship with food and cooking.

Although white mainstream culture stereotypes African-American cooking and cooks in dismissive and degrading ways, there is a more positive side to this culinary tradition. Black women use cooking and cooking literature to build and strengthen their culture. In the process, they subvert mainstream white society's assumptions about blacks and cooking.[3] First, these authors question racist stereotypes about blacks and cooking, including the mammy stereotype. They reveal that this racist image has little in common with the real lives of black women. The writers show how white culture has used this icon to affirm that blacks "naturally" wish to serve whites, a deeply disturbing racist idea that still circulates in U.S. society. Second, the authors use cooking literature to convey cultural and historical facts about African and African-American lives that are commonly left out of mainstream history books. Third, the writers emphasize the importance of community formation, for black women especially, through the medium of cooking literature. Fourth, the writers pass on traditional African and African-American recipes, showing their continued relevance to black culture. The authors also demonstrate, however, that these recipes can evolve, since African-American cooking is a living and changing tradition. In these ways, the writers undermine white stereotypes about blacks and cooking.[4]

This chapter unravels some of black cooking's political elements. As are all art forms, cooking is also political. In her essay, " 'I Yam What I Yam': Cooking, Culture, and Colonialism" (1992), Anne Goldman observes, "Precisely because art—in this case, the art of cooking—is produced . . . within a specific social context, it encodes a political problematic" (171–172). What she suggests is that *all* art forms are influenced and shaped by the cultures that create them; society brings certain assumptions about a work of art and its creator. There is always a political dynamic involved between those who produce art and those who receive it. This dynamic is driven by many different forces, including gender, age, and socioeconomic status. The web of relationships is made yet more complex if cooks or writers of cooking literature are from a different race or ethnicity; here that political dynamic is influenced by a host of stereotypes related to race. This chapter addresses some of these stereotypes about blacks and how African-American authors combat them. Cookbooks become a political venue for blacks to rewrite their experiences. Such books allow black women to take an active role in creating their own identities, an important way for them to gain political and personal identity in a society that often, at least historically, has not allowed them a voice.

A Cultural Fantasy: Mammy and Racist Stereotypes

Among the stereotypes that black women confront, one of the most culturally influential and damaging is the mammy image that no black woman can entirely escape. "[An image] of black women in American culture that has persisted since the early days of slavery is that of the quintessential cook and housekeeper. . . . The Mammy's legendary creativity with preparing foods is attributed to her 'magical' powers with blending just the right foods and spices," historian Alice A. Deck writes (69). This stereotype is one of the most ubiquitous images of black womanhood, and it is particularly troublesome because it suggests that black women (and men) are only too happy to serve whites. Hidden behind the mammy's smile is the ideology that blacks desire to serve whites and do not mind their servile roles. Mammy and Uncle Tom stereotypes continue to linger in the twenty-first century, justifying a service economy where millions of less affluent blacks are still "servants" to middle- and upper-class whites. The stereotype remains common in mass culture that blacks, even today, wish to serve whites, just as their black predecessors did before the Civil War. This assumption works to shore up a culture of racial discrimination, with blacks at the social hierarchy's bottom rung.

The mammy stereotype has its historical roots in slavery, when African-American women typically played important roles as mammies or house servants in the larger plantation houses. They served as liaisons between blacks and whites and as nursemaids to white children. Mammies also performed countless other roles. The black mammy often cooked for the whites.[5] The hardworking mammy was presented as an antithetical figure to the refined white woman, creating a social system where the two could be treated dramatically different because black women were not regarded as fully female or human.[6] Today, it is difficult to uncover the reality of mammies in the South. They frequently lacked writing skills, so they did not write about their experiences. Thus, we are left with secondhand accounts, often by whites. In the 1890s, Annie Laurie Broderick of Mississippi wrote, "We had the greatest love for [our mammy]" (qtd. in Genovese 354). In the same decade, Edward A. Pollard described his mammy as "an aged colored female of the very highest respectability" (qtd. in Genovese 355). Broderick, Pollard, and other whites wrote about mammies, but it is difficult to determine how shaded by nostalgia some of these accounts were. In addition, they were frequently written by Southerners who wished to justify the slave system and the Southern way of life. In such nostalgic accounts, the mammy and her love for her white owners—and their love for her—was a common stereotype that was used to support a whole ideological system.[7]

Scholars interpret mammy and her historical roles in different fashions. In his influential book, *Roll, Jordan, Roll: The World the Slaves Made* (1976), Eugene D. Genovese perceived the mammy as the white woman's "chief executive officer" whose power was never questioned by whites or blacks (355). He described her as a "surrogate mistress—neatly attired, barking orders, conscious of her own dignity, full of self-respect" (356). She was "loyal, faithful, efficient" (356). Rather than perceiving her as a sellout to other blacks, Genovese understood her as trying to ensure her family's safety since mammies and their families were rarely sold. In addition, mammies were allowed access to more food and other resources than slaves who worked in the fields. Unlike Genovese, Deborah Gray White questioned the notion that the mammy performed all of a plantation's domestic work as the "surrogate mistress" (50–53). White argued that Southern plantations had too much work for any one individual, so mistress and slave both had to cook, wash, sew garments, and care for children (52). Other historians in the 1960s and 1970s, influenced by the Black Power movement, interpreted mammy as a closet militant who schemed to overthrow white households from within (Manring 48). Scholars interpret mammy in a gamut of ways, ranging from lackey to her white mistress to black revolutionary.

Although we do not have an adequate record of mammy and her real life on Southern plantations, we have a better cultural record of how she was depicted in popular culture, which transmogrified the historical mammy into something very different. Her popularity "transcended the plantation kitchen and entered the American psyche" (Kern-Foxworth xix). In other words, the mammy of historical reality became the stereotyped media image with which almost every American is familiar from childhood and one that lingers in our collective subconscious. In the second half of the nineteenth century, an image of mammy emerged that connoted many things. In her book, *Slave in a Box: The Strange Career of Aunt Jemima* (1998), M. M. Manring observes, "mammy" became a "shorthand for a set of behaviors used to explain diverse concepts such as slavery, love, service, motherhood" (59). What emerged from the historical reality of plantation life and its mammies was a white cultural fantasy in which the days of slavery were romanticized as superior to the post–slavery era. One aspect of this mythology was the image of the mammy who wanted to help her kind white owners. It was this myth to which the Daughters of the Confederacy referred in 1923 when they tried to make Congress set aside a site in Washington, D.C., to build a memorial to the black plantation mammy (Genovese 353). The Daughters were not interested in praising the black women who had served as mammies. Instead, they wished to keep alive the fantasy of the always help-ful and obedient servant, which was crucial for the Daughters and other

Southerners to perpetuate since they supported the notion that the blacks were better off under slavery.

In the late nineteenth and early twentieth centuries, the image and myth of Mammy permeated popular culture. After the Civil War, such figures were reassuring to whites, suggesting that blacks enjoyed their secondary positions in society and did not mind serving whites, which explains the countless mammy images that filled books, magazines, films, and advertisements.[8] The first mammy was Aunt Chloe (Uncle Tom's wife) from Harriet Beecher Stowe's novel, *Uncle Tom's Cabin* (1852). A heavyset woman with a kerchief tied around her head and a beaming smile, she is a mother to all the plantation's children but always privileges her white charges. Another well-known mammy defends her master's home against invading Union troops in D. W. Griffith's film *The Birth of a Nation* (1915). When soldiers take away her former master, Dr. Cameron, she springs into action, knocking together two black soldiers' heads and beating them up, allowing the Cameron family and their faithful retainers to escape. Other film mammies followed; the most famous was Mammy (Hattie McDaniel) in *Gone With the Wind* (1939), the fierce and protective woman who guards Scarlett O'Hara during the Civil War and the antebellum years. Mammy is almost single-handedly responsible for saving Tara, Scarlett's beloved plantation. Bold and outspoken, she is more than a match for her raven-haired mistress. McDaniel played numerous mammy characters in other films, including *The Gold West* (1932), *The Story of Temple Drake* (1933), *Judge Priest* (1934), and *Alice Adams* (1935).[9] Louise Beavers also played many mammy roles in films, including *She Done Him Wrong* (1933), *Bombshell* (1933), *Wings over Honolulu* (1937), and *Made for Each Other* (1939). Her most famous role was as a cook in *Imitation of Love* (1934); in the movie, she teams up with a white acquaintance to sell pancakes, making both women wealthy. (Ironically, although Beavers was repeatedly portrayed as a cook, she despised cooking, so white chefs prepared the food off screen and then she served it on screen [Bogle 63].)

Along with Mammy, images of Aunt Jemima were also popular. She first appeared at the Columbia Exposition in 1893 when black cook Nancy Green served up pancakes made with a new mix, which has been famous ever since (P. Turner 49). Aunt Jemima was so popular at the fair that afterward she traveled across the United States promoting her pancakes. She was given a make-believe history, becoming a "former slave with a love for the Old South and devotion to the whites she served" (M. Harris 88).

Supposedly, she had been a slave on Colonel Higbee's plantation. After the war ended, she stayed and cooked her famous pancakes for him and his guests. She did not tell anyone her recipe until he died. Then she gave it to the Davis Milling Company, which developed a mix so everyone could enjoy her pancakes (Deck 75). Aunt Jemima became the "ultimate symbol and personification of the black cook, servant, and mammy" (M. Harris 84). Other companies used mammy images to sell their products, including Aunt Dinah molasses, Luzianne coffee, Dinah black enamel, and Fun to Wash laundry soap (P. Turner 51). Mammy images were "imprinted on virtually every possible accessory for the . . . kitchen" (51).[10] Such images assured a white audience that black women "naturally" enjoyed cooking and other household tasks. From this could be extrapolated the idea that all blacks "naturally" enjoyed serving whites, which had roots in the Southern stereotype that slaves loved serving their "benevolent" masters. The real labor was concealed for a reason, as Patricia Yaeger observes in her article, "Edible Labor" (1992); the fantasy camouflaged the grueling hours of black women's work that actually went into cooking for whites (152). Today, when black women cook, they still must address the stereotype that they are "natural" cooks who wish to serve whites.

A number of scholars have written about the mammy stereotype and how it shapes racist ideology. Rafia Zafar describes the black woman cook as "too well inscribed in the collective American unconscious"—a disturbing image that overshadows the labor of countless real black culinary workers, both in the past and today (449). She continues, "Popularly held misconceptions about black cooks haunt, consciously or not, the African-American woman, whether she is a chef or an author" (450). As she observes, this image is both "gastronomic and historical," shading and influencing how others perceive blacks' culinary and historical past (450). In her article about mammy figures in the popular media, Deck points out that these images reassured whites that blacks would remain servants, catering to the needs of whites, and they would do so willingly because they enjoyed their work (69–74). Mammy served as a "spiritual guide" in the kitchen through her depiction on products such as pancake mix (Deck 70). She went home with the white women who bought the items, acting as a culinary helper. She represented the black servant whom few whites could afford at a time when servants were rapidly disappearing from all but the wealthiest white households. Like Deck, Doris Witt links the mammy image to the whites' desire for blacks to serve them. She writes that Aunt Jemima and other mammy figures are "one axis of U.S. desire for African-American women to be the ever-smiling producers of food, to be nurturers . . ." (23). In this fantasy, whites want black women to have no needs of their own but to be all-giving and asexual mothers and caregivers. As Witt mentions, the sexless mammy is possible only because she is linked to a very different image of black womanhood: Sapphire, the sexually promiscuous black woman (24). Thus, Mammy/Sapphire operate together as two influential stereotypes that shape how U.S. society perceives African-American women. Zafar, Deck, and Witt observe that the mammy or Aunt Jemima image has influenced the ways whites interpret black women and cooking. But, as the three argue, this image shapes much more, including general social stereotypes about black women being nurturers and caregivers for whites; far beyond the kitchen, this racist idea has cultural reverberations at every level of society.

Rewriting Mammy, Reclaiming Identity

Given the prevalence of Mammy and Aunt Jemima images, no black woman can ignore this stereotype, especially when she cooks or writes about cooking. How do black culinary authors rewrite Mammy? One strategy they use is to make their books pass on black history and culture, something that Mammy never possessed and something on which her myth depended. Providing information about black lives transforms cookbooks into unofficial history books, which convey lessons that traditional books slight. In addition, black cookbooks also discuss and privilege women's contributions to black history. Again, most textbooks fail to pay adequate attention to females; black cookbooks subvert the traditional historic narrative found in the mainstream United States and rewrite the story so black voices can be heard.

It is not only in recent decades that black cookbook writers have been concerned about passing down historical and cultural facts. Earlier authors also included such information. For example, *The Historical Cookbook of the American Negro* (1958), published by the National Council of Negro Women, combined historical facts about African-American accomplishments with recipes. The book included information about many black women: Biddy Mason, a nineteenth-century philanthropist in Los Angeles; Clara Brown, among the first African-American women to settle in Colorado; Lucy Diggs Slowe, Howard University's first Dean of Women; Susie Ford, a prominent Arkansas educator who devoted a lifetime to educating youth in Little Rock and around the world; Lola M. Parker, who founded Iota Phi Lambda in 1929, an organization of professional women that encouraged high school females to pursue business careers; and other narratives about both famous and lesser-known figures. The authors of *The Historical Cookbook* and other early cookbooks recognized the significance of writing their own history during a time when black concerns, especially those of women, were often ignored. Black cookbooks asserted that women's issues deserved to be heard as much as men's.

In recent decades, African-American cookbooks continue to pass on historical facts about black women and men and their history. For example, *The Black Family Reunion Cookbook* is dedicated to Mary McLeod Bethune, "one of the most significant forces of her era in the emerging struggle for civil rights," and the book is filled with historical facts about her life (*Black* v). The National Council of Negro Women's *The Black Family Dinner Quilt Cookbook* (1994) teaches readers about Malcolm X, Mary McLeod Bethune, Harlem's history, and Langston Hughes. Similarly, Jessica B. Harris's *A Kwanzaa Keepsake: Celebrating the Holiday with New Traditions and Feasts* (1995) includes recipes interspersed with historical accounts of famous blacks, including Thurgood Marshall, Chaka Zulu, Fannie Lou Hamer, Jomo Kenyatta, Frantz Fanon, Julius Nyerere, and John Merrick. Phoebe Bailey's *An African-American Cookbook* (2002) is also filled with historical observations about past African-American lives. She writes, "Most enslaved Africans did not have the opportunity to eat fresh vegetables. . . . If an African were caught eating a piece of fruit from the Massa's orchards, he or she was whipped" (115). The book contains other comments from slaves or former slaves. For example, Solomon Northrup describes the slave's ration of "three-and-a-half pounds of bacon, and corn enough to make a peck of meal. That is all—no tea, coffee, sugar, and, with the exception of a very scanty sprinkling now and then, no salt" (qtd. in 117). Another slave, Charles Ball, describes his meals as "nothing . . . but yams, which were thrown amongst us at random—and of these we had scarcely enough to support life" (qtd. in 24). Harriet Tubman describes slavery as "the next thing to hell" (qtd. in 60). Bailey's book is not solely about cooking, but also about keeping black history alive. As mentioned earlier, in the 1950s Chinese-American women included history lessons in their cookbooks because the experiences of Chinese Americans or Chinese rarely found mention in traditional history books; in a similar fashion, history books leave out African-American experiences or cover them in a cursory manner. It is common at primarily white high schools across the United States to mention black accomplishments very briefly, often only during African-American History month, or reduce them to the achievements of a few famous blacks, such as Harriet Tubman, Sojourner Truth, or George Washington Carver. Rarely is black history covered in the same depth and complexity as white history is. There remains a need for blacks (and all people) to learn about African and African-American accomplishments in places other than the classroom, and cookbooks are one resource to help accomplish this.

Along with providing black cultural and historical facts that show real mammies possess a history, black cookbook authors find other ways to question the mammy stereotype, such as showing how cooking, rather than being solely a way to feed whites, solidifies ties with other blacks, including women. African-American cookbooks privilege female community. Food scholar Sally Bishop Shigley describes a specific African-American cookbook, but her words also apply to others: "In this nexus of recipes and quilts and memories and nutrition sits a reminder that possibility and hope and power lie within the patchwork of mind, body, heart, and head that makes up all women" (124). She observes that cookbooks play a special role in women's lives, remembering their lives and privileging their contributions. She suggests that cooking is more than a way to feed people; it is a way to pass down cultural lessons that might otherwise be forgotten. For black women, cooking plays a vital role in helping their community thrive. As Josephine A. Beoku-Betts notes, African-American women draw strength and support from female-centered networks (536). One of the most central female networks is established in the kitchen, where, for centuries, blacks have gathered. Although the kitchen and domestic work is stereotyped as a place where conservative gender roles thrive, this is not always true. The kitchen gives many minority women, including blacks, a place to build a unique and powerful female community, despite a mainstream society that is often hostile to minorities. "We as a people have for generations communed in the kitchen," Jessica B. Harris observes. "We have for generations gathered around scarred wooden tables shelling peas and picking pieces of meat off a chicken or turkey carcass. . . . We have come together at thousands of wedding banquets, christening feasts, and family reunions. . . . We have danced with friends, mourned lost loves, advised children, and planned protests around kitchen tables" (*A Kwanzaa* 21–22). Cooking has been a means for black women to raise money and to gather women together (Schenone 131). The centrality of food and cooking in black life has allowed women to have a prominence in African-American culture that they lack in other racial and ethnic groups.

Cookbooks specifically emphasize the importance of black women's traditions. The books highlight women's daily lives, which are not included in traditional history books. Black cookbooks show that female experience, including culinary ones, are a part of the black experience.[11] Women's traditions help build African-American society, as Cassandra Hughes Webster observes in *Mother Africa's Table: A Collection of West African and African American Recipes and Cultural Traditions* "Why does Cousin Mae give the family recipe for caramel cake to her co-worker but leave out that one special flavoring or spice? Tradition. Only family members are privy to the complete recipe, passed down from generation to generation. . . . Tradition helps us tell our story . . . It provides a cultural base, as well, that keeps us connected to the past, the present, and future generations" (166). Webster's book is not alone in stressing the importance of women's culinary contributions. The National Council of Negro Women's *The Black Family Reunion Cookbook* (1991) also includes women's culinary memories and traditions. Mayme L. Brown describes the basket dinners that her church served when she was young (3). Susan L. Taylor writes about her grandmother's talent at making black-eyed peas and rice and how local community members would stop by when she prepared this recipe (57). Helen E. Baker describes her first Kwanzaa in Nigeria and how she has celebrated the festival for the last thirteen years (125). Jacqui Gates describes her weakness for chicken wings (123). These cookbooks and others share women's culinary traditions, demonstrating that Cousin Mae's caramel cake recipe and Taylor's grandmother's black-eyed peas and rice are significant. Too often, recipes are downplayed as unimportant to the cultural record, but black cookbooks demonstrate that recipes and culinary issues are essential for understanding black women's lives, African-American culture, and, more generally, U.S. society.

Whether in the form of Cousin Mae's caramel cake or any other recipe, women's cooking has been at black culture's center. Psyche A. William-Forson observes, "Through their culturally sanctioned roles as nurturers and caretakers, African-American women make food a major aspect of the expressive culture of the black community" (188). Cooking has held together generations of families and friends. Ruth L. Gaskins acknowledged this in her book, *Every Good Negro Cook Starts with Two Basic Ingredients: A Good*

Heart and a Light Hand (1968). She wrote that when visiting black friends, she knew that there would always be food and that she was welcome to eat it because "for our family, the pot is always waiting" (viii). She discussed how the kitchen and cooking were essential to developing what she calls "the Negro Welcome," the sense of welcome and comfort in an African-American home (viii). Similarly, in 1978, Norma Jean and Carole Darden wrote in their cookbook, *Spoonbread and Strawberry Wine: Recipes and Reminiscences of a Family,* "Our mother used to tell us that good food inspires good thoughts, good talk, and an atmosphere of happiness and sharing" (xiv). Whether in the 1960s, 1970s, or the present, cooking has unified the black community and demonstrated how women help the culture grow and thrive. Gaskins, Jean, Darden, and others have used their cookbooks to strengthen and energize African-American society—a vital task in a racist world that often ignores the achievements of blacks. By creating a feeling of community, the writers show other African Americans that they are not stigmatized at home but welcomed.

African and African-American Recipes and Cultural Pride

Along with passing on black history and culture and building black women's community, another strategy that cookbook authors use to undermine the mammy stereotype is to include African recipes and describe African cultures, highlighting that slavery brought many African foods to the United States originally; in this fashion, the writers challenge the myth of Mammy happily preparing white dishes for whites. They also question the stereotype that blacks have given nothing to American food traditions. In addition, by writing cookbooks specifically addressed to other blacks and aimed at preserving African and African-American foods and food traditions, authors show that black women cook because they want to nurture blacks, not whites—a radical reworking of Mammy that puts blacks at the center. It is subversive because it suggests that blacks do not "naturally" wish to serve whites but have been forced to do so because of a socioeconomic system that offers few other options.

One way that contemporary black authors challenge the mammy stereotype is by including African and African-influenced international recipes.[12] For example, *The Black Family Reunion Cookbook* includes a number of such recipes: Bahia-style collard greens and okra, *ndiwoa za mandanda* (curried eggs with onions and tomatoes), *moui nagden* (rice and beef stew), and Caribbean meat pie. Angela Shelf Medearis's *Ideas for Entertaining from the African-American Kitchen* (1997) has many recipes for African dishes, such as Kenyan chicken with coconut milk, Ethiopian lentil salad, North African orange salad, and Ghana plantain appetizer. She writes about one menu: "I designed this menu so that your guests will learn a little more about African and African-American history" (35). A typical menu in her book includes recipes for Nigerian roasted pepper chicken, West African–style spinach with okra, and Nigerian-style *munko*; she strives to give her readers a wide survey of Africa's different cultures and their foods, so many recipes include short paragraphs about their origins. Cassandra Hughes Webster's *Mother Africa's Table* (1998) also contains diverse African recipes: *sidio* with *gari* (Ivory Coast), *osu tsinalo* (Ghana), coconut shrimp and rice (West Africa), *moi-moi* (Nigeria), and *bajia* (Kenya). Such African recipes are predominantly written by blacks and for blacks—a different vision from that of Aunt Jemima flipping pancakes for an audience of whites at the World's Fair.

Including African recipes serves two important functions for these cookbooks. First, it preserves traditions that otherwise would have been lost. In slave culture, cooking was one of the few ways that blacks could remember their African past. In her *African Heritage Cookbook* (1971), Helen Mendes observes, "Throughout the history of African Americans, food has provided more than physical sustenance" (11). By remembering African culture, authors teach African Americans about African foods and traditions. For instance, Webster's *Mother Africa's Table* contains brief descriptions of African ceremonies, including the Naming Ceremony, Bone House day, and Watch Night. Cookbooks teach blacks about Africa's rich cultures, traditions, and peoples. Second, including African recipes exposes a common myth about black cooking. In effect, it rewrites the Aunt Jemima myth, which lacks a history connected to slavery or Africa. Mammy was part of a fantasy where master and mistress were always good, and mammy could not wait to serve them. As mentioned, this myth about slavery is troubling because, even today, it functions as ammunition for a racist ideology. Including African recipes shows that a much more covert history hides beneath mammy's smiling face.

African recipes are subversive because they suggest a different food legacy than Aunt Jemima willingly giving up her pancake recipe so more whites could enjoy it. Instead, African recipes point to a culinary tradition that was stolen from blacks, often with little or no reward. Medearis writes, "Many Africans were put to work as cooks, and they deserve much more credit for the ways foods are seasoned and prepared than many cookbooks have given them" (*The African-American* xii). She continues, "My African ancestors are an invisible but strong presence in my kitchen. Part of their legacy to me and to America can be found in a simmering pot of spicy okra gumbo, in a delicious handful of peanuts, in a steaming bowl of black-eyed peas and rice on a cold New Year's Day, and in freshly baked rolls, warm from the oven and covered with sesame seeds" (xiii). Africans' contributions to America's culinary culture are visible in countless ways, but Africans are rarely given credit. Instead, such contributions are overlooked or regarded as the creation of a different racial or ethnic group (such as okra gumbo being identified as Cajun, without acknowledging that okra originally came with the slaves and that slaves influenced this dish and others). When African-American authors include African recipes and discuss how Africa contributed to America's cuisine, the writers show the significance of recognizing those contributions and acknowledging the racist system that ignored them in the past and that frequently continues to do so. Ignoring African foods is part of a much larger racist belief system about how white Americans perceive Africa as "primitive" or uncultured. Including African foods challenges this false assumption.

Along with passing on African recipes, black cookbooks convey traditional African-American recipes, including hopping John, ham hock and red beans, mixed greens, and other recipes that have powerful roles in black culture. Zafar writes, "Each recalled or recreated dish in a community's cuisine signifies mightily, and the multiple readings of a simple dish of rice, greens, and meat reveal past and present worlds in which race and culture define our very taste buds" (450). Thus, African-American dishes are a crucial element of black society and pass down cultural as well as culinary lessons. While African recipes remind blacks of their past before slavery, African-American recipes remind them of their lives in the United States and the role that food has played. In addition, authors use such recipes to fight the dominant white society's perception of African-American foods as worthless because they are stereotyped as lower class, lacking the cultural prestige attached to other ethnic foods.

African-American heritage recipes are frequently simple. In 1993, food writer Joe Crea noted: "[Blacks] started with scraps. Today, the legacy of African-American cooking is a phenomenal array of flavors—from crusty barbecue smoldering with sassy sauce to the wild taste of bitter greens boiled to mellow tenderness with salty-smoky meat to melt-in-mouth yams and buttery-tender pies" (L27).[13] Black women used scraps because they had no other choice. As slaves, although they often were allowed to till and harvest small plots of land for their own personal use and many learned how to fish, trap, or forage off the land for other wild foods, they commonly had to accept the discards or inexpensive foods that whites did not want. For planters, the best financial idea was to feed blacks whatever food was most economical, so cheap and monotonous staples and limited quantities of meat were the norm. After slavery, countless blacks still had to cook with whatever foods were least expensive. Although traditional heritage dishes might have been born out of necessity, they have long helped to unify blacks, so contemporary cookbooks include many. For example, Kathy Starr's *Soul of Southern Cooking* (1989) includes traditional African-American recipes from the Mississippi Delta, such as chicken and shrimp gumbo, fried chicken feet and legs, Delta fried catfish, cabbage and salt pork, and hock bone soup. *The Black Family Reunion Cookbook* includes recipes for buttermilk hush puppies, black-eyed pea soup, okra and tomatoes, and navy beans with pig tails.[14] Bailey's *An African-American Cookbook* contains many traditional recipes: ham and red-eye gravy, chitlins and maw, collard greens with ham hocks, mustard greens and ham hocks, Carolina red rice, fried sweet potatoes, and black-eyed peas. These books and others pass on traditional African-American recipes that form the heart of black society. In addition, as do African recipes, these recipes point to the centrality of a uniquely black food tradition, a tradition that questions the assumption that blacks cook only to nurture whites. By including heritage recipes, the authors demonstrate that Mammy is more interested in cooking for other blacks than whites.

When cookbook authors include traditional African-American foods, they rebel against a white mainstream that stigmatizes such foods. In the United States, people's relationships to food mark them, and this is more visible when people from different racial and ethnic groups prepare and eat foods associated with their race or ethnicity. Mainstream white American eating preferences (a burger and fries, for example) go unnoticed by many Americans because they are judged to be "the norm." But nonmainstream foods are interpreted differently, and the interpretations often convey negative connotations about their consumers. For example, a Chinese woman preparing Chinese food has to contend with the stereotype of Asians being exotic Others, consuming foods that some whites would shun. (A number of my white midwestern university students will not eat at a Chinese restaurant because they fear that they will be fed a cat or dog. When I asked them if they had the same fear about fast food restaurants, none did.) An Indian woman preparing Indian food also has to contend with white stereotypes that Indian food is not palatable because whites are unsure what ingredients compose the different dishes. Indian women have to address stereotypes about their food being mysterious. (Again, many of my students avoid Indian food because they are worried that the meat, vegetable, and starch are not neatly separated. They do not express any concern about eating a casserole.)[15] Chinese and Indian women are not alone in this predicament. Women from other racial and ethnic backgrounds, including blacks, have to consider how their food habits are evaluated by the white American mainstream because those stereotypes influence how people from different backgrounds are perceived, judged, and stereotyped. Rebelling against such stereotypes, disenfranchised minorities strengthen their sense of cultural identity by cooking their native foods (Beoku-Betts 536). Although some whites view ethnic foods with suspicion, the members of a particular minority group interpret such foods differently. For example, blacks' traditional heritage foods help to form a sense of shared identity. Thus, studying such foods reveals how marginalized racial and ethnic groups maintain strong and vibrant culinary cultures, despite a dominant society that might not always be accepting of difference.

While Chinese and Indian people face stereotypes about their foods being "exotic" and "strange," blacks confront the stereotype that their traditional foods are lower class.[16] They lack the cultural capital and prestige of French or Italian foods because African Americans have long been at the bottom rung of the American social hierarchy, and so have their foods. Fried chicken, chitterlings, and other traditional African-American foods do not possess the same societal prestige as traditional French or Italian foods.[17] Black cooks acknowledge this stereotype and point out that African-American foods are judged at this culinary hierarchy's lower rung. Zafar observes, "Black women and their cookbooks come across as less 'high culture' than the popular American guides to French or Italian cuisines" (453). African-American cooks must struggle with this stereotyping since it can subtly—or not so subtly—perpetuate the notion that black people, like their foods, are lower class.

Black cooks rewrite such negative stereotypes. Their "lower-class" foods are a reminder of the economic discrimination that blacks have confronted for generations, so sharing them reminds African Americans of their history. In addition, women use traditional heritage foods to rebel against the negative mainstream stereotypes associated with them. For example, in her essay, " 'Suckin' the Chicken Bone Dry': African-American Women, Fried Chicken and the Power of a National Narrative" (2001), Psyche A. Williams-Forson explores the power of one food, fried chicken, that has been used to stigmatize blacks in the past and present. A famous instance of this occurred when golfer Fuzzy Zoeller made his comment about serving fried chicken "or collard greens or whatever the hell they serve" to Tiger Woods when he won for the first time at the U.S. masters tournament in Georgia (qtd. in Witt 3–4). Although there was a public outcry against Zoeller's remark, it points to a deep-seated racial hostility in the American white mainstream toward blacks and other nonwhite races and their foods.[18] Williams-Forson demonstrates how black women use food as an ideological weapon against racism. She observes, "Black women have manipulated fried chicken to serve as a weapon of resistance in repudiating the negative connotations and denigrating ideologies espoused in the image of 'chicken eating black folks' " (188). Among these women are churchgoers, who take part in rescripting the negative stereotype of "chicken-stealing darkie." In the church, chicken is a celebratory food for women's day, youth day, revivals, and other festive occasions (179). Williams-Forson writes, "African Americans have used fried chicken to symbolize self-definition, self-expression, and celebration" (181). In the process, blacks rewrite white stereotypes about fried chicken on which Zoeller draws. Black women use traditional "lower-class" African-American foods to subvert white stereotypes and reveal that these foods play a crucial part in unifying blacks and have done so for years.

Such traditional black foods also serve as a bridge between African Americans and others who appreciate their food. Heritage recipes, often known as soul food, have long been used as culinary ambassadors, as Mary Jackson and Lelia Wishart demonstrated in their book, *The Integrated Cookbook; or the Soul of Good Cooking* (1971); the book "is meant for everybody. Young blacks who have been away too long from Mother's cooking may revive the old flavors of their ancestors and take pride in their origin. White people may enjoy the unique taste, the tantalizing savor and solid nourishment of the soul dishes. It is our hope that more 'integrated' participation in soul food will lead to a deeper, better understanding for us all" (3).[19]

Like Jackson and Wishart, other authors used their books to provide a bridge of understanding between whites and blacks. In *Soul Food Cookery* (1968), Inez Yeargen Kaiser writes, "It is my hope that this book will help you to develop an appreciation for food that has been prepared and enjoyed for years by minority people, especially Negroes. The recipes may in some way bridge the gap in our society" (n.p.).[20] In the 1960s, 1970s, and more recent decades, traditional African-American food has served to build ties between blacks and other racial groups.

Cookbook writers share traditional African-American recipes to perpetuate a vibrant food culture that has been central to black life and one that continues to thrive. But these recipes can change, as Jessica B. Harris writes in *The Welcome Table: African-American Heritage Cooking* (1996): "My desire . . . is not to preserve African-American heritage cooking in amber as a dead fossil, but rather to press it gently between the pages of the cookbook as a fond remembrance of a living tradition, one that is still growing" (35). Harris and others not only seek to preserve traditional black recipes, but they also wish to show how they change because black culinary culture is living and growing today. Black heritage cooking thrives because its creators are willing to adapt to new influences, while not forgetting its historical roots.

Cookbooks are not static; they evolve with the times, reflecting larger culinary and cultural changes in society. Black cookbook authors, for instance, have become more aware about how the African-American diet needs to adjust to new food trends, including the emphasis on healthy eating. Now contemporary cookbooks include numerous recipes that reflect the national trend toward healthier eating. *The Black Family Reunion Cookbook* includes recipes for oat bran muffins, bran muffins, and vegetarian black-eyed peas and rice. In the National Council of Negro Women's *Black Family Dinner Quilt Cookbook* (1994), Geneva's quick gumbo contains boneless skinned chicken and turkey sausage; creamy macaroni-and-cheese uses skimmed milk and nonfat sour cream; Melba's collard greens includes smoked turkey wings and no sausage; hot and spicy black-eyed peas includes turkey ham; and many of the recipes include low-fat ingredients. Angela Shelf Medearis's *Ideas for Entertaining from the African-American Kitchen* (1997) contains healthy recipes for updated versions of traditional recipes, including porkless mixed greens and macaroni salad with feta. Similarly, Ruby Banks-Payne's book, *Ruby's Low-Fat Soul Food Cookbook* (1996), includes recipes low in fat, sugar, and salt, so that "[blacks] can truly nourish our souls with a rich culinary history while also nourishing our bodies with healthful and delicious foods" (xii). Black women use their culinary authority to suggest that blacks need to alter their diet, with its traditional emphasis on foods high in cholesterol and fat. This is a significant move when much of America, including blacks, is confronting skyrocketing rates of obesity. Changing the traditional African-American diet is imperative, especially because blacks are still more likely than other ethnic minorities to eat poor-quality food and have a variety of health problems, ranging from diabetes to high blood pressure, due to their diet (Basiotis, Lino, and Anand 61).[21] Blacks, especially from urban areas, are also more likely than other ethnic groups to patronize fast food restaurants (Raloff 381). When authors of cookbooks include healthy foods, they play a part in changing the negative components of African Americans' relationship to food.

Another way that black cookbooks stress the need for change and adaptability is by including recipes that are not traditionally black. This is not a recent phenomenon, as a number of earlier African-American cookbooks included dishes from different nationalities, demonstrating that black cooking was not composed solely of Southern or black heritage recipes but had a variety of culinary influences. For example, Bertha L. Turner's *Federation Cook Book: A Collection of Tested Recipes Contributed by the Colored Women of the State of California* (1910) included recipes for oyster bisque, coquilles of sweetbread, fish timbales, lobster cutlets, and Boston steak.[22] In her book *A Date with a Dish: A Cook Book of American Negro Recipes* (1948), Freda De Knight wrote, "Like other Americans living in various sections of the country [blacks] have naturally shown a desire to branch out in all directions and become versatile in the preparation of any dish, whether it be Spanish in origin, Italian, French, Balinese, or East Indian" (xiii). The book contained recipes, including tamale pie, New England fried clams, Boston baked beans, and Yorkshire pudding, from a number of culinary traditions. It also included recipes for elegant dishes, such as asparagus on toast, lobster and shrimp Newburg, cocktail oysters, and filet mignon with chicken livers. Similarly, the National Council of Negro Women's *Historical Cookbook of the American Negro* (1958) incorporated varied recipes, including lobster in curry sauce, codfish and potato casserole, pistachio parfait, Middle East–style stuffed chicken, and wilted Pennsylvania Dutch salad.

This same cultural mingling appears in contemporary books as well. For example, *The Black Family Dinner Quilt Cookbook* includes recipes of many different cultures: honey Mandarin chicken toss, chicken veggie pasta, classic lasagna, pizza garden style, and ground beef tostadas. Phoebe Bailey's *An African-American Cookbook* includes an especially eclectic group of recipes: sweet and sour chicken, chicken parmesan, Grecian lamb, Indian meatloaf, risotto with spring vegetables, linguini with asparagus, pasta Mexican, Chinese beef with broccoli, and baked lasagna. Some might interpret the inclusion of these recipes in a negative light: namely, as African Americans being forced to cater to a nonblack audience. However, these recipes, whether in De Knight's early work or more contemporary ones, have a more subversive role. Black women know all too well how mainstream white culture stereotypes them in derogatory and racist ways due to their traditional food preferences. Stereotypes, such as the watermelon-loving or chicken-stealing black, are used in popular culture to support an ideology that blacks are "simple" and content with their lives, just as long as they have the foods that they love. Thus, by including a wide range of dishes from different ethnic and racial backgrounds, cookbook authors demonstrate that black culinary culture is not circumscribed by watermelon, fried chicken, and chitterlings alone. These traditional foods are highly significant, but so are other foods, including those that are not commonly identified as African American. Like any other racial group, blacks cook and eat a wide range of foods, including lobster in curry sauce, sweet and sour chicken, and ground beef tostadas. Too often, society believes that minorities consume just their heritage foods (e.g., Chinese people eat Chinese food). Black cookbooks challenge this racist assumption.

The Kitchen: From Slavery to Social Change

As we have discovered, African-American cookbooks perform many roles both in and out of the kitchen, including questioning racist stereotypes about black culture and cooking. The authors address these questions and show how they function to subordinate blacks, especially women, in white society. Among the most influential stereotypes is the one of mammy as the nurturer and caregiver for whites who even disregards fellow blacks because of the desire to help whites. African-American authors rewrite Mammy by depicting blacks as cooking for other blacks, not whites. Through the inclusion of traditional African and African-American recipes, black cookbook writers subvert the mammy image of someone who cooks whatever whites wish, just as the mythical Aunt Jemima originally prepared the white colonel's favorite pancakes. Black cookbooks decenter the image of mammy caring for whites. This stereotype needs to be challenged because it still lingers in America's popular imagination; for generations, this icon has served as a justification for black service to whites. Mammy (and her male counterpart) enjoys her work, so she should be allowed to do it without whites feeling guilty about their privilege. Her shadow darkens mainstream society, where many blacks remain trapped in poorly paid and low-status service jobs while whites are the ones served.

One way that cookbooks undermine Mammy is by showing that she (and all blacks), has a historical past. By being a respository of African and African-American recipes as well as cultural and historical facts, cookbooks refute the notion that blacks have no culture or have one that is less significant than that of whites. This pervasive and long-lasting stereotype has been used by whites to justify the inferior social position of blacks, both in the past and today. As well, blacks recognize that mainstream white society has neglected to record African-American history, so they need to tell their own histories and stories. Cookbooks pass on lessons, demonstrating that blacks have a culture that is as rich and complex as that of any other racial or ethnic group.

In addition, the cookbooks rewrite stereotypes that are associated with many African-American foods. They are at the white culinary hierarchy's bottom rung in terms of social class, and this is connected to the low socioeconomic place of blacks, too. In the United States, the low status of black foods is intermingled with other assumptions about the presumed inferiority of African Americans. Black cookbooks challenge the stereotype that traditional black foods are lower class by representing a diversity of foods from various cultures as "at home" in an African-American cookbook. In addition, authors privilege supposedly "lower-class" African-American foods and show that they have played, and continue to play, an essential role in building black community. The art of preparing and eating such traditional foods develops a sense of shared identity for African Americans today.

Finally, African-American cookbooks question the image of black women always cooking for whites, not blacks. On the contrary, black cookbooks celebrate the role that black women play in building and perpetuating a feeling of community for African Americans, which is crucial to their survival in a mainstream society that is frequently deeply racist. The kitchen table and the rituals of eating have long been central to black culture. Even when blacks possessed little in terms of economic or social status, they counted on the kitchen's pleasures to bring them together as a people. This space became a vital area where blacks could draw emotional, physical, and spiritual sustenance. It was also a place where women could do more than just cook; they could ferment rebellion, including during the Civil Rights movement, when many black activists were women. Whether during the antebellum period, the Civil Rights movement, or today, black women used and continue to use the kitchen to agitate for social change and build a strong community. Although some black women have, no doubt, felt confined by their culinary roles, others have used the kitchen to shape and alter American society.

Chapter 6

"You Can't Get Trashier"[1]:
White Trash Cookbooks and
Social Class

We have created an American dumping ground. Americans use the terms "rednecks," "trailer-park trash," "white trash" and others to create a semantic repository of the collective "unfortunate." Through such branding, anything and everything can be blamed on these people who are stereotyped as being on the social ladder's lowest rung. They are disparaged as dumb and ignorant, allowing different socioeconomic groups to feel securely distant and insulated. Making fun of white trash helps other groups assume that, despite any problems that they face, they are not as low as white trash or trailer-park trash. The popular media frequently disparages this underclass, too. Writing for the *New York Times Magazine* in 1994, Lloyd Van Brunt observed that poor whites are "the one group everybody feels free to belittle, knowing that no politically correct boundaries will be violated" (38).[2] Since white trash are commonly looked down upon in U.S. society, it is acceptable to make jokes about them in ways that are not acceptable while joking about African Americans, Latinos, Asian Americans, and other minorities. White Americans may make jokes about these other groups, but the humor is generally concealed; people rarely try to camouflage jokes about white trash or hillbillies. What is the difference? Why is it that white trash are ridiculed openly? One reason for this attitude is that poor whites have become convenient scapegoats for any dissatisfaction. Few people question society's attitudes toward white trash because of the assumption that this group is genetically and socially inferior, which makes their position at the social ladder's bottom rung only "natural."

Although they are frequently the butt of racist humor, people who are considered white trash have found ways to fight back, using humor to gain a voice in a middle-class society that either ignores them or condemns them. In the last twenty years, being "white trash" has lost some of its stigma, because many popular film stars, authors, and other media celebrities have stated that they are proud of their redneck/white trash roots.[3] Often these individuals have used humor in their work to teach others about what it means to be lower class and white in the United States. For example, in her novel *Bastard Out of Carolina* (1992), Dorothy Allison effectively uses humor to convey the painful experiences faced by the poor white trash main character, Bone. Cookbook authors have also used humor to convey white trash experiences. They have discussed white trash food with pride, not disdain. They have had an impact on U.S. cooking culture, showing that white trash food deserves to be embraced because it is as much a part of America's cooking past as any food tradition. More broadly, these authors have conveyed what it means to be poor and white in a society that regards this as the worst affront to the American dream. Focusing on Ernest Matthew Mickler's *White Trash Cooking* (1986) and Ruby Ann Boxcar's *Ruby Ann's Down Home Trailer Park Cookbook* (2002), this chapter explores how these books and their sequels use humor in a transgressive way to help explain what it means to be white trash in America. Like Allison, Mickler and Boxcar use humor to convey a darker image of being poor and white today. Although Mickler is a man, I include his books since his recipes came predominantly from women, and their contributions should be acknowledged.

Before going on to discuss white trash culture, we should first define "white trash," since it is an especially malleable term. Some consider "white trash" and "redneck" to be identical, while others draw distinctions (Bledsoe 69). According to two southern researchers, "redneck and white trash are synonymous terms," except when the label "white trash or trash is reserved for the more disreputable, irregularly employed, allegedly immoral and lazy" (Roebuck and Hickson 2). In other words, "redneck" and "white trash" both describe the bottom stratum of poor whites, especially those living in the South or rural regions. But "white trash" is more than just a term for poor whites, as Annalee Newitz and Matt Wray point out in their book, *White Trash: Race and Class in America* (1997): "It refers to actually existing white people living in (often rural) poverty, while at the same time it designates a set of stereotypes and myths related to the social behaviors, intelligence, prejudices, and gender roles of poor whites" (7). Thus, white trash refers to a complex range of stereotypes and myths about what it means to be poor and white—a taboo combination in the United States. "White trash" and "redneck" are used to indicate whites who have not succeeded economically and remain at society's bottom, so "white trash" remains a vitriolic term because it links whites with poverty:

> Americans love to hate the poor. Lately, it seems there is no group of poor folks they like to hate more than white trash. . . . In a country so steeped in the myth of classlessness, in a culture where we are often at a loss to explain or understand poverty, the white trash stereotype serves as a useful way of blaming the poor for being poor. The term white trash helps solidify for the middle and upper classes a sense of cultural and intellectual superiority. (Newitz and Wray 1)

As Newitz and Wray observe, Americans hate the poor because it is a way to justify a cultural and economic system that is crucial to maintain the more elevated status of the middle and upper class. This hatred is also a way to justify the feeling of the elites that their position is "natural" because they are "naturally" superior to the poor.

In addition, the American upper and middle classes hate poor whites, as well as other groups lower on the socioeconomic ladder, because such distinctions are essential to perpetuating society and the hierarchy on which it is built. All cultures depend on differentiating between the high and low, as Peter Stallybrass and Allon White suggest in their book, *The Politics and Poetics of Transgression* (1986): "The human body, psychic forms, geographical space, and the social formation are all constructed within interrelating and dependent hierarchies of high and low" (2). Human society is based on a multitude of interconnected hierarchies that structure every element of culture, from human bodies to different geographical regions. The differentiation between high and low is "dependent upon disgust. The division of the social into high and low, the polite and the vulgar, simultaneously maps out divisions between the civilized and the grotesque body" (191). In other words, groups use disgust as one way to separate themselves from those lower on the ladder. Such a physical and emotional reaction serves as "proof" for why the others deserve their low status. Stallybrass and White show a key reason why upper- and middle-class Americans hate poor whites and disparage them openly as vulgar and not civilized: doing so justifies the privilege of the higher socioeconomic groups.[4] More broadly, hating the poor is a means by which elites establish themselves as "civilized" and white trash as "not civilized," a divide that helps to form the structure of American society.

Despite its deeply negative associations, white trash also possesses positive connotations. In the 1980s and 1990s, the media created a new image of white trash, and being white trash was suddenly all the rage. Musicians, actors, authors, comedians, and other celebrities wanted to flaunt their white trash roots, the same ones they had been careful to conceal in earlier years. If they did not have those roots, they invented them. No matter how blue-blooded their background actually was, people could buy white trash fashions. Everyone wanted to appear as though she or he came from the "wrong side of the tracks." Looking, dressing, talking, and acting like white trash was hip. Why were poor whites thrust into the media spotlight? Kathleen McDonald views the media attention negatively. "The American culture industry perpetuates the fascination with white trash. . . . The one-dimensional nature of most cultural representations of white trash allows consumers to overlook the painful aspects of poverty" (17–18).[5] Although she acknowledges one side of the popular media's depiction of poor whites, it is also equally important to recognize the other. White trash authors, television actors, and celebrities use comedy in a subversive way to convey what it means to be poor and white.

With white trash's growing popularity over the last two decades, it has gained a new meaning that it lacked in earlier years. White trash has become a transgressive term to refer to white bodies that fail to conform to upper- or middle-class norms. In his essay, "Unpopular Culture: The Case of 'White Trash,' " (1997), John Hartigan, Jr., writes, " 'White trash' is used to name those bodies that exceed the class and racial etiquettes required of whites if they are to preserve the powers and privileges that accrue to them as members of the dominant racial order in this country" (320). He continues, "It is possible to read images of 'white trash' as a carnivalesque aesthetic, a transgressive celebration of the 'grotesque' body . . . that will not be restrained by the constraints of (white) middle-class social decorum" (326). In other words, it is possible to interpret white trash as a positive and transgressive term that writes poor white bodies into being, so some have embraced it. "[White trash] is passing very rapidly from an unambiguously derogatory label to a transgressive sign under which certain whites are claiming a public speaking position" (Hartigan 317). Claiming a speaking voice is vital for white trash individuals because, for generations, the mainstream has ignored them and assumed that they had nothing to express about their lives or lacked the intelligence to speak. Thus, claiming a voice helps white trash to adopt an active role in shaping how people understand them and enables them to rebel against a culture in which others have spoken for poor whites.

If we are to understand how class, gender, ethnicity, and race function in the United States, one starting point would be to understand what it means to be white trash, a term that combines poverty and whiteness. To determine how whiteness is constituted in American society, we need to consider how being poor influences it.[6] Newitz and Wray observe, "White trash is 'good to think with' when it comes to issues of race and class in the U.S. because the term foregrounds whiteness and working-class or underclass poverty, two social attributes that usually stand far apart in the minds of many Americans" (4). In other words, most Americans find it difficult to link whiteness and poverty because doing so brings up the disturbing notion that whites are not superior to other races. Thinking about white trash makes it clear that not all whites "naturally" move to America's socioeconomic top.

It is also important to consider what constitutes white trash because it helps to make whiteness visible, which is vital in a culture where whiteness is regarded as the "norm," and thus invisible. Wray and Newitz write, "The invisibility of whiteness is an enabling condition for both white supremacy/ privilege and race-based prejudice. Making whiteness visible to whites— exposing the discourses, the social and cultural practices, and the material conditions that cloak whiteness and hide its dominating effects—is a necessary part of any anti-racist project" (3–4).[7] When discussing racism, mainstream society primarily considers conflicts between different races, such as black and white or Asian American and white. Whites find it disturbing to recognize that racism can be as intense when it is between whites as between people with different racial backgrounds. To understand how whiteness and its different variations are constructed in America, one has to start with white trash, who highlight the hatred felt between different white groups. The modern hatred of white trash, however, cannot be understood without recognizing that the United States has had a long tradition of hating lower-class group. Only if we understand this history can we recognize that hating the poor has been an essential feature of America's past since the nation's beginnings.

"Little Better than Animals"[8]: White Trash Stereotypes in the Past

To understand society's modern hatred of white trash, one has to go back in American history, since this antipathy has roots that have existed for centuries. "Poor whites have been seen as one of America's groups of 'savages' for a long time" (Thomas and Enders 37). Wherever poor whites lived, more affluent whites tried to distinguish themselves by using racist stereotypes. One place this happened was the South, where poor whites were segregated as "hillbillies." This stereotype has been used for centuries in literature and real life to distinguish the poor from the wealthy. "Whether as lubber, cracker, po buckra, redneck, hillbilly, or white trash, the Southern poor white character has been a popular literary figure at least as far back as the eighteenth century" (K. McDonald 15–16).[9] Such stereotypes flourished in the South and helped support and strengthen a sharply stratified white socioeconomic system.[10] Today, no matter what term is used, the hillbilly or white trash stereotype persists in the South despite the national acceptance of diversity (Foster and Hummel 157). The image of a hillbilly is as "recognizable as the Colonel Sanders and Mickey Mouse icons" (Foster and Hummel 159).[11] We take the hillbilly or redneck stereotype for granted, seldom stopping to think about how it would hurt those being referred to, imposing "psychic and material costs . . . beyond being the brunt of jokes or humor" (Foster and Hummel 170). This image of the ignorant Southern hillbilly or redneck continues to shape American perceptions of the South and its inhabitants. The assumption is widespread that anyone from a rural southern region is a hillbilly.

In earlier centuries, it was not only the poor Southern whites who were labeled as white trash, but also many poor whites from the West, Southwest, Midwest, and New England. The expressions used to describe poor whites might have varied, but what did not alter was the antipathy felt by others toward the poor. One reason that the white mainstream despised white trash was because they looked like other whites, raising the horrifying idea, at least to the white elites, of a world turned topsy-turvy. To separate the haves from the have-nots, an entire science, eugenics, developed. It was based on demonstrating that white trash were not identical to other whites, but were as much a distinct, separate group as blacks, Latinos, or Chinese. Their speech patterns, living environments, and genes marked them as poor whites. Nineteenth- and early twentieth-century scientists labored to separate and distinguish the poor from other whites, reassuring elites that the chasm between themselves and white trash was a deep one that could never be transgressed because the poor lacked the mental, physical, and emotional capabilities.

Scientists used "genetic inferiority" as a convenient ploy to explain the disturbing presence of whites at the bottom rung of the social ladder.[12] Social scientists throughout the country sought the reasons for entrenched pockets of poverty among whites from the West Coast to the East. Typical of the "scientific" accounts influenced by eugenics was Florence H. Danielson and Charles B. Davenport's account, "The Hill Folk: A Report on a Rural Community of Hereditary Defectives" (1912). The authors reported about Neil Rasp's progeny, who lived in a small rural Massachusetts village. They dwelled on the "Hill"; most of "their wages go for hard cider, or, if handed to the wives, are spent in other equally foolish ways. They move frequently from one shanty or tumbled down house to another. So long as food and shelter are furnished by some means, they live in bovine contentment" (87). Rasp's descendants were charged with arson, incest, adultery, rape, perjury, murder, assault, and other crimes (103). Although such accounts could describe every region of the country, it was more common that they focused on the South or regions close to the South, such as rural Ohio. For example, Mary Storer Kostir's essay "The Family of Sam Sixty" (1916) described a typical no-account white trash family, Sam Sixty and his family members, who lived in rundown hovels in the "river hills of Ohio" (185). Over generations, members of the family were constantly charged with different offenses, including "burglary, larceny, destruction of property, bootlegging, operating houses of ill-fame, intoxication, riot, perjury, incest, rape, homicide, shooting to kill, and attempting to poison" (189). Discussing Sam and Pearl Sixty, Kostir wrote, "Such *physically vigorous but mentally feeble persons* are a social menace today. . . . Their children threaten to overwhelm *the civilization of the future*" (208). Yet another account was Mina A. Sessions's essay "The Feeble-Minded in a Rural County of Ohio" (1918), which was first published by Ohio's Bureau of Juvenile Research. She described the

poor living in the "hills of southeastern Ohio" (253). One family she
discussed at great length was the Hickories, who lived "in one of those isolated townships, cut off in almost Himalayan fashion by 'inaccessible
ridges' " (254). She observed that the family took "pre-eminence because of
the fecundity of its members, the anti-social nature of their habits and mode
of living, their utter dependency, and the large amount of inbreeding that
promises to perpetuate the defective traits" (288). She was especially critical
of the women, describing them as "little better than animals" (292). These
three essays were typical of the pseudo-scientific research published in the
late nineteenth and early twentieth centuries that eugenicists used to suggest
that poor whites, due to their high levels of imbecility and presumed
prolific inbreeding, should be forcibly sterilized to protect "the human gene
pool" (Bledsoe 71).

These attitudes existed even in reputable scholarly journals. Writing
in 1919 for *The New Orleans Medical and Surgical Journal,* a Louisiana
physician was adamant about sterilization for the insane, noting they "were
permitted to marry among themselves; these morons, these imbeciles, these
maniacs, are procreating their kind. . . . No crystallized public opinion [pro-
hibits] such unclean unions" (Carruth 184–185). The "insane" were taken
largely from the ranks of poor whites and people from races other than
white. To control their breeding, the doctor argued for passing strict laws.
Similarly, in the 1930s an Atlanta physician, W. L. Funkhouser, wrote an
article titled "Human Rubbish" for the *Journal of the Medical Association of
Georgia* that was about the high societal cost of taking care of Southern
white trash or "rubbish"—"the product of the physical and mental unfit"—
and provided a solution: "Sterilize all individuals who are not physically,
mentally, or emotionally capable of reproducing normal offspring" (199).
He had a sweeping definition of who was "feebleminded," estimating that
15 percent of the American population, more than eighteen million people,
should be included (197). Such attitudes were common among even upper-
and middle-class whites, including physicians and other medical profes-
sionals, who assumed that poor whites were subhuman and did not possess
"normal" moral reasoning skills. In order to understand how American
society perceives poor whites today, it is necessary to recognize these earlier
attitudes and their lasting influence.

These pseudoscientific ideas still haunt our society. Poor whites make
mainstream society uneasy because they are white, yet are at the bottom of
the social hierarchy, which is deeply disturbing because U.S. society is based

on the supposed superiority of whiteness and white individuals. At the top of the ladder are whites, with other races and ethnicities ranked below and with blacks at the bottom. Below even the blacks are white trash, which raises the disturbing idea that whites do not "naturally" belong at the top, and that they could slip at any time, a profoundly troubling notion and a major reason that white trash receive so much disdain. One way to address the anxiety that white trash evoke in upper- and middle-class people is by suggesting that they belong to a genetically inferior group. As shown, generations of whites have argued that the South's poor whites are genetically inbred, making it impossible to judge them by the same standards as other whites. Thus, white trash remain at society's bottom rung because they are not "real" whites. This argument reassures upper- and middle-class whites because they understand that a genetic difference exists between themselves and the white trash, so whites at the top do not need to worry about helping poor whites, who are "naturally" where they should be.

The American Dream and White Trash Humor

White trash also make upper- and middle-class people uneasy because the poor suggest to them that the United States is not a classless society, a fiction that many like to believe. Americans wish to assume this because it keeps alive a myth that is central to the U.S. ethos: the American dream. According to this ideology, any person can succeed in America, as long as she or he possesses sufficient willpower and determination. The American dream is based on a notion of a classless democracy where everyone, no matter his or her socioeconomic, racial, or ethnic background, can succeed. White trash show that this is not true, since, for generations, they have not achieved the American dream, remaining stubbornly at the bottom of the American hierarchy.

A period when the American dream seemed achievable by any (white) person with enough grit and determination was during the go-go years of the 1980s and 1990s. During these decades, when it appeared as though computers and technology were going to solve all social problems, many Americans' wealth soared. Suddenly it seemed as though upper-middle and middle-class people had a chance to grow enormously wealthy. Bill Gates and Steve Jobs were two examples of the new ultrawealthy, but numerous others existed. It seemed that anyone who had enough gumption and grit could form a dot-com and end up a millionaire, and the media was filled with such technological success stories. But the truth is that millions did not succeed. The 1980s and 1990s brought prosperity to some, but others, lacking the technological acumen to make their way in a dot-com universe, sank further in debt. During this period, it was not surprising that white trash humor gained media attention. Less fortunate whites used it to express their anger against a society where they were never taught the skills to succeed, at least at the level of Bill Gates. Paradoxically, white trash humor lulled middle-class whites into thinking, "Well, it could be worse." Humor offered a way for the middle class to separate themselves from the bottom and distance themselves from it, so they had less time to recognize the bleak fact that they were as economically distant from the ultrawealthy as poor whites were from them; actually, the gap was greater.

As mentioned, although it seemed as though anyone could reach the American dream, in reality, it was a period when poor and uneducated whites were hurtling ever farther away from that dream. In these years, white trash/redneck/trailer trash humor was widespread; television shows and movies commonly used white trash or redneck jokes, and the redneck or poor white character appeared frequently in comic skits. What explains the prevalence of such humor and its popularity when other forms of racist humor have died out or at least lost their acceptability? One reason white trash humor survives is because our society needs a scapegoat. White trash play that role, allowing other Americans to blame their problems on them.

By depicting white trash as ignorant, sexist, and uneducated, racist humor depicts them as deserving to be treated as inferior. Although some white trash individuals are in fact racist, sexist, and uneducated, it is disturbing that society stereotypes *all* members of this group as sharing the same traits. Be it about blacks, Latinos, Asians, or rednecks, all racist humor operates in a similar fashion, portraying every member of a particular group as possessing the same denigrated features. People who are made the butt of racist humor, however, find ways to use humor to fight oppression. For example, white trash use humor that relies on society's jokes and stereotypes about white trash, but also show that such stereotypes do not convey the whole truth about their lives. When different races and ethnicities use humor, they transform something that can be belittling into something potentially empowering. Poor whites have discovered that humor can be used to question society's stereotypes about them. For example, the humor used in white trash cookbooks helps writers share their experiences with a wider audience, and under the humor, serious messages about class inequity are conveyed.

For centuries, poor and working-class people have used humor to give voice to their experiences; this was especially important because in many societies they were seldom heard. In medieval times, humor was viewed positively as a way for all of society's members, from the highest to the lowest, to let off steam. Sense went hand in hand with nonsense. In the nineteenth century, this changed; reason was highlighted, and folly "lost all the positive connotations it had had in medieval culture" (Palmer 127). As comedy grew more marginalized, modern society gained a new relationship to humor: "Civil polite manners dictate[d] a certain decorum which exclude[d] those forms of humor or mirth creation which come to be regarded as vulgar" (129). In this environment, vulgar or bawdy humor became increasingly associated with the lower classes, who used it to express a sensibility different from more elite classes. Whether in the Middle Ages, the nineteenth century, or today, humor expresses a working-class sensibility that frequently is at odds with upper- or middle-class standards of behavior. Often bawdy or slapstick, humor is used to express working-class lives that might not be articulated in other ways. In addition, humor gives a voice to experiences that, if not laughed about, might erupt in anger. Humor provides an outlet for working-class rage.

In the last few decades, white trash humor has done exactly this. At a time when many working-class people, especially those living in the South, recognized that they were not going to benefit from the affluence of the 1980s and 1990s, poor Southerners (and other poor people) needed a way to verbalize their resentment about being overlooked. They needed to express the anger they felt about being social pariahs in America. Poor whites found an outlet in white trash humor, whether through a white trash cookbook or Roseanne Barr's blue-collar humor on her popular television show, *Roseanne*. Popular culture offered "a 'licensed space' for the expression of working-class humor" (Arthurs 140). One reason for this might have been that white trash was simply the next trend that existed for the media to exploit; however, white trash's popularity also stemmed from the fact that the humor expressed the feelings of America's working class. Although the media would not have been receptive to open rebellion, they were open to humor. It became a way to discuss blue-collar issues, which found a voice by being concealed as comedy. Beneath this façade, however, lie serious, concealed issues.

Whiskey Pie, Fried Okra, and Baloney Roll-ups

White trash humor appeared in novels, short stories, and cookbooks. One cookbook that used humor to convey what it meant to be poor and white was Mickler's *White Trash Cooking*, which, when originally published in 1986, was an instant hit from California to New York. A writer for the *New York Times* observed, "Although an unlikely candidate for success, except perhaps in the Deep South, it is currently one of the fastest-selling books on either side of the Mason-Dixon line" (McDowell 11).[13] This was ironic because many publishers had refused to publish the work unless the author changed its title to something "innocuous" like *Poor Southern Cooking*, but he refused and found a publisher that was willing to publish the book with its original title (McDowell 11). Mickler's book was a success with a wide audience, and critics praised it. Bryan Miller observed in the *New York Times* that it "was the most intriguing book of the 1986 spring cookbook season" (BR13). He continued, "Even if you rarely make Four-Can-Deep Tuna Pie (except perhaps after a Legion Hall sing-along) this book is a delight to peruse. It is one of the few unvarnished regional cookbooks around" (BR13). Readers were equally enthusiastic, and Mickler's book became a best-seller, selling over 350,000 copies by 1988 (Anderson 8). By 2002, it had sold 500,000 copies ("Puttin' " 73).[14] Featuring "down-home recipes, part loving re-creations of family heirlooms, part tongue-in-cheek inventions," it was a tremendous success because it was one of the first books that stated that all of America's cooking traditions, including those of poor whites, needed to be remembered (Anderson 8). Mickler also created a space for poor white voices, especially women's, to be heard. Radically, he suggested that white trash culture, including its cooking, should be embraced and not shunned. American society would never be the same again.

The impact of Mickler's book was dramatic. Food writer Mason Lemuir observed, "When the first *White Trash Cooking* appeared, it kind of marked the moment that American cooking lost its snobbery and started to embrace the vast traditions that were out there just waiting to be discovered" (qtd. in

"Puttin' " 73). This was the first cookbook to praise the culinary contributions of white trash and suggest that they were as vital as the contributions of other American cultural groups. In this fashion, Mickler used his cookbooks to demonstrate how poor Southern whites have positively influenced America's cooking culture, a revolutionary notion in a middle- and upper-class society that always ignored entirely or disregarded poor whites' contributions as trivial and insignificant. More broadly, Mickler's book implied that other "lower-class" traditions might be as important as upper-class ones. This challenged generations of American thinking about which groups should be regarded as positive contributors to America and which should be ignored and forgotten.

Mickler also revealed the significance of women's contributions to white trash cooking, and many of his recipes feature women's names. For example, he includes Edna Rae's smothered potatoes, Mammy's mashed potatoes, Betty Sue's fried okra, Mary Beth Boney's collard greens, Brenda's black bean soup, Dana Pullen's chicken feet and rice, Loretta's chicken delight, Aunt Donnah's roast possum, Aunt Cora's coleslaw, and Retha's Ritz pie. His *Sinkin Spells, Hot Flashes, Fits, and Cravings* (1988) includes recipes such as Aunt Sarah's stepped-on corn bread, Marlene's honey pumpkin pie, Aunt Bimmie's meat and beans, Chestine Butler's meatloaf, Lucille Collins's whiskey pie, Aunt Calliope's mixed-up beans, Big Molly's cracker pie, Aunt Evie's pickled peaches, and Rose Pink's baloney roll-ups. These names make readers aware that Mickler, when he discusses cooking, is recalling primarily a women's history. It is not only important to remember the recipes; it is equally essential to remember the individual ways that different women personalize their recipes. For example, Mickler shares the secret of Clara Jane's unforgettable peach pie: "[she] used Watkins' pure vanilla extract, Watkins' pure almond essence, and mace only" (*White Trash* 110). In her recipe for Ritz pie, Retha Faye cautions, "One more cracker and you'd ruin the whole thing!" (qtd. in *White Trash* 107). Tutti's fruited porkettes are composed of sliced sweet potatoes, canned sliced pineapple, bacon, pork chops, and brown sugar, but she adds her own sense of style: "She learned to make her porkettes by using a Hawaiian recipe combined with Southern ingredients. You can't get trashier than that" (*White Trash* 29). Describing her recipe for smothered potatoes, Edna Rae observes, "Let them get a real brown crust on bottom without burnin', that's the trick" (qtd. in *White Trash* 22). Clara Jane's, Retha Faye's, Tutti's, and Edna Rae's individual touches are as crucial to recalling their recipes as Julia Child's unique touches for a chocolate

mousse. Mickler shows that Retha's Ritz pie or Edna Rae's smothered potatoes deserve the same praise as more upper- or middle-class recipes. This is a
radical move because in the past, the culinary establishment ignored such
recipes. Now Mickler suggests that they are an important element of
American food traditions.

Not only do the recipes make a difference, Mickler suggests that it is
equally vital to remember how women's stories and traditions have shaped
this culture. For example, readers learn about different women, including
Mickler's mother and Big Reba Culpepper, and their experiences. In earlier
years, Edna Rae Mickler was always ready to help others by cooking "a big
dinner of fried chitlins, a mess of turnip greens, enough hoe cakes for a Bible
story, a wash pot full of swamp cabbage stew, and two large Our Lord's
Scripture cakes"; then everyone would have a celebration and fill a cigar box
with money for the people whose trailer burned down or had suffered
another accident (2). Today, Reba is famous for her rainbow ice cake. Once
she wished to clean a weed-filled local cemetery where a relative was buried,
so to coax others to help she prepared a meal of "fried chicken, hoppin' John,
biscuits, ice tea, and, of course, [her] famous Rainbow Icebox Cake, enough
to kill us all" (2). Similarly, in *Sinkin Spells*, recipes are intermingled with
stories about the lives of white trash women. The chapters focus on a variety
of events: prayer meetings, funerals, wakes, family reunions, barbeques, pic-
nics, holidays, sewing parties, and quilting parties. Women are at the center of
many of these activities, and Mickler suggests their traditions should be
remembered because "telling stories, laughing, and enjoying good food are all
deeply rooted in our southern White Trash background. We'll tell any story to
make it funny. And we'll bend over backwards to make a good meal" (*White
Trash* 3). His books are as much history books as cookbooks, recalling poor
women's contributions and celebrating how they hold their community
together. Like the 1950s Chinese-American cookbooks or contemporary
African-American cookbooks, Mickler's books let an alternate history be heard
that mainstream society had ignored because it revolved around poor women
and their domestic lives.

Mickler affirms that poor white Southern traditions are significant and
includes many recipes from this culture, such as fried squirrel, perlow, sweet
potato pone, corn pone, hush puppies, country-smoked ham, turnip greens,
and mustard greens. *Sinkin Spells* includes other Southern recipes: corn
pudding, sweet fried pies, fried chicken, head cheese, fried chitlins, grits, and
greens. The sequel, *More White Trash Cooking* (1998), written by Mickler's

cousin, Trisha Mickler, contains other Southern recipes, including baked possum and sweet taters, hog jowl with turnip greens, okra succotash, drunk sweet potatoes, Beulah Mae's corn pudding, grits casserole, corn fritters, and sweet potato pie. These recipes give a voice to poor Southern whites, a group that rarely has had one in the past, and shows that their contributions make a difference. Ernest Mickler challenges centuries of stereotypes that depict "rednecks" and "hillbillies" as adding nothing to American society. He proudly demonstrates that Southern white trash culture is as significant as that of any other racial or ethnic group.

Although Mickler defends white trash culture, he also creates a hierarchy that establishes some white trash as superior to others. "The first thing you've got to understand is that there's white trash and there's White Trash. Manners and pride separate the two," he notes (*White Trash* 1). *New York Times* writer Edwin McDowell observes that Mickler "wears the White Trash label, which he says is cultural rather than economic, with considerable pride" (11). Mickler's distinction is disturbing because it makes some poor whites "acceptable" and others not. Similar reasoning establishes some blacks as "acceptable" because they conform to middle-class white norms of behavior and others as not acceptable because they reject these norms. When Mickler distinguishes between White Trash and white trash, he accomplishes something similar, making some white trash more acceptable than others. This strategy to seperate whites into different classes is dangerous because, historically, it has been used to separate whites from different classes. Even though Mickler is arguing for the inclusion of some poor whites, he is not suggesting that all should be included. For a writer who has a broader view of including all poor whites, we have to turn to Ruby Ann Boxcar and her books about trailer-park life.

"A Tool of Comfort"[15]: Cooking and Trailer-Park Life

"A typical resident will get up, work like a dog for nine hours at minimum wage, come home, eat, maybe have a drink, watch some TV, and go to bed. Then you got the folks who get up, eat, get drunk, watch game shows or talk shows or soaps, pass out, cook somethin', get drunk, watch TV, and go to bed. Every once in a while the police show up and arrest a neighbor," writes Ruby Ann Boxcar in *Ruby Ann's Down Home Trailer Park Holiday Cookbook*, describing her trailer park's residents (xi). Like Mickler's, Boxcar's books focus on lower-class people and the significance of food for them. Not all media critics are as enthusiastic about her work as they are about Mickler's, however. One writer for the *Irish Times* observed, "These days, sadly, the White Trash kitchen revolution ignited by Mickler has got a little campy. Authors such as Lisa Miller and Ruby Ann Boxcar are huckstering what they've dubbed 'Trailer Park Cuisine,' most of which is a gimmick and involves Spam-and-jelly desserts set in breast molds. . . . Pay it no heed" ("Puttin' " 73). Although Boxcar's culinary accomplishment might be considered inferior to Mickler's, readers should not ignore her work, since it conveys serious messages about the grim opportunities that white trash individuals confront. Millions lead identical lives, working at minimum-wage jobs, watching television, and getting drunk. Boxcar uses humor to convey a bleak lesson about the lack of opportunities for poor whites. Although she writes about trailer-park life, in this book and others she also criticizes American society in general and, particularly, its socioeconomic system that leaves out the poor.

Boxcar's books focus on the inhabitants of High Chaparral Trailer Park. In the first volume, *Ruby Ann's Down Home Trailer Park Cookbook*, we are introduced to the people who live in the twenty trailers. Lot two is Anita Biggon's; she is a cocktail waitress at a local bar (12). Lot seven belongs to Ben and Dora Beaver, who own Beaver Liquors (19). Lot nine belongs to Juanita and Harland, who work at the Piggly Wiggly (21). Kitty and Kyle Chitwood own lot eleven. She is a convenience store clerk and can "really pull a good RC slushy" (22). Although some of these people move or die over the course of Boxcar's books, they are replaced by similar down-and-out individuals, living on society's margins, surviving from paycheck to paycheck, and struggling to exist. Ruby Ann is a "well-known temptress of song, confidante to the jet set, a former beautician extraordinaire, and world traveler" (xi). She records the lives of the park's inhabitants and their recipes. Since she focuses on a trailer park—a strongly stereotyped place in American culture—readers already have preconceptions about the inhabitants of High Chaparral.

In the United States, the middle class have a love/hate relationship with trailer parks. On one hand, they think of trailer parks as outside of society's "respectable" boundaries. It is a common stereotype that, when crime strikes a community, the one place to look for the criminals is the trailer park, where miscreants of all kinds supposedly lurk. Not every city or town has a trailer park filled with criminals, but this makes little difference; the cultural myth continues to thrive. Trailer parks have become symbols for everything negative about the United States. If a television show or film shows a character living in a trailer park, it is sufficient to make the audience view that person negatively. This dark image is upheld by the fact that most trailer parks are set off from the rest of town, in nebulous spaces on a town's edge or on a semi-industrial area where deteriorating warehouses and half-empty strip malls serve as neighbors. This geographical location, at least according to the stereotype, sets trailer parks apart as places where people live because they have something to hide.

One reason for the ubiquitous nature of this dark image of trailer parks is that the United States needs it in order to feel secure, since it is too frightening for mainstream America to think that evil people could live just anywhere, including down the street. It is reassuring to assume that they live in an entirely different location, a place separated from everyone else, in other words, a trailer park. In this way, the American mainstream scapegoats trailer-park dwellers for society's ills. If a town possesses no trailer park, a slum or the "other side of town" serves the same purpose of acting as a place to separate the "bad" from the "good." This is common across the United States. Even if a town has only a few streets separated by a railroad track, the people on the "other side of the track" are disparaged as lower class. In a major city such as New York, multiple regions, including Harlem, are stigmatized as the "ghetto." No matter where we dwell, Americans desire to separate the evildoers from everyone else. The trailer park, the area on the other side of the tracks, or the ghetto does this, creating a mirage that the bad can be separated from the good.

On the other hand, not all American images of trailer parks are negative. Although they are associated with evil, they also are stereotyped as sites where redneck culture is embraced. At least in our cultural mythology, they are a place where no one cares if you repair your '74 Chevy in the front yard; make planters out of old tires sprayed with garish colors; build the largest, gaudiest rhinestone-covered shrine to Elvis outside of Memphis; or have such a huge collection of plastic flamingoes stuck in front of your trailer that your yard looks like a bastardized Audubon preserve. The trailer park is a place where redneck society is assumed to flourish, without the restrictions and regulations that it confronts elsewhere. Although this cultural stereotype might not always be true, the media stereotype creates space for working-class resistance to and subversion of middle-class norms.

In the trailer park, middle-class aesthetics and rules of behavior are turned upside down.

Certainly, Boxcar's books discard any sense of upper- or middle-class culinary norms. "I've gathered all the recipes from my family and neighbors who all live at the High Chaparral Trailer Park in Pangburn, Arkansas. . . . These are the recipes that we all use at the High Chaparral. And bein' the star and world traveler that I am, I know that most of these recipes are used every day at trailer parks across the globe," Boxcar writes (*BBQ* xiv–xv). Her recipes proudly show their white trash roots. In *Ruby Ann's Down Home Trailer Park Cookbook*, the recipes include Eula's string bean delight, Ollie's vivacious vinegar pie, Spamcakes and syrup, Donna Sue's Spam muffins, mayonnaise cake, Lulu Bell's lemon tree cake, sweet tater cake, Jell-O divinity, two-timin' beer cookies, Dr Pepper salad, Aunt Violet's sausage bread, and Dora Beaver's blue ribbon peanut butter fudge. The *Holiday* cookbook includes recipes for good-luck collard greens, chili-dog bake, Christian carrot cake, Kitty's lemon beer cake, and Tammy's green bean bake. Her *Ruby Ann's Down Home Trailer Park BBQin' Cookbook* (2002) includes recipes for a variety of trailer park classics: trailer park kabobs, Baptist burgers, Laurie's one hot sexy momma BBQ sauce, Dr Pepper can chicken, and numerous ambrosia recipes. The book also includes a recipe for the infamous trailer park green Jell-O salad. Boxcar writes, "I'm only puttin' this recipe out there so that y'all can suffer just like the rest of us in trailer parks around the world have suffered" (114). (The recipe's ingredients include a box of lime Jell-O, miniature marshmallows, shredded cabbage, crushed pineapple, walnuts, mayonnaise, and evaporated milk.) In Boxcar's books, middle-class culinary notions are discarded; she exalts poor white trash recipes and demonstrates their importance in the trailer park's working-class culture. She takes pride in trailer-park cooking, something that people from other class backgrounds do not. She observes, "There just ain't nothin' like good trailer park cookin'! I know that for some of y'all this is hard to believe. It seems like every time I tell this to people, they always think that I'm kiddin' " (*Cookbook* xi). She rebels against a culture in which white trash tastes, especially in cooking, are dismissed. Mainstream society disparages trailer-park aesthetics, whether in food or any other area, and assumes they should not be taken seriously. Boxcar suggests such attitudes need to change, especially where food is concerned. American society privileges a meal cooked by Julia Child, but not one cooked by Boxcar or any other trailer-park woman. Boxcar scoffs at such a pretentious attitude and shows that trailer-park cooking can be superior to more elite traditions.

Although Boxcar's books are tongue-in-cheek, they convey serious messages about poor lives in America. In her first book, she writes, "There are three things that trailer park women are good at: holdin' our liquor, jackin' our hair to Jesus, and cookin' " (*Cookbook* xii). She continues, "Bein' able to slam together a great tastin' meal with whatever happens to be in the fridge is somethin' that's in our blood. It's a gift that the Almighty has seen fit to bestow on us common folks" (xii). Although Boxcar takes pride in trailer-park cooking, she also shows its darker side. She describes BBQ as something with a taste that can "only be beat by the tender lovin' from one's spouse," but observes, "BBQin' is about as common in a trailer park as a visit from the cops" (*BBQ* xiii).[16] This is a world where cooking offers fleeting relief from poverty, but that respite is apt to be destroyed by visits from the police or other officials. Poor women are great cooks, despite meager and inexpensive ingredients, because they have no other options; cooking is a "tool of comfort, which we folks turn to in times of need. Your son's been arrested . . . whip out the skillet! Your husband's cheatin' on you . . . fire up the stove! A tornado's been spotted a few trailers down . . . grease up a pie pan. . . . Yes, dear reader, trailer park cookin' plays a very large role in our everyday lives" (*Cookbook* xii–xiiii). Despite the limitations that confront them in trailer-park life, women have found ways to express themselves in the kitchen. Boxcar praises how women use this space in creative ways, despite limited ingredients, but she also shows the bleak social reality that makes women turn to the stove.

The emphasis in Boxcar's books on the joy of trailer-park cooking is an attitude shared by Jill Conner Browne's *The Sweet Potato Queens' Big-Ass Cookbook (and Financial Planner)* (2003). This cookbook is also filled with rich and delicious recipes that show no concern for waistlines, including bitch bar bacon shrimps (bacon wrapped around shrimp and pepper jack cheese), Twinkie pie, fatten-you-right-up roll pig candy (bacon coated in brown sugar and baked), praline sweet potatoes, and queen-style coconut caramel pie (a pie crust filled with a mixture of a large package of cream cheese, a can of sweetened and condensed milk, a tub of Cool Whip, seven ounces of coconut, and a cup of chopped pecans, then topped with a jar of caramel sauce). Browne remarks about the pie, "There is absolutely no way on earth to cram any more fat into a single food item" (257). These white trash recipes are unlikely to appear in a middle-class cookbook, such as Betty Crocker's.[17] Browne's recipes, like Boxcar's, rebel against any sense of upper- and middle-class limits. The poor white authors glory in the excessive and no-limits nature of their cooking, recognizing that it is a rare respite from the grim realities that the poor confront on a daily basis. This is a world where poor women are worried that they cannot afford any food for their families, so they do not fret about losing weight. "If you can spend enough money in diet books . . . and joining gyms and exercise classes you never go to, eventually you will not have enough money to buy actual food and you will lose weight—at last" (Browne 71). Browne and Boxcar show very different sensibilities from upper-class women who support the diet industry.

Since poor white trash never know if they will have sufficient food, they glory in its plentitude, when they have it, and prepare it in mouthwatering ways. Despite the creative ways that trailer-park women use inexpensive foods to make interesting recipes, Boxcar demonstrates how poverty limits their choice of food. Food historian Jessamyn Neuhaus writes in her book, *Manly Meals and Mom's Home Cooking: Cookbooks and Gender in Modern America* (2003), "For those people living in poverty, cooking meals can mean reckoning with deprivation, not creative opportunity" (3). This is true in Boxcar's trailer park. In her *BBQin' Cookbook*, she writes, "In my party recipes, when they had cheese in 'em, I put Government cheese and told y'all that if you don't get it, then you could use somethin' else like cheddar, Swiss, American, or Velveeta for that matter, if you got that kind of money. Well, I just found out recently that Government cheese ain't as easy to get as it used to be. . . . Needless to say, my heart sank all the way down with disbelief. I can't imagine a trailer or even an old home that ain't got a slab of Government-approved cheese, which even the mice won't touch" (xv). This is a universe where Velveeta is a luxury, and even government cheese has become scarce. Boxcar reveals that trailer-park dwellers and other poor whites live in a world where they sometimes are forced to subsist on food that mice would not eat, and countless similar poor women across the United States are forced to survive on government handouts.

Challenging Culinary Elitism

In previous generations, the lower classes used humor to express a sensibility that rebelled against upper- and middle-class restraints and notions of correct decorum. In addition, comedy was an opportunity for working-class people to give voice to their resentment against a system of which they were at the bottom. Today, white trash authors use humor for the same subversive purpose. In the 1980s and 1990s, a time when the working class fell ever farther behind socioeconomically, white trash authors used humor to express what was happening to them in a society that wished to forget about the poor, especially those who were white. Hidden under the humor were serious lessons about what it meant to live on society's margins. Writers might have been humorous in describing recipes with government cheese, but their text contained a sobering message about what it means to live in poverty in the United States.

More broadly, white trash authors show that poor whites have always lived in the United States, no matter how much the mainstream ignored them. The authors give this underclass a voice that they have not had in earlier epochs. In the past, middle-class reformers, scientists, and other outsiders wrote about Southern white trash, trying to find a reason for their position at the bottom of the social hierarchy. These outsiders created an image of poor whites being morally depraved and mentally slow-witted, so, at least according to reformers, they had to be saved and raised to the level of the middle class. The outsiders failed to recognize that poor whites possessed a culture that was as rich and vibrant as that of upper- or middle-class whites. White trash cookbooks acknowledge that white trash culture deserves attention.

Along with using humor to express poor whites' anger at a system that offers them little and that suggests white trash culture is no culture at all, white trash cookbooks also play another covert role, rewriting American culinary history and suggesting it is not confined to an elite tradition handed down by culinary figures (such as James Beard or Julia Child) who pass on an upper-class cooking tradition strongly influenced by French, Italian, German, and other Europeans. White trash authors demonstrate that different voices need to be heard, including ones that have been ignored in the past. They demonstrate that American culinary culture originated from many sources. This is a radical shift because in previous generations mainstream culinary culture considered white trash cooking not worth preserving. Now white trash writers show it should be, recognizing that it is as much a valid part of American cuisine as other more elite food traditions.

Finally, white trash cookbooks reveal how difficult it is to change societal attitudes about white trash. Other racial and ethnic stereotypes have changed, but the image of white trash has altered more slowly. It will take more than a few decades to shift cultural views about white trash that have developed over such a long period. "While other derogatory terms for lower-class whites have been transformed, it seems that 'white trash' . . . will remain an improper name" (Hartigan 336). This term will exist as long as the American dream is a central myth in our society. White trash show that this dream is not available to all people, even if they are white. White trash also demonstrate that the United States is not a classless society where everyone has a chance to succeed but, rather, is a rigid class system with poor whites at the bottom. It is easier for upper- and middle-class Americans to assume that white trash "deserve" this position because of their genetic makeup than to explore how American culture fails to offer white trash the same advantages as more affluent whites.

Chapter 7

"Dining on Grass and Shrubs"[1]: Making Vegan Food Sexy

The media are filled with anti-vegan statements, grouping vegans together with other left-leaning activists who are portrayed as radical extremists, too unusual, too radical for anyone to accept.[2] One recent *Toronto Star* writer observed, "If you're like me . . . vegans, yoga nuts, and people who eat only organic food might as well be from another planet" ("The Week" D16). When taken to a vegan restaurant, another commentator grumbled, "I hate hippie food" (Musgrave G6). If writers do not complain about "hippie food," they sneer at the presumed superior attitude of vegans. In an article in the *San Francisco Chronicle* in 2004, Jon Carroll observed he felt contempt for "the concept of veganism and vegans themselves. Vegans . . . were people who were too snotty to be vegetarians" (D10). Writing for *The National Review* in 2003, Jonah Goldberg was similarly negative as he described his experiences when he tried veganism for one week: "From either ethical or health motives, vegans don't eat anything remotely associated with the meat-industrial complex. This means not just beef, fish, chicken, etc., but all forms of dairy, including butter, cream, and cheese. This qualifies vegans as an orthodox sect of the wider religion of vegetarianism and, hence, often a bit arrogant toward their lesser brethren. . . . Many of them are indistinguishable from the nuttier animal-rights crowd" (36). He described the vegan food industry as "large, booming, and strange" (36). These different writers' negative perceptions about veganism and vegans are representative of a culture in which veganism has not become as popular as vegetarianism, something that is visible in many ways. In most grocery stores, foods labeled vegan are difficult if not impossible to find—although one can discover vegan foods if one carefully reads prepared foods' labels—unless one is visiting a health food store; few restaurants include vegan menu items; school cafeterias, too, rarely include vegan items. And people are less likely to be familiar with veganism than vegetarianism. If familiar with veganism, people typically view it askance, as a radical movement that attracts only the oddest people. Many share Goldberg's attitudes toward vegans and their food, categorizing them as "nuts." Why do vegans receive so much vitriol in the press? How do vegans address this negative attitude? How do they rewrite cultural stereotypes about what it means to be vegan?

This open hatred is unusual because other food faddists, vegetarians, for example, rarely receive the same negative reaction, at least in recent decades. One reason vegans are perceived as "nuts" is that they ask for greater changes in the American diet than merely giving up meat. Vegan activists want Americans to give up all animal products, including eggs, honey, cheese, leather, and other items that use animal by-products. Obviously, this is a major reason that mainstream Americans feel uneasy, as most do not wish to make this tremendous shift in their diet and lifestyle, no matter how healthy or ethical such a change might be.[3] But Americans' uneasiness about vegans has other roots too. As Goldberg suggests, Americans assume that vegans are no different from the most radical fringe of animals' rights activists. Therefore, vegans and People for the Ethical Treatment of Animals (PETA) supporters tend to be clubbed together.[4] Although this is sometimes true, it is not always. The media depict members of both groups as strident, self-righteous, and smug because of their political and ethical views. Due to this negative image, vegans have confronted a difficult challenge in recent decades. They have had to change this stereotype if they desired to spread their movement and move it out of the radical fringe. Vegan activists hold different ideas about what should be done to spread veganism. In a more unusual approach, when lecturing about veganism, Dr. Neal Barnard promotes the idea that a vegan diet leads to better sexual prowess for men and consuming a diet with meat leads to impotence.[5] One commentator observed, "Equating meat-eating with sexual dysfunction is the latest tactic used by vegans and animal rights extremists to advance their radical agenda. . . . Vegan groups target men in their twenties, telling them that a meat-eating lifestyle will make them a flop with chicks" (Agren 15). Although not every member of the medical establishment agrees with his views, Barnard has discovered that talking about sexual potency makes almost any male interested in a vegan diet. The doctor is not alone in his crusade, as vegan activists have found different ways to make veganism appealing to people who are not necessarily moved by issues related to animal welfare.

Other vegan activists have adopted approaches less controversial than Barnard's. For example, a number of women cookbook authors have transformed vegan food into something hip, trendy, and tasty. If people could not be lured to veganism by animals' rights and ethical issues, they could possibly be lured if vegan foods tasted better than anything else, including filet mignon or roast beef. Vegan cookbook authors have to include recipes so tempting that they will challenge the assumption that any good meal has to start with a slab of meat, chicken, or fish, a belief that has been engrained in the United States from its earliest years. Vegans were not the first faddists to try to make their foods chic and fashionable. They borrowed their ideas from vegetarians who changed the plain fare of the 1970s, such as whole-wheat bread, vegetable soup, and lentil burgers, into something more hip, in the process welcoming more people to the vegetarian lifestyle. In a similar fashion, vegans have recognized that, if they wish for their movement to appeal to more people, they have to make vegan foods more appealing to mainstream tastes.

A number of women-authored cookbooks appearing over the last few decades have tried to do exactly that, including Jeani-Rose Atchison's *Everyday Vegan: 300 Recipes for Healthful Eating* (2002), Tanya Barnard and Sarah Kramer's *How It all Vegan! Irresistible Recipes for an Animal-Free Diet* (1999) and *The Garden of Vegan: How It all Vegan Again!* (2003), Susann Geiskopf-Hadler and Mindy Toomay's *The Complete Vegan Cookbook: Over 200 Tantalizing Recipes* (2001), Myra Kornfeld's *The Voluptuous Vegan: More than 200 Sinfully Delicious Recipes for Meatless, Eggless, and Dairy-Free Meals* (2000), Leslie McEachern's *The Angelica Home Kitchen* (2003), Robin Robertson's *Vegan Planet: 400 Irresistible Recipes with Fantastic Flavors from Home and around the World* (2003), and Lorna Sass's *The New Vegan Cookbook: Innovative Vegetarian Recipes Free of Dairy, Eggs, and Cholesterol* (2001).[6] These authors and others have played an important role in changing how American society views vegans.[7] The writers take different approaches to promoting veganism. Some show that eating vegan food is "fun," fighting the stereotype of vegan food being something that someone would eat only under duress. Other authors emphasize the versatile nature of vegan foods, suggesting that they can be combined in as many exciting gourmet ways as their nonvegan counterparts; these authors transform vegan foods into something that would be at home on the pages of *Gourmet* magazine. Still other writers emphasize that vegan foods can be used in countless international recipes, showing that vegan cooking offers an opportunity for culinary exploration. Although the writers use different approaches to make vegan foods appeal to a mainstream audience, they share a common concern in discussing the ethical side of vegan eating, an issue that lies at the heart of most books. Using different strategies, cookbook authors reinvent vegan food; in the process, they seek to show their audience the appeal of a vegan diet and, more generally, a vegan lifestyle to both vegans and nonvegans.

"Absolutely Uninviting"[8]: The History of Vegetarianism

To understand the spread of vegetarianism and veganism in the United States, one must first understand how the movements spread in Great Britain and then were transported to the United States.[9] In 1807, the Reverend William Cowherd, founder of the Bible Christian Church in Britain, declared that Christians should not eat flesh, following in Christ's footsteps. Despite the reverend's belief in complete abstinence, his group attracted many working-class followers because he provided vegetable soup and medical aid at a time when crops were poor and unemployment was widespread (Spencer 255). A follower of Cowherd's, Joseph Brotherton, founded the national Vegetarian Society in 1847 to spread ideas about a nonmeat diet.[10] Due to the groundwork laid by early vegetarians, including Cowherd and Brotherton, the British vegetarian movement has a more robust and longer history than does America's.

From its inception, the British movement was aided by many women. For example, Brotherton's wife, Martha Harvey Brotherton, published *Vegetable Cookery: With an Introduction Recommending Abstinence from Animal Food and Intoxicating Liquors* (1829). If more people were vegetarians, she declared, it would "prevent much cruelty . . . and disease, besides many other evils that cause misery in society" (xiii). Another woman, Mary Pope, wrote *Novel Dishes for Vegetarian Households: A Complete and Trustworthy Guide to Vegetarian Cookery* (1893). She aspired to make vegetarian cooking less insipid: "It has been said, vegetarians are bad cooks, and that one reason why [vegetarianism] makes little headway . . . is because one's repasts are so absolutely uninviting" (6). Her book included recipes for savory specialties, such as artichokes au gratin, aubergine fritters, maize curry, lentil fritters, endive with poached eggs, and asparagus loaves. These two women and others sought to alter the British diet. For some, these changes were part of their Christian responsibility since the Bible Christian Church and similar institutes preached abstinence from animal food and alcohol. Some were drawn to vegetarianism because a number of noted intellectuals, writers, and artists in Britain, including Percey Bysshe Shelley and George Bernard Shaw, were vegetarians for ethical and moral reasons. These two traditions, the Christian and the ethical, helped build a firm foundation in Britain for vegetarianism at an early stage.

In the United States, vegetarianism spread more slowly. Americans have always been wary of vegetarianism because, since our nation's earliest centuries, meat has been a crucial part of the U.S. diet. On the frontier, it was not always possible to grow crops, but meat was available to any good shooter or trapper.[11] "Game made the settlement of America possible," Dale Brown wrote in his book, *American Cooking* (qtd. in Root and de Rochemont 68). Although this was perhaps an overstatement, game was a crucial element of the American diet in the seventeenth and eighteenth centuries and remained important until the Civil War. Whether game or any other form, most commonly salt pork, America was a nation of heavy meat-eaters, a custom that "astonish[ed] many European travelers" when they visited the United States (Root and de Rochemont 68).[12] Meat was perceived as the highest form of sustenance, so meals featured a dizzying array of meats in huge quantities. One reason for our dependence on meat was that, since our nation's beginnings, meat has been associated with mas-culinity. It has been considered to be the male food par excellence, and gen-erations of men have eaten it to increase their vigor. In her book, *The Sexual Politics of Meat: A Feminist-Vegetarian Critical Theory* (1990), Carol J. Adams writes, "According to the mythology of patriarchal culture, meat pro-motes strength; the attributes of masculinity are achieved through eating these masculine foods. Visions of meat-eating football players, wrestlers, and boxers lumber in our brains in this equation" (33). Since meat has been equated with masculine strength, athletes have been fed meat to prepare for competition. Males have sometimes existed on nothing but meat because it has such a highly esteemed place in our society as increasing men's strength. Adams observes, "The literal evocation of male power is found in the concept of meat. . . . Meat is upheld as a powerful, irreplaceable item of food" (33). Due to the association between male power and meat—an association that many people in modern society continue to make as restaurants still feature large slabs of beef aimed at an audience primarily, although not exclusively, of men—vegetarians have appeared suspect, as lacking virility. They have also seemed suspiciously effeminate, the worst possible trait for males.

Despite widespread fears about a vegetarian diet demasculinizing men and not supplying them with adequate nutrients to maintain their strength, some Americans, influenced by the British movement, embraced vegetarianism in the nineteenth century. The Reverend William Metcalfe, a Cowherd follower, sailed to the United States and established a Bible Christian Church in Philadelphia. Even though the local press denounced him as "an infidel," he gained a number of followers, including the food reformers and philosophers Sylvester Graham and Bronson Alcott (qtd. in Spencer 273). Metcalfe, Graham, and William Alcott organized and formed the American Vegetarian Society (AVS) in 1850. (Alcott was the first president and Metcalfe the second.) As did many British vegetarians, Alcott, Graham, and Metcalfe believed that vegetarianism was the responsibility of all Christians. Metcalfe's *A Conversation on Abstinence from the Flesh of Animals as Food* (1821) and Alcott's *Vegetable Diet: As Sanctioned by Medical Men and by Experience in All Ages* (1838) helped spread their views to a larger audience. Although the followers of the AVS and different groups embraced vegetarianism, mainstream America has never felt entirely comfortable with it, assuming such a diet is aligned with society's extreme fringe of health fanatics.[13] The reason for this attitude stems from the fact that U.S. society has always been meat-oriented. Whether it is a chicken in every pot or a steak on every grill, meat has a long association with images of success, of having achieved the American dream. Thus, vegetarianism is suspect because it casts aspersions on our love affair with meat.

It was only in the 1960s and 1970s that vegetarianism became more widely accepted as something other than a fringe movement in the United States. As mentioned previously, this was a time when many Americans experimented with natural foods. With the popularity of *Diet for a Small Planet*, *Laurel's Kitchen*, and other cookbooks that focused largely or exclusively on vegetarian dishes, the vegetarian movement no longer appeared as unusual as it had in earlier decades. Now eating a vegetarian diet seemed to be the wise choice for individuals and the world. Numerous people decided to become vegetarians, a choice made easier because vegetarian meals began to appear on restaurant menus across the United States and a growing number of natural foods grocery stores catered to vegetarians with a plethora of products. Suddenly it was positive to be a vegetarian. It demonstrated that one cared about one's health but, more important, also cared about the world's. Although only a fraction of Americans decided to become vegetarians, the movement impacted countless others, mostly people who lived on one of the coasts or in a university or college town. Being vegetarian was no longer considered unusual. It became a practical choice for some, and millions were introduced to vegetarianism in this era.

In the 1980s, the vegetarian movement shifted its stance. The emphasis on feeding the world's booming population was no longer hip or trendy. In the 1980s, the emphasis shifted from saving the globe to saving the self. People wanted to consume a vegetarian diet because it was healthy, and they were obsessed with health. During this period, vegetarian dishes went mainstream. Most major restaurant chains began to include at least some vegetarian selections. Frozen foods companies featured a number of vegetarian items. School cafeterias at universities and high schools offered vegetarian selections. During this decade vegetarianism increased greatly in popularity. This growth continued in the 1990s as vegetarianism spread, either because people desired healthier diets or were concerned about the ethical problems attached to a diet based on meat.

Today, vegetarianism is more mainstream than it was in earlier decades. From coast to coast, people have become vegetarians, and it is no longer a rare choice. The movement's spread, however, is uneven. Although it has become more popular in some regions, in others it is still less widely accepted. In rural areas, being a vegetarian is still an oddity, as it is in many small towns across the United States. Most grocery stores are likely to stock a variety of vegetarian foods, and frozen food aisles at major grocery chains usually include a number of vegetarian selections, from enchiladas to vegetarian burgers. Not all people who eat these foods and other similar items are necessarily vegetarians, but such foods suggest the higher profile that vegetarianism has gained. Restaurants offer vegetarian selections, although they might be limited. School cafeteria offerings also include vegetarian selections, although, again, they can be limited. While vegetarian foods have become mainstreamed over the last few decades, and vegetarian food selections are no longer unusual, this greater acceptance is still limited. For example, fast food restaurants add one or two vegetarian items to their menus, but they do not change their primary reliance on beef and chicken.

Veganism has taken longer to spread both in Great Britain and the United States, although, again, it has spread more rapidly in Britain. In 1942, the British Vegan Society, led by Donald Watson, broke away from the national Vegetarian Society (Leneman 219). Before this time, however, other British had spoken in favor of a vegan diet, although their numbers were limited. Rupert H. Wheldon published *No Animal Food,* the first vegan cookbook, in 1910. It supported eschewing animal foods for "ethical, aesthetic, and economic reasons" (Leneman 220). The book was forgotten over the course of time, so many people considered Fay K. Henderson's *Vegan Recipes* (1946) to be the first British vegan cookbook. In addition to these two books, there was a flourishing discussion among British vegetarians in the 1920s and 1930s about whether a vegan diet was desirable (Leneman 221). Although British vegetarians discussed the importance of a vegan diet, they were divided about pursuing such a diet. Watson broke away from the Vegetarian Society because it was not willing to have a nondairy section in its national magazine (Leneman 227).

The American Vegan Society was founded in 1960 in New Jersey by H. Jay Dinshah. It was preceded by an earlier vegan group in California—founded by Catherine Nimmo and Rubin Abramowitz—the Vegan Society, but it lasted only from 1948 to 1960. The AVS still thrives and works with a number of other groups that support a vegan diet, including the Physicians Committee for Responsible Medicine, Vegan Action, and Vegan Outreach. Since 1969, the AVS has sponsored many outreach activities, including cooking courses at its New Jersey headquarters.[14] Veganism has never attracted as many adherents as vegetarianism, perhaps because it demands a greater change in lifestyle. Only since the 1970s has veganism gained more popularity among a more general public, although vegans are still a minority of the population compared to vegetarians.

Not Just "Hippie Food": A New Image of Veganism

In recent years, a hip new image of veganism had appeared.[15] One recent writer observed: "Here's a novel recipe for today's modern vegan: subtract eggs, dairy, and meat. Add a dash of sass, a cup of punk, and a pound of conscience. The result: a stereotype bashing image that is gaining ground" (Yim E01). In England, too, vegans struggle to present a hip and modern image to challenge old-fashioned stereotypes. For example, Oxford's Healthy Living Supper Club focuses on having meetings and dinners to demonstrate that vegan food is not solely for "sandal-wearing bearded types" (Jones 34). In the United States and England, being vegan is suddenly "cool," at least in some circles, and has moved beyond being a movement for "hippies" to encompass a variety of people who hold different philosophies. Although they might have different ideas, these people are bringing a trendy new image to veganism. In the United States, there are between two and three million vegans, and the number is growing rapidly (J. Robertson C1).[16] One reason for this growth is because vegan writers, chefs, and activists have given veganism an appeal that it lacked in earlier decades, spreading vegan foods and philosophies to many who would not have considered them previously.

Among the groups who are attracted to the new image of veganism and vegetarianism are young people, who are becoming vegans and vegetarians in growing numbers.[17] The number of vegetarian teenagers in the United States doubled from 2001 to 2002, and one-third to one-half are vegans (Baca 1E). How does one explain this explosive growth, especially when many teenagers, at least in the past, have shown little interest in dietary reform? (Despite the sharp growth in the number of teen vegans, the vast majority of teens are meat-eaters and would be aghast at the thought of giving up their weekly runs to McDonald's or other fast food places for cheeseburgers and milkshakes; such eating patterns remain an entrenched part of American culture for countless people, young and old.) In 2003, *Wall Street Journal* writer Katy McLaughlin observed, "While teens have long flirted with vegetarianism, it lately has in many ways become a mainstream fad. The reasons range from health concerns, to marketing campaigns by animal-rights groups to rock music" (D1). Similarly, a teenage writer for the *Buffalo News* in 2002 explained why teens should become vegetarians: "People will think you're cool. . . . Unlike the '70s, when the only vegetarians around seemed to be spaced-out hippies, vegetarianism has become a respected and decidedly 'cool' way to live" (Burke N6). This is a dramatic shift in how youth view vegetarianism and veganism, transforming them into something cool and hip. Although still more likely to be found in a variety of East or West Coast cities and college towns rather than in the

South or Midwest or rural areas, these food trends are influencing young people's attitudes across the United States. Many of them might not become committed vegans, but they might become more open to including more vegan (or vegetarian) foods in their diets.

Despite the popularity of veganism with young people, the general population does not always respond positively to it, especially when their children are the ones transforming their diets. In the *Wall Street Journal* in 1995, one journalist observed, "Vegans, who outdo vegetarians by half, won't eat meat, fish, poultry, or dairy products and won't wear silk, leather, or wool. Teenage vegans follow all of these strictures . . . and drive their parents crazy" (Coleman B1). Parents are concerned that veganism is a "wacky teenage phase. But then it starts wreaking havoc on households. . . . Parents are harangued about cooking ingredients, annoyed by mealtime lectures, and often feel compelled to prepare two sets of meals" (B1). Parents are apt to have ambivalent attitudes toward veganism, particularly when it means that family life needs to be redesigned. They also worry that veganism is not a healthy diet choice for anyone, especially children and teenagers. The rift between some parents and their teen vegans suggests the uneven acceptance that veganism has had. But even parents are being brought into the fold. Vegan cookbook writers and activists are trying to broaden the appeal of veganism. Gradually, the attitude that veganism is only a "wacky teenage phase" is being questioned. Vegan cookbook writers challenge and change the negative image of veganism by showing that a vegan diet is a healthy decision for teenagers, parents, or anyone else.

Contemporary vegan authors fight the stereotype that veganism is a "wacky" diet for teens and a few radical extremists by showing that a vegan diet is something that anyone would find hard to resist because vegan food is so tempting. If one becomes vegan, one does not have to limit oneself to a life of barely palatable foods, so veganism should appeal to everyone. In *How It All Vegan! Irresistible Recipes for an Animal-Free Diet* (1999), Tanya Barnard and Sarah Kramer observe: "There is a popular belief that by removing animal products from one's diet, food will become necessarily boring, a life of dining on grass and shrubs. But let us assure you: vegan food is fabulous food . . ." (11). In their sequel, *The Garden of Vegan: How It All Vegan Again!* (2003), the authors note, "A vegan lifestyle doesn't always have to be about sprouts and sandals" (13). In their two books, the writers wish to "make veganism a fun and easy place to be. So that you can spend less time worrying about how to be vegan and spend more time just enjoying being a vegan" (17). Barnard, Kramer, and other authors have played a crucial part in showing that vegan food can be as exciting as non-vegan food. In addition, they have shown that vegans can also be jocular, an image far removed from bleak mainstream stereotypes that depict vegans as humorless.

"A World of Choice"[18]: Beyond Brown Rice and Lentils

One way that vegan authors have challenged vegan stereotypes is by creating recipes that rebel against the image of vegan food being as appealing to eat as a bowlful of shredded cardboard. In past decades, vegan food was stereotyped as boring and unexciting. But this has changed. The vegan diet's image has now been refurbished dramatically, and vegan writers create recipes that would be at home in any gourmet restaurant. These delectable, rich recipes are a far cry from the plain vegan recipes of earlier decades. One author observes, "There is a world of choice in the vegan diet. In fact, I hesitate to use the word *diet* because it means austerity or deprivation, and a vegan diet is anything but that" (R. Robertson xiv). Similarly, Kornfeld in *The Voluptuous Vegan* writes, while the recipes in her book are healthful, they are also "unequivocally rich in taste and attractive in presentation" (2). By creating dishes that anyone would wish to eat, these activists rewrite the idea that a vegan diet is only for "nutty" animal activists and other extremists.

The dishes in contemporary vegan cookbooks often appear as though they would be at home in *Food & Wine, Saveur*, or any other glossy, upscale food magazine. For example, Sass's *The New Vegan Cookbook* and McEachern's *The Angelica Home Kitchen* have beautiful full-color illustrations of recipes that look irresistible, and the recipes that accompany the photographs are equally luscious. Kornfeld's book includes many gourmet recipes: wild mushroom and rice soup, asparagus potage with garlic cream, chickpea crepes with wild mushrooms and roasted cauliflower filling, pumpkin, sage, and pecan ravioli, and gingerbread with blood-orange sauce. Geiskopf-Hadler and Toomay's *Complete Vegan Cookbook* also includes gourmet recipes, such as tofu-stuffed squash blossoms, avocado-tomato bisque, summer squash and apricot soup with fresh basil and pine nuts, and pumpkin-stuffed shells with jalapeno-rosemary sauce. Similarly, *The Angelica Home Kitchen* includes recipes for many gourmet recipes: chickpea tart with potatoes and onions, ragout of white beans with gremolata, lemon-almond tart with raspberry sauce, and mocha cheesecake with chocolate brownie crust. The authors of these cookbooks and others rewrite veganism by borrowing the recipes and aesthetic style of gourmet food writing.

In addition, vegan cookbooks also borrow the opulent description and language found in gourmet magazines. Kornfeld uses lush evocative language when describing a recipe for smoky chestnut and sweet potato soup: "This soup has all the soothing comfort of mashed potatoes, while a splash of rum . . . adds grown-up relief. Best of all, the dried chestnuts . . . give the soup a smoky anchor" (29). In *The New Vegan Cookbook*, Sass describes phyllo triangles filled with kale, pine nuts, and currants: "These flaky phyllo packets get rave reviews. . . . For the unusual filling, cooked kale is combined with allspice-scented leeks, toasted pine nuts, and chewy grains" (75). She describes carrot, bean, and caramelized shallot puree as "an attractive, pale, autumn orange color. Caramelized shallots add earthy depth and balance the carrots' sweetness, while white beans contribute their buttery smooth texture" (87). Like Kornfeld and Sass, Robertson uses rich language to describe her recipes in *Vegan Planet*. Her potato gratin with pineapple and coconut milk is "a delicious way to prepare sweet potatoes . . . an opulent gratin"; rosemary-lemon potatoes with black olives and sun-dried tomatoes is described as "a perfect backdrop for a wide range of Mediterranean flavors, from fragrant rosemary and refreshing lemon to the salty depth of black olives and the smoky richness of sun-dried tomatoes"; and sautéed tofu with shallots, almonds, and Amaretto is described as "decidedly decadent. The crunch of toasted almonds amplifies the flavor of the liquor" (360, 205, 340).[19] The recipes in the different cookbooks use language that would be at home in any gourmet magazine. The writers, though, are borrowing the language for a subversive purpose: trying to make people more interested in a vegan diet and veganism in general. In a media-saturated universe where people are fed pictures and descriptions of food twenty-four hours a day from myriad sources, including television and magazines, those who wish to change the American diet need to consider how to make their recipes and food philosophies acceptable. One tactic is to create recipes so luscious that anyone, vegan or not, would wish to try them.

Gourmet vegan food is not limited to cookbooks alone. Chefs have rushed to create fancy, upscale vegan meals at restaurants from coast to coast. In the last twenty years, a number of such elite dining places have appeared, where the cost of an entrée rivals that of filet mignon or lobster at more traditional restaurants. Although making vegan food into a chic, gourmet experience has given it a new prominence in American culture it would not have gained otherwise, such an approach possesses limitations.[20] Due to the high cost of many vegan foods at expensive restaurants, not everyone is able to afford them. These swanky restaurants expose more people to vegan foods, but the diners are apt to be upper- and middle-class whites, who can afford the high prices. The restaurants are also limited in geographical range, with the majority located in New York City, San Francisco, Los Angeles, or other East or West Coast cities. Again, only a limited group of people is exposed to such cooking. Some of the restaurants' owners write cookbooks to share their ideas with others, but not many people can afford to devote the time and energy required to make the often highly elaborate and expensive recipes.

Perhaps because vegan authors recognize that not everyone who wishes to experiment with vegan cooking can necessarily afford the funds, time, or effort required to make gourmet recipes, they have tried to present less costly choices, so that vegan food does not need to be limited only to elaborate and expensive meals. These authors have rewritten the image of vegan food being boring by making it seem hip, cool, and global, but also, at the same time, affordable. These cookbooks include a wide range of foods and recipes from around the world. This emphasis on international vegan dishes is important because it helps to show that a vegan diet is cosmopolitan. The authors demonstrate that a vegan diet can be as multi-cultural and international as a nonvegan one, destroying the stereotype that a vegan diet is centered on only a few tasteless foods. Vegan authors also include international foods to demonstrate that vegan foods are not as unusual as some people might think. By including vegan recipes from around the world that have been for centuries in existence, such as hummus, tamales, and risotto, vegan authors imply that being a vegan is not as odd as some might assume.

Geiskopf-Hadler and Toomay's *Complete Vegan Cookbook* has recipes for wasabi mashed potatoes, risotto with saffron, peas, and pine nuts, spicy Chinese eggplant with tempeh and baby corn, and polenta porridge with hot fig compote. In *The New Vegan Cookbook*, Sass includes kabocha squash and spinach with Moroccan spices, Thai-inspired broccoli in coconut-cilantro sauce, and West Indian pumpkin with jerk-spiced tempeh. Atchison's *Everyday Vegan* includes recipes for South American jicama and orange salad, Thai vegetables, chipolte and white bean pasta, and coconut curry mélange. McEachern's *Angelica Home Kitchen* includes recipes for lentil-walnut pate ("It is . . . multicultural with a hint of Japan from the umboshi and miso and a Mediterranean influence from the olive oil. . . ." [113]), Moroccan-style tangine, enchiladas with mole, and Greek phyllo casserole with beets, spinach, and potatoes ("With its delicious, flaky baked phyllo topping and smooth layer of mashed potatoes underneath, it is a study in balance and contrast" [184]). Barnard and Kramer's *Garden of Vegan* includes numerous international-inspired recipes: cinnamon apple quesadilla, huevos ranchero, tamale pie, spicy Asian noodle soup, squash and sweet potato soup with chipotle sauce, coconut curry vegetable bake, and oyster mushroom sauté. Clearly, these authors and others challenge the stereotypical notion that vegan food is "hippie food" composed of nothing more international than brown rice and lentils. The writers create a whole new image and style for vegan recipes being as international as nonvegan recipes. This is a new universe where being vegan does not mean limiting oneself to a particular ethnic food tradition; all food traditions, the authors demonstrate, are vegan.

Again, we find that vegan activist writers use a strategy they borrowed from the world of gourmet cooking in which the media feature a wide assortment of international recipes to attract readers. The language used to describe such food is similarly exotic. The cover of Robertson's book notes, "*Vegan Planet* is comfortably global in its culinary reach, traversing the globe from hearty dishes, and from hip Southeast Asian food to regional American favorites." In *The Voluptuous Vegan*, Kornfeld also uses rich embellished language to describe the dishes in her book. They "fuse flavors and ingredients from around the world. For instance, a French chickpea crepe with a robust, earthy, Eastern European filling is paired with bright red beets and a pungent, creamy horseradish topping. Spicy Mexican tamales are paired with side dishes such as cucumber and jicama salad and sweet glazed squash" (51). After reading such delectable and descriptive prose, anyone would wish to try a vegan meal, and this is exactly what Kornfeld hopes. She and other vegan writers need to make their recipes twice as appealing so that countless skeptics will forget the absence of meat, fish, cheese, milk, and other animal-based products.

No matter how gourmet or international some vegan cooking has become, authors have not forgotten recipes that are simple and basic, too. They include numerous vegan versions of old standard favorite recipes, suggesting that one's diet does not have to change entirely if one becomes a vegan. Atchison's *Everyday Vegan* includes simple recipes for garlic and mushroom soup, primavera pasta, fruit mousse pie, strawberry mousse, and Black Forest cake. Robertson's *Vegan Planet* includes a number of recipes that are standard favorites: chili-macaroni bake, backyard barbecue chili, and macaroni and cheese. Barnard and Kramer's two books are filled with a number of traditional favorites that are transformed into vegan versions. The authors observe, "Many people can't imagine a main meal without the presence of a meat dish. These exciting vegan recipes offer nutritious alternatives to that old-fashioned idea" (*How* 101). *How It all Vegan!* includes a number of revised vegan versions of old favorites, including Greek scrambled tofu, fabulous French toast, faux eggs Benny, banana pancakes, vegan sloppy joes, and classic spinach lasagna. The authors are especially interested in challenging the notion that vegan desserts are boring and that vegans cannot eat the desserts to which they have grown accustomed. "What could be more satisfying after a meal than a delectable dessert? Some people think that vegan desserts are lackluster and tasteless; *au contraire*, they're zesty and full of taste," Barnard and Kramer write (133). *How It all Vegan!* includes recipes for many old-favorite desserts: chocolate pecan brownies, classic chocolate chip cookies, maple walnut brownies, creamy coconut pie, apple cinnamon matzo kugel, and chocolate bourbon pecan pie, formerly "referred to as 'orgasm pie.' One bite and you will understand. This pie is so elegant and rich, it has a reputation" (143). *The Garden of Vegan* also contains numerous revised vegan old standards: banana-nut muffins, voluptuous vegetable soup, garden carrot soup with fresh ginger, curried vegetable pie with chickpea crust, death by chocolate pie, and chocolate mint mousse. These writers show that a vegan diet is every bit as exciting as a nonvegan one. Just because someone is a vegan does not mean that he or she has to give up macaroni and cheese, French toast, chocolate bourbon pie, chocolate-chip cookies, spinach lasagna, and other traditional favorites. With the new vegan diet, there is room for all of these dishes and others. A reluctant, hesistant newcomer does not need to feel that veganism demands too many sacrifices. If chocolate-bourbon pie and other similar delicacies are also constituents of vegan fare, who wouldn't wish to become a vegan then?

Ethical Issues and Veganism

Although many vegan writers strive to make vegan food appear gourmet and global in order to attract a larger audience, the authors do not forget the importance of ethical issues connected with veganism. The writers lure people unfamiliar with vegan philosophy into their cookbooks through their luscious recipes, but once lured in, the readers are introduced to the philosophies associated with being vegan. The authors use their cookbooks as stepping-stones for readers to learn more about veganism and ethical living. Vegan writers demonstrate how activist groups can use cooking literature to discuss more than cooking. Ethical concerns lie at the heart of the majority of vegan cookbooks, including even those that do not insist that everyone must be a vegan.[21] In a similar fashion, African-American cookbook authors attract readers who are interested in learning about how to cook African and African-American recipes, but the writers also teach about history and black cultural beliefs. In both cases, cookbooks focus on much more than just conveying recipes.

Not everyone views veganism as an ethical ideal. For example, in *Animal, Vegetable, or Woman? A Feminist Critique of Ethical Vegetarianism* (2000), Kathryn Paxton George observes: "The 'vegan ideal,' . . . is a vision of human beings or the world to which some persons think we should all aspire. Those who endorse it currently believe it is a moral ideal, rather than a non-moral, psychological, or aesthetic ideal" (4). George dismisses veganism for a number of reasons, including that such a diet might not provide adequate nutrition for children. She does not spend enough time exploring the fact that for many vegans, their choice is a deeply moral choice, one that seeks to reduce suffering in the world. Despite some people's negative perception of vegans, vegetarians generally view veganism as morally desirable. Colin Spencer observes in his book, *The Heretic's Feast: A History of Vegetarianism* (1995): "Veganism is much respected by vegetarians for many feel that it must be the next step forward. Veganism is an ideal to aim at . . ." (318). A key reason that vegetarians think about veganism as an ideal is because it is a philosophy that promotes and encourages broader changes than only altering one's diet. If one becomes vegan, one must strive to follow a lifestyle that impacts every aspect of life, including how one treats other people, animals, and the world.

A vital aspect of the vegan ideal is to strive to be a compassionate and caring person. Geiskopf-Hadler and Toomay write in *The Complete Vegan*

Cookbook: "To walk the vegan path is to consider all the consequences of how to eat and to make food choices that are . . . compassionate" (xi). This ethic takes in more than food. Compassion must seep into every aspect of one's existence, as Joanne Stepaniak discusses: "People who are vegan attempt to imbue every aspect of their lives with an ethic of compassion. This influences their day-to-day choices and colors their political perspectives, social attitudes, and personal relationships" (*Being* 5). Barnard and Kramer in *The Garden of Vegan* also discuss the centrality of compassion to being vegan: "Compassion isn't sissy; it isn't hippie dippy. It's a way to change the world, and it can change you at the same time" (17). The writers give a new spin to compassion, implying it is something that anyone can use to change the globe. In this cookbook and others, compassion is integral to being an ethical person. The authors wish for their readers to alter their perception of vegan foods as boring, but, more important, to change how they interact with the world and recognize that compassion is a key element for anyone who desires to have a positive impact on the globe.

This compassionate attitude is apparent in how people, whether vegan or not, treat other people and animals. Geiskopf-Hadler and Toomay write: "For many, the vegan decision goes beyond concerns about personal help. They realize that the livestock industry depletes and degrades the environment and that inhumane treatment of animals is common at large-scale 'factory farms' " (xi). In a similar fashion, Kornfeld points out the importance of considering animal welfare and being concerned by how animals are treated at farms (1). These three authors use their cookbooks to argue that being concerned about animal welfare issues is central for any moral individual, whether vegan or not.

Another aspect of being a compassionate person is to feel responsible for the larger global community. "In order to practice veganism, it is not sufficient to simply avoid specific foods and products; it is necessary to actively participate in beneficial selfless action as well" (Stepaniak, *Being* 2).[22] Veganism resonates far beyond the dinner table and impacts every aspect of people's interactions with both their local communities and the world. In *The Angelica Home Kitchen*, McEachern includes profiles of people who help to make Angelica Kitchen possible, among them Paul Breneman, former owner of Clear Spring Organic Farms; Gary Abramowitz, owner of Fresh Tofu Inc.; and Elizabeth Ryan, owner of Breezy Hill Orchard.[23] McEachern wishes to demonstrate that every vegan needs to be concerned about the local farmers and other suppliers who provide them with food.

More broadly, vegans also need to be concerned with the fate of the planet and every living being. In *Everyday Vegan*, Atchison writes, "People need to take responsibility for their actions, whether it is how they treat their neighbor, how they use the resources of our Earth, or what they choose to eat" (xiii). Like Atchison, Stepaniak adopts a global view of what it means to be a vegan: "Embracing veganism compels practitioners to live moral lives . . . while minimizing their impact on the Earth and its resources" (*The Vegan* 129).[24] Atchison and Stepaniak challenge readers to change how they take the world's resources for granted and acknowledge that being a vegan means adopting a more mindful and long-range view of the world's limited resources.

Although the majority of vegan writers focus on limiting consumption and saving the planet, not all do. Vegetarianism and veganism, for some people, can be more about following the new hip diet than about leading a more ethical and compassionate life. In *Vegetarian Times* in 1997, Barbara Haspel and Tamar Haspel describe Madonna and other followers of the low-fat vegetarian diet designed by Dr. Dean Ornish as participants in "me-decade vegetarianism—nothing about saving the planet or your fellow creatures, but, hey, the food's good" (84). Although the writers are describing vegetarianism, it could have been veganism, especially since vegan foods have been revamped into something delicious, gourmet, and trendy. Some people who eat vegan foods are more concerned about its gustatory pleasure than saving the world. Some vegans are primarily concerned about how their diet could make their bodies as lean, trim, and desirable as Madonna's. Not everyone who plunks down the money for a twenty- or thirty-dollar entrée at the latest vegan hot spot in New York City or San Francisco is concerned with saving the environment. Nor is every vegan cookbook author. However, many cookbook authors, as we have discovered, are interested in not only changing the plain Jane image of vegan food but also influencing how people can lead more compassionate and humane lives, not just in how they treat animals. Ultimately, the goal of many vegan cookbooks is global change.

Rewriting Veganism

Using the popular media, vegans have revamped how many Americans perceive veganism. By depicting vegan food as chic, exciting, and tasty, culinary writers have altered how it used to be perceived as unappealing, except to the most zealous fans who did not care if their food tasted as appetizing as a plate of twigs. Writers and chefs have transformed vegan food into something that is both delectable and hip. Vegan activists have used the popular media to show that vegan food is as appealing as nonvegan food, a radical shift from earlier decades when vegan writers were more concerned about the ethical importance of eating a vegan diet than the pleasure it afforded. This approach, however, proved difficult to promote to the American mainstream, making veganism spread up slowly in the 1970s and early 1980s. To attract a larger audience, vegan activists recognized that they had to make vegan foods as appealing as their nonvegan counterparts. Using gourmet and international recipes that would be at home at any high-quality restaurant, authors transformed the image of a vegan diet being dull at best, unpalatable at worst. At the same time, the writers used their delicious and interesting recipes to convey a serious discussion of ethical issues connected to a meat-centered diet.

Like black women cookbook authors who rebel against mainstream stereotypes of the African-American woman as mammy, vegan writers rebel against a stereotype of the vegan being an ultraradical whose ideas should be ignored by more moderate individuals. Vegan authors show that modern vegans are as diverse as any group. Some vegans choose their lifestyle for ethical reasons, others for health reasons. Some choose it because it is the latest "hip" diet, and they are little concerned with ethical issues. Yet others are not vegan but enjoy eating vegan recipes. Both blacks and vegans show how disenfranchised groups can use cooking literature to speak against stereotypes that assume all blacks or vegans are identical. In this fashion, cooking literature becomes a powerful platform for minorities to question mainstream cultural stereotypes.

Vegan writers demonstrate how a media-savvy activist group can play a crucial part in rewriting society's stereotypes. In a nation flooded with media images of food and cooking, any group that wishes to make significant changes to America's eating habits has to consider how to make its views appeal to a mass audience. One way to accomplish this is through the utilization of the same strategies—glossy and beautiful pictures of perfectly prepared meals and enticing prose—that are successfully used to promote and sell recipes and foods in *Gourmet* and similar magazines. In a world where culinary media has grown increasingly slick, polished, and professional, some activist groups have recognized that they have to adopt similar strategies for their philosophies to be heard beyond a limited group of adherents.

Vegans have been one of the most successful of these groups, recognizing that they have to use the media to fight the sharply negative views of them as fanatics who are unwilling to compromise. Vegans have actively engaged with this image in cookbooks, newspaper articles, magazines, and Internet sites, showing that they are as varied as any group. In addition, vegans have used the media to demonstrate that vegan cooking can be as "fun" as cooking with nonvegan foods. By knowing how to depict vegan foods so that they appeal to the largest audience, vegans have changed how many view their movement. Vegans have demonstrated to other activist groups how the popular media can be a power tool to sway public opinion.

Finally, vegan writers (and other vegan activists) have changed the American diet. This is visible at the University of California, Berkeley, where students petitioned so that vegan food choices would be available at all meals (Parr 19).[25] That is not such an unusual switch; California has always been a state where alternative food traditions have thrived. What is more striking is that a number of universities and colleges across the United States have followed Berkeley's lead and tried to include vegan choices. For example, my midwestern institution, Miami University, in 2004 won first place in a National Association of College and Food Services competition. The recipe was not for another new way to disguise "mystery meat." The winning recipe was for a vegan entrée, grilled tofu "steak" with orzo and sun-dried tomatoes and artichokes. Miami has vegan and vegetarian selections for lunch and dinner. This is a remarkable change for a school where in the 1970s an official called vegetarian diets a "fad, one which can be dangerous to health and well-being" (qtd. in "Two" 32). Our cultural attitudes to veganism have undergone a major shift, although such changes are still more likely to appear in college and university towns than other areas. Vegan food writers have played an influential part in encouraging Americans to grow more accepting of vegan and vegetarian foods.

Chapter 8

Thin Is Not In: Two Fat Ladies and Gender Stereotypes on the Food Network

Stars of the late 1990s hit television series *Two Fat Ladies*, Jennifer Paterson and Clarissa Dickson Wright, broke a major social taboo by being fat. They did not just have an extra few pounds; they were fat, appearing as though they spent more than a little time indulging at a dinner table groaning with hearty British dishes. These women did not try to conceal their fatness but, instead, reveled in it. This was a first for food television to depict fat women positively. Why is this unusual? After all, cooking is an industry where fat or heavy set men have been embraced. James Beard's rotund form did not slow down his success, and Chef Paul Prudhomme's and Chef Mario Batali's shape has not hampered their success. It has always been acceptable for a male cook to be fat, and this does not prevent him from becoming a culinary superstar. In this context, his extra pounds are proof of his success. This situation, however, is different for women. Almost all successful female culinary stars look as though they are movie actresses. The Food Network features many such women, including Sara Moulton, star of *Sara's Secrets*, and Gale Grand, star of *Sweet Dreams*. On television's Style network, Nigella Lawson is equally glamorous. Similarly, Martha Stewart—at least before her prison term—never looked like she nibbled one of the treats that she produced by the score. Sleek, sophisticated women who look like they spend more time at the gym than in the kitchen are typically culinary stars.

This reflects a society in which the ultimate sin is for women to grow fat, but men do not face the same pressure. Heavy males are considered successful, mature; heavy females are considered slovenly, sloppy. Rebelling against a culture that assumes women have to be thin in order to star in the media, the Fat Ladies delighted in their fatness. Unlike Oprah and her repeated attempts to slim down, the Ladies did not try any drastic weight reduction plans, and they were definitely not feasting on carrots and celery sticks for dinner. The Fat Ladies' weight did not hinder their enjoyment of food or life in general—a subversive idea when women are obsessed by the thin ideal, which helps explain the Ladies' success.

One reason for the Fat Ladies' popularity was that their show originally aired at a time when Americans, including women, were becoming noticeably heavier.[1] Despite Americans' growing girth, fat people rarely appear in the media, which are filled with beautiful, stick-thin female figures, ones that have little connection to many women's real bodies. The Fat Ladies enjoyed their stockier figures, sending out a message that being heavy was acceptable, despite what most other female stars look like. For millions of women, this was reassuring and revolutionary. In addition, the Ladies challenged the stereotype that it is taboo on television to be middle aged or older. Jennifer Paterson was in her sixties and Clarissa Dickson Wright in her fifties when their show aired. They did not depict middle age as negative but, instead, as something that did not slow down their pursuits at all. They questioned a society that expects women to be young, thin, and glamorous and showed how unrealistic such standards are.

The Ladies, however, accomplished more than just suggesting that it was acceptable for women, including media stars, to be fat and older. In their television show and cookbooks, the Ladies spoke out about a number of important social issues related to food and the people who provide it. First, Clarissa and Jennifer emphasized that it was acceptable to enjoy food, even if it was rich and high in calories and cholesterol. They condemned a society that seemed to have forgotten the delights attached to old-fashioned cooking. In a land of nouvelle cuisine, this was a radical message. Second, the Ladies suggested it was important to remember the past and its food traditions, so they repeatedly focused on cooking traditional English meals. Although some people might perceive this as a conservative move, the Ladies had a more progressive reason for their reliance on historical British recipes. They sought to remember and preserve a culinary past that helped make Britain's culture unique; in this way, the Ladies questioned a world where everything, especially food, had grown increasingly homogenous and bland. Third, the Ladies stressed the significance of recognizing where various foods originate, as well as patronizing small local suppliers. They questioned how large agribusinesses have taken over supplying food because it is profitable, not because it is best for consumers.

"A Moral Panic"[2]: Anti-Fat Attitudes in the United States

The Fat Ladies rebelled against a society that despises fatness. The American mainstream hates fat people and seems to feel little or no need to hide that emotion. U.S. society belittles fat people of all genders, socioeconomic backgrounds, races, ethnicities, and ages. If someone is fat, this is sufficient for that individual to become a victim of vicious jokes and name-calling. The treatment is worse for women, who are repeatedly told by others that they should lose weight or are asked why they do not. American culture scapegoats fat people in much the same way that it scapegoats white trash. Redneck jokes reassure the middle class that they have not fallen that low. Similarly, jokes about fat people reassure less-fat individuals that they have not gained as much as heavier people. Whether in real life or the popular media, fat women and men are ridiculed. In this environment, the Fat Ladies showed that overweight people deserve the same respect as everyone else does.

Along with disparaging fatness, Americans are scared of fatness because it can sneak up on anyone. Our culture depicts fatness as something that demands constant vigilance, so that one does not become fat oneself. In 2004 in the *New York Times*, Sander L. Gilman wrote, "We are in a moral panic about obesity" (qtd. in D. Smith 7). It is nearly impossible to read a newspaper or watch a television program without hearing something new about the growing rates of obesity in the United States. It is not, however, only the obese who concern society. American culture has a deep-rooted fear of fatness in any form, so we go to any extreme, even plastic surgery, to lose extra pounds.[3] Why are we scared? Why is it such a phobia to gain weight? Many reasons exist for this fear, including health concerns. Excess weight has been shown to be a reason that both women and men live shorter lives, so we wish to lose weight to be healthy, but other reasons exist for our phobia. Another reason is that American society is based on action. To succeed in our economy, we believe that we have to appear slender and fit, as though we visit our local gym on a daily basis. Americans esteem the lean-and-hungry look, so we fear gaining weight, which society perceives as a sign of failure. For women, especially if they are upper or middle class, this is particularly true.

Women are supposed to feel guilty if they gain a few pounds because it is a sign that they, at least according to social stereotypes, lack discipline and willpower. These extra pounds carry a heavy price. In her book, *Body Image: Understanding Body Dissatisfaction in Men, Women, and Children* (1999), Sarah Grogan observes, "In affluent Western societies, slenderness is usually associated with happiness, success, youthfulness, and social acceptability. Being overweight is linked to laziness, lack of will power, and being out of control" (6).[4] She continues, "People who do not conform to the slender ideal face prejudice throughout their life" (7). Even as children, fat individuals face discrimination, including having their peers tease them. As adults, overweight people are stereotyped as not as intelligent or popular as slender people (Grogan 7). This prejudice is worse for women, who are supposed to be slender and fit in a society where, as gender researchers Jane Arthurs and Jean Grimshaw note: "Discourses of health, fitness, and beauty have become scarcely separable from each other. The body that is most commonly coded for sexual attractiveness is the 'fit' body—toned, lightly muscled, and gleaming" (5).[5] In a culture that emphasizes a vision of attractiveness that is unobtainable for countless women, they are supposed to feel guilty about each bite they consume because it could lead to extra pounds. Every nibble is suspect. This is worse if a woman eats something high in fat or carbohydrates because they are closely linked to weight gain. American society teaches women that food is potentially dangerous, so they must never relax for a moment. The Ladies fought the social stereotype that women were supposed to feel guilty about everything they consumed. The television show hosts declared that one did not have to feel guilty about eating, even if the foods were high in fat and calories, and, instead, should glory in such food and enjoy it as one of life's joys. The Fat Ladies rebelled against a culture that assumed every woman had to be slender.

Fantasy, Fatness, and Females: Media Images

It is odd that women who are food celebrities on television are typically slender because, like some of the famous male chefs with their extra pounds, one would expect some of the women to show a few pounds around their middles. But the typical woman looks as though she owns a crunch machine, maybe one that sits right by the pasta machine in the kitchen so she can squeeze in a few sets between preparing crème brulee and cooking a veal roast stuffed with brie. No matter how elaborate, fanciful, and rich the meals are that they prepare, not an ounce appears on the women's bodies. Why are their figures so sleek and toned? They represent a fantasy, one in which a woman can indulge in all foods and not gain weight. Of course, we know too well that real life does not work in this fashion, but on the Food Network, it does. Food television is popular with women because it creates a fantasy universe where eating that éclair does not mean you have to spend another hour on the treadmill.

The fact that few fat women appear in the world of cooking-culture stardom is one example of a popular culture phenomenon I refer to as "the missing fat woman." The media contain remarkably few, certainly not in a number that recognizes their real presence in the United States.[6] Despite these millions of real women, fat women rarely appear in the media and, in some cases, vanish entirely.[7] For example, women's magazines and teen girls' magazines typically include no fat women. Occasionally a story might describe someone who was fat, but she always loses fifty or a hundred pounds, in the process finding true happiness and a hunky boyfriend. Celebrity magazines, such as *People*, rarely feature fat celebrities, unless it is discussing Oprah's or some other star's new diet.[8]

This fantasy world where no woman carries any extra weight impacts how real women perceive their bodies. They see so many unrealistically slender bodies that they begin to assume that their bodies should be similarly thin. This feeling is aggravated because American culture is inundated with ways to slenderize, many focused on women. Every diet food imaginable crowds the shelves of grocery stores. Every diet book possible fills bookstores. Health clubs and gymnasiums inundate cities and towns from coast to coast. Television shows and tabloids are replete with ways to diet. Losing weight obsesses our culture, and the media add to this by depicting thin, beautiful bodies that few women can actually acquire, so they feel that they must strive for thinness, whatever the cost. Anorexia and bulimia are rampant because women feel such a desire to lose weight. Even if a woman is not anorexic, she is still apt to wish to lose five or ten pounds.

Like magazines, television shows and movies rarely depict fat women. It is a strange world in which every woman is tall, slender, and no one needs to lose a pound or two, a remarkable contrast with reality. In this universe where no female carries an added ounce, let alone a pound, the Fat Ladies rebelled against the culture of thinness. Like Roseanne Barr, they were fat and unapologetic about it. Such women provide a needed corrective to the scores of shows that star thin leggy beauties—although a caveat is that the Ladies and Roseanne are allowed to be fat because they are funny, so they are not supposed to be taken too seriously. Despite this, the popularity of the Ladies and their show, points out that females wish to see figures in the media that better represent their own bodies and experiences.

It is difficult to understand the Ladies' fame unless one also discusses the Food Network's popularity. The tremendous growth of food television has created a new space for celebrity chefs, including the Fat Ladies, but many other names could be added, including Martha Stewart, the Iron Chef, Paula Deen, Emeril, and the Naked Chef. In the United States, it is unusual that people do not recognize these names from cooking shows on the Food Network. Even if viewers do not watch the network, they are still likely to be familiar with the chefs and the shows in which they star because of the popularity of food television.[9] There is no question that the network is an important part of American popular culture, which is a major accomplishment since the network had a modest start, beginning in 1993 with six million subscribers (Brown 27). At first, some commentators worried that it might not survive. Who could be interested in watching twenty-four hours of people cooking, an experience vastly different from turning on Julia Child for an hour? But, apparently, millions were. By 1998, the audience had risen to 33 million homes (Grimes TV5). In 2000, the Network reached 50 million households (Slatalla F13). In 2004, it reached 80 million households (Aikman A32). In the last decade, food television has grown tremendously. Why have millions tuned in to the Food Network?

Food television is "hot." Director of the Center for the Study of Popular Television at Syracuse University Robert Thompson observes, "The Network has managed to take food and turn it into a glamorous hobby. . . . It has the same effect as rock 'n' roll on a whole generation of viewers. We've gotten to a point in our culture where you're hip if you've discovered the latest hot program on the Food Network" (qtd. in Slatalla F13).[10] Another commentator observes, "For millions of households, the Food Network has become as much a staple as bread and butter, though ten years ago the idea of a twenty-four-hour cable channel devoted to . . . food was a little hard to swallow" (Littlejohn 5D).[11] Today, the network "has become a pop-culture fixture, featured in movies and television shows . . . and has been parodied on *Saturday Night Live*. . . . And the appeal has been far-reaching, with everyone from kids to college dorm buddies and from husbands and wives to singles, novice cooks and experts" (5D). One of the reasons for the success of food television is, as David Rosengarten, a Food Network host, observes, "There's been a 'Hollywoodization' of food TV" (qtd. in Puente 2D). In other words, the network has adopted some of the same styles and techniques of other media hits, such as talk shows or real-life adventure shows. Recipes and their creation have become "hot" and sexy, which is evident in all the attractive women and men featured on many food shows. It is also apparent in shows, such as *The Naked Chef*, that emphasize sexuality or at least sexual puns. With the Food Network's focus on Hollywood glamour, the Fat Ladies' success was more surprising. The British duo provided a much-needed corrective to the large numbers of slender female bodies crowding other cooking shows.

Despite its nontraditional female stars, *Two Fat Ladies* was a great success when it was first aired. One writer for the *New York Times* observed that the Ladies "took off in the United States. . . . In the blink of an eye, they developed a cult following among those who have an innate fondness for British eccentrics in the tradition of Miss Marple and 'Fawlty Towers' " (Hamlin F1).[12] Another commentator noted that the show "made the Food Network worth watching" (Schrambling F1). The program was a hit in other countries, including Canada and Australia. One journalist for Montreal's *Gazette* in 1998 observed, "Squeeze over Spice Girls, make room for the Two Fat Ladies. The latest British sensations are whetting appetites not with music but with their straight-talking, calorie-unwise, and politically incorrect approach to cooking" (Petosa W4).[13] When the Ladies visited Australia, they were treated like a "mixture of the Queen Mother and the Beatles," as Paterson remarked (qtd. in Mack E5). What explains the women's appeal around the globe?

One reason was that their shows and cookbooks allowed the audience to look at rich and decadent food. The Ladies provided what I refer to as "food pornography." In a culture where such food is taboo to consume, especially for women, we like to look at food. Even if we do not cook or seldom do, we still enjoy looking at images and reading descriptions of food that fill the media. Whether television, films, newspapers, cooking articles, or cookbooks, our culture is saturated with images of food. Much of the food imagery is glamorous and upscale, depicting meals that few real people would actually make and serve. Elaborate recipes are accompanied by photographs that show equally perfect images. These lush words and pictures are literally food pornography, created to be gazed at by the audience but not actually consumed. Like traditional pornography, food pornography is about desire but never allowing that desire to be fulfilled, so the viewers wish to have more.

We seem to enjoy gazing at food as much as eating it, which is a reason that food pornography has grown so popular, especially with the women viewers it targets. Some women would even say that looking at food is better than eating it because one does not gain a pound, no matter how luscious a recipe is. Women long for food in a society where eating has become the ultimate crime, so they turn to food porn to fulfill their desires, knowing they can vicariously savor the chocolate gateau or seven-layer lemon torte. Food pornography feeds women's craving, and one place to seek satisfaction is food television. The Ladies' show was a classic example of food pornography, as the two created innumerable rich recipes for their viewers' pleasure. However, the Ladies challenged the food pornography stereotype that a beautiful slender woman prepares decadent dishes but, obviously, never indulges herself with anything more fattening than half a Ry-Krisp cracker. They indulged in their recipes and suggested that it was acceptable for women to do the same.

Another reason for the Ladies' success is that they questioned a society where being thin and young are considered essential attributes if a woman wishes to be successful. The Ladies fought the stereotype that a woman's happiness is directly related to how beautiful, youthful, and slender she is. The show's producer noted in her introduction to *The Two Fat Ladies Ride Again* (1997): "In an industry where women's success in front of the camera is mostly defined by youthful good looks and anodyne personalities, Jennifer and Clarissa's success is an enormous achievement" (8).[14] Similarly, another commentator observed, "On television, the realm of the pert and the blond, [the stars] were revolutionary. In a world that fears fat on the body as much as on the plate, here were two women who were not afraid to revel in excess" (Schrambling F1). The Ladies were a radical change in a media universe where every woman has to be blond and youthful. They possessed neither of these traits and, more important, they did not strive to appear as though they did. They took pleasure in their fat older bodies and displayed them proudly as the two roared around the countryside on their motorcycle; they conveyed a subversive message that being fat was not as negative as the popular media suggested.

In a society obsessed by the necessity of women being thin, no matter what the cost might be to physical health or emotional well-being, the

Ladies were resolutely anti-diet, as the cover of their videotapes made clear: "If you're fed up with faddy diets and supermarket blandness, take a lesson from the Ladies." In their world, one did not have to worry about following the latest diet. Clarissa expressed her views in an article in the *Financial Times* in 2004 when she wrote about the death of Robert Atkins, the diet guru. She observed,

> The legacy of today's ultra-thin "heroin chic" models—and of celebrity diet gurus—is anorexia. The popularity . . . of our television food program, *Two Fat Ladies*, and our cookery books may point to an era where people worry more about inner well-being than their outer image. . . . I shall . . . go and eat my perfect breakfast of Christmas ham and fried eggs. . . . Do not make a resolution to diet but learn to love yourself—fat and all. (Wright 15)

Jennifer was no less anti-thin fascism. She remarked, "It's the last taboo, isn't it—fat? . . . It's all the fault of the Duchess of Windsor. She came up with that stupid line, 'You can never be too rich or too thin.' And America took it to their heart" (qtd. in A. Woods A9). The Ladies shook up America's deeply entrenched belief that the only content woman is ultra-thin. They questioned the idea that thinness equates happiness and that fatness equates unhappiness. This challenged a media world where being fat was the ultimate sin, suggesting that fat women actually enjoyed their lives.

"Cream, Bacon, Grease, and Other Shocking Ingredients"[15]: The Fat Ladies Rebel

One way that the Ladies found joy in eating was by being proponents of rich and high-calorie cooking. In their world, there was never a reason not to throw another cup of cream or another rasher of bacon into a recipe. A commentator observed in 1997 that the Ladies "roar around the British countryside on a motorbike and sidecar, commandeer kitchens, and rustle up meals made with cream, bacon, grease, and other shocking ingredients" ("Have" F3). Another writer noted, "It takes more than a stick of butter to scare Jennifer Paterson and Clarissa Dickson Wright. They are undaunted by eggs and cream, unruffled by meat marbled with fat" (Mack E5). A reason for the Ladies' appeal was that bacon and cream have become "shocking" ingredients in a society obsessed with eating food because it is healthy, even if it is not that tasty. The soy craze is one example of this; every food from chips to cereal now seems to contain soy solely because it is supposed to be good for one's health. The Ladies questioned a culture based on eating food merely because it is healthy.

The Ladies were staunch believers in the emotional and psychological benefits of high-fat cooking. The back cover flap of their book *The Two Fat Ladies Ride Again* states: "The Ladies laugh in the face of the fat-fearing fanatic and are proud to share some decadent gems such as spare ribs and whiskey chocolate pie." Repeatedly, the Ladies emphasized the importance of taking pleasure in high-calorie recipes and foods. In this book, Patterson was resolutely against healthy desserts: "I like my puddings to be lavish. Not for me the insipidity of a fruit salad made with tasteless 'nuked' tropical fruit, or some healthy concoction based on yogurt" (63). Both the Ladies were pro-cream, bacon, and other high-fat ingredients. Clarissa raved about cream in all its varieties from liquid cream to whipped cream to clotted cream, commenting, "Forget all that health and hygiene nonsense. Real cream is far better than that tasteless pasteurized rubbish you get in supermarkets. The antidote to stress is serotonin, and dairy fats stimulate natural serotonin production. . . . Half a pint of double cream will do you more good than a Prozac tablet" (qtd. in J. Lee 78). A journalist observed, "In the high-caloric life Jennifer Paterson viewed through black-rimmed glasses, there was never a reason to go easy on the bacon" (K. Johnson 2D). One reason for the high-calorie ingredients is that the Ladies questioned a culture that told people to avoid them.

The Ladies' recipes were filled with bacon and other rich ingredients. For example, *Two Fat Ladies Full Throttle* (1999) includes recipes for lobsters with latkas, lobster with mayonnaise, duckling with green grapes, duck in red wine sauce, cream-smothered pheasant, and Christmas pudding ice cream bombe. *Two Fat Ladies: Obsessions* is also filled with rich recipes: spaghetti with sour cream, lobster en casserole, lobster Newberg (one cup of heavy cream, two egg yolks, a glass of sherry, and one lobster), and chicken Jerusalem (one chicken, one stick of butter, artichoke bottoms, sherry, two and a half cups of heavy cream). Similarly, their television show included countless decadent and high-cholesterol recipes. When they made appetizers for a party at the Brazilian embassy, Jennifer prepared deep-fried Portuguese cod cakes and Clarissa prepared blinys, topped with sour cream and caviar. The Ladies' recipes were filled with similar decadent ingredients.

The women demonstrated that such cooking should not be abolished, despite what medical doctors argue, because it is one of life's great pleasures.

Along with rich recipes, the Ladies included many hearty and old-fashioned recipes. For example, *Cooking with the Fat Ladies* contains recipes for marinated mackerel, roasted conger eel, marinated Loch Fyne kippers, and Yorkshire gingerbread. *Obsessions* has recipes for eel pie, jellied eel, and eels fried in breadcrumbs. *The Two Fat Ladies Ride Again* includes many old-fashioned recipes: pikelet (a "small, flat crumpet"), mitton of pork (a Northumbrian dish), haggis Waldorf, and George pudding. Like all the recipes that are heavy in cream, butter, and other high-fat ingredients, the old-fashioned recipes break cultural assumptions about what women should eat. These cookbooks show the importance of recognizing how some recipes, albeit old-fashioned, still deserve recognition and resurrection. In our modern culture, it is easy to forget them because they do not seem as fashionable or trendy as new recipes, but the Ladies demonstrated that it was a mistake to simply eat whatever is new. This was a subversive reworking of much contemporary culinary writing, which commonly features whatever is in vogue, whether it tastes delicious or not.

Along with providing high-calorie or old-fashioned recipes, the Ladies also include many that emphasized meat and game. Again, the women rebelled against a culinary establishment that emphasizes eating food that is slenderizing and light. Meat and game are foods typically thought of as "for men," but the Ladies suggested that they are equally for women. In this fashion, the Ladies called into question how society constructs women's light and feminine eating as the antithesis of men's hearty and masculine eating.

One way that the Ladies questioned the ideology that a woman's eating should be light, delicate, and feminine was by being staunchly pro-beef, despite social pressures for women not to eat such heavy fare. In *Two Fat Ladies Full Throttle*, the women observe: "One of the great mysteries of life is why so many people refuse to eat beef because of the BSE scare . . ." (102). In *Two Fat Ladies: Obsessions*, the authors write, "The title of this book, *Obsessions*, was chosen in part as a rude gesture to mimsy journalists who, content with . . . irradiated, badly raised meat, reared without fat, suggest that we are obsessed" (8). The Ladies continue, "In the UK, the Labour government banning of beef on the bone in 1998 not only hardened [our] stance against Mr. Blair's . . . government, but it also made [us] realize how important beef on the bone was. . . . Buying beef on the bone is now rather more difficult than buying heroin" (36). This pro-beef attitude rebelled against the notion that women should not eat it because it is unhealthy. The Ladies suggested that women should eat meat, game, and other heavy, decadent fare even though the "nutrition police" might frown.

The Ladies' cooking is filled with other meat and game, as well. *Cooking with the Two Fat Ladies* includes recipes for boiled squab and ham, pheasant Normandy, rabbit with anchovies and capers, and duck in honey sauce.[16] *Two Fat Ladies Full Throttle* also has many substantial meat and game recipes: pot roast of beef, pickled beef with soda scones, leg of lamb with chicken liver stuffing, venison pie, and baked rabbit. *Obsessions* has recipes for oxtail casserole, veal shanks with garlic, steak and kidney pie, and enveloped kidneys in suet. Their shows also commonly featured meat. In one episode, the Ladies prepared a menu for the guests at the Duke of Hamilton's castle in Scotland that featured partridge with cabbage, Duntreath roasted grouse, medallions of venison, and rabbit with anchovies and capers. In another episode, the Ladies cooked a dinner for a group of Gurkha officers that features stuffed quail with white wine, coq au vin, and beef with chestnuts, peas, and almonds. The Ladies demonstrate that they could still be "ladies" even though they took pleasure in food. In addition, they also undermined the cultural stereotype that associates all women with eating habits that are light, refined, and delicate and suggest that the image has little to do with real women, who struggle to adhere to a cultural stereotype that does more damage than good.

If it is taboo for women to eat meat, it is equally taboo to be anti-vegetarian, when women are supposed to enjoy such light dining. But the Ladies had little patience with vegetarians, an attitude that they freely express in their books and show. In *Cooking with the Two Fat Ladies*, the Ladies observe that the "rise of the vegetarian" is a threat to the meat industry (40). In *Two Ladies Full Throttle*, the authors note: "Since our last volume, I am happy to report a number of vegetarians have been restored to the fold of meat eaters" (71). In *Obsessions*, the Ladies disparage vegetarians: "It has always fascinated me that . . . vegetarians [have] . . . rather strange habits of making vegetable and grain products look like meat. . . . The most horrible of cheap meat products is probably safer" (84). Their shows were also filled with anti-vegetarian comments. When the cooks visited Westonburt School in Gloucestershire to prepare a dinner for the girls' lacrosse team, Jennifer grumbled, "In this day and age, they will probably be vegetarians." In another episode when the Ladies visited the Lake District for a vintage motorcycle rally, Clarissa commented, "More vegetarians relapse on bacon than any other substance." In yet another episode when the two prepared a dinner for the Colyn Male Voice Choir, Jennifer quipped: "It's 'be kind to vegetarians' week, as long as they can eat an anchovy." She prepared tartine, which she described as "delicious, despite its vegetarian undertones." The Ladies made a number of meat recipes in the episode, including mitton of pork and Welsh lamb pie. Clearly, they would not have found some of the vegan activist writers discussed in the last chapter to be good dinner guests. Despite their different perspectives, however, both groups were attempting something similar: they wanted to use their writing to alter how we think about our diets and, ultimately, to change how we eat.

Nostalgia and Social Commentary

As well as questioning a society where women are not supposed to indulge themselves with heavy eating because it might detract from their pursuit of slender, toned bodies, the Ladies also fought other aspects of society. The women were antimodern because, for them, being modern meant that one had to purchase tasteless groceries at huge stores that care little about what is best for the consumer. The Ladies viewed this modern system with disdain and demonstrated how it has negatively impacted small food purveyors. Along with focusing on the delights of eating old-fashioned, substantial meals, the show was about recapturing a vanishing way of life, one that is disappearing rapidly. The Fat Ladies used their cooking show and cookbooks to re-create an almost lost way of life and try to preserve its remnants. It was a universe where everything was fresh and natural because it was just pulled from the garden or fished out of the sea. The Fat Ladies wished to save these small producers, showing how much better tasting their food supplies were than those available at major grocery stores. By purchasing supplies at such small shops, the Fat Ladies sent a subversive message to viewers that fought the notion that bigger is always better. The Ladies showed that smaller is sometimes better.

The Fat Ladies' message is relevant beyond the kitchen. They were also concerned with how our large-scale modern culture makes us strive for whatever is new. The Fat Ladies suggested to their audience that they have to reflect on their relationship to mass society in general. Whether we are in the kitchen or another arena, the Ladies wished for us to slow down and take pleasure in our daily lives and not just rush through them with the aid of newfangled conveniences. Cooking one of the Ladies' meals demands more time than popping a frozen dinner into the microwave, but it is more pleasurable; they are interested in making us embrace both the process of cooking and the end result.

Ironically, the Ladies' philosophy shared some similarities with 1970s natural foods activists. Both wanted people to utilize small food suppliers and thought this was a healthy move for consumers. Both thought that larger was not always better when it came to the places where people purchased food and other supplies. Both wished that people would slow down and embrace the process of making food, although the natural foods fans would have been kneading a loaf of homemade whole-wheat bread while Clarissa and Jennifer would be preparing roasted pheasant. They would not be ideal dinner guests at the same party, but they shared similar belief systems about how the modern food system needed to be changed. More broadly, they thought that society needed change, too, and that people's embrace of all that was new was not always the best strategy for their own benefit or the world's.

One aspect of modern culture that the Ladies rejected was the huge supermarket. Instead, they wholeheartedly supported small suppliers and used their television program to promote them. Much of the show featured the Ladies as they explored the British countryside and bought local ingredients from small farmers or other small-scale providers. The gathering of the ingredients was equally as important as the cooking, and the Ladies demonstrated that this was part of the pleasure of cooking. For example, in one episode, they visited fishermen and purchased fish directly off the boat.[17] They bought crabs, lobsters, mussels, and other fish and the audience members were taken along on the trip, experiencing everything, including the bad weather. "It looks murky and wet out there. Maybe we should put on our wellies?" Jennifer commented before they met a local crabber in his boat. Later, the Ladies prepared fish pie, scallops with leeks, and gigot of monkfish and rosemarin with anchovies, using the fish that they had just caught. They also cooked mussels that they had picked alfresco on the local beach. In another episode, the Ladies cooked for Father Mark and the other fathers at Westminster Cathedral. Clarissa prepared bubble and squeak and stuffed artichokes. After gathering their vegetables and fruits from a nuns' convent garden, Jennifer made tomato summer pudding and peaches for Cardinal Hume. In another episode, the Ladies prepared a meal of corn griddlecakes, deviled kidneys, kedgeree, and jugged kippers for the brewers at the Black Sheep Brewery in North Yorkshire. Before cooking this meal, they visited a local smokehouse where they saw the fish being smoked and purchased smoked kippers. A different episode featured the Ladies visiting a British village and helping women at a local fair raise money to preserve a church. The Ladies walked to a local farm to gather eggs directly from the hens before preparing chopped walnut coffee cake, Yorkshire gingerbread, Danish prune cake, and other delicacies. Similarly, the women depended on local ingredients in another episode when they prepared a Christmas dinner of roasted goose with pâté and prune stuffing, Swedish cabbage, and Christmas pudding ice-cream bombe for a choirboys' celebration. Visiting myriad local shops for local ingredients is a radically different approach to shopping than simply taking a single trip to the closest major supermarket. Therefore, the Ladies gloried in visiting a vast range of farms, fisheries, and butchers, and showed that such experiences are part of the pleasure of cooking and eating. Although visiting local shops might take more time, the Ladies demonstrated that it added immeasurably to the recipes that they later prepared from freshly gathered ingredients.

The Ladies' visits to small suppliers were designed to make viewers rethink whether a grocery trip to the nearest mega-superstore was always the best idea. The Ladies wrote, "We hope that over the years a bit of our obsession has rubbed off on you, that you take the choice to travel that bit further to a good butcher or fishmonger, that you look for the best local sources of supply" (*Obsessions* 9). Another time, Clarissa observed, "I don't sell out. . . . I have turned down hundreds of thousands of pounds. My attitude has always been resolutely anti-supermarket" (qtd. in McCann 55). She disliked their "greedy" attitude toward the farmers who provided them with goods (55). Not only did the Ladies demonstrate that small farmers, fishmongers, and others provided healthier food, the two women also suggested how much more fun and interesting it was for consumers to speak with and buy from such small suppliers rather than hunt for food in sanitized aisles of a large corporate store.

The Ladies did not only use their culinary skills to argue for the importance of buying food from small local providers; they also critiqued agribusiness in general and how it has had a negative impact on our food supply in countless ways. For example, the Ladies discussed problems of over fishing around the globe and suggested stores that did not know how to sell fish properly should be banned from selling it. They also observed: "Mass-produced frozen fish concoctions should be banned too, to prevent waste of this diminishing asset" (*Obsessions* 40). In addition, the Ladies condemned the corporate greed that has made food flavorless. For example, in one episode when the two are preparing game for guests at the Duke of Hamilton's castle in Scotland, Clarissa observes, "A piece of polystyrene has a better taste than the average supermarket chicken." Throughout their cooking show and cookbooks, the Ladies were openly disdainful of the food produced for the majority of large grocery stores. In another video, the Ladies lamented about how much apples have changed and blame it on the Americans:

> "It's extraordinary how they breed flavor out of apples," Clarissa observes.
> "They breed flavor out of everything they can lay their hands on now-a-days," Jennifer comments.
> "I blame the Americans. They seem afraid of strong flavors. Strong flavors. Strong emotions."

The Ladies sought to change how large corporations have taken over the food system in Britain and the United States, resulting in the flavorless apples about which they complained. In this industrial setting, no one cares about the flavor of an apple or a tomato; all that corporations are concerned with is designing food that will increase their profits. If these foods are tasteless, it does not make a difference as long as profits stay the same or increase. The Ladies showed that consumers could make a difference by rejecting such flavorless foods and by visiting small suppliers who care that their foods are bursting with flavor. The Ladies wanted their audience to nostalgically recall how they used to buy foods in the past and to return to such shopping patterns. Even if viewers were too young to remember such experiences, the Ladies resorted to their loving and nostalgic encounters with small suppliers to encourage *everyone* to change the way they shop.

The Fat Ladies resorted to nostalgia for more than making readers rethink how they purchased foods. They used it to recall a way of life that has nearly vanished. Food does not exist in a vacuum, so consuming it recalls memories of the past. For different people, different foods convey varied messages about the past. The writer who best expressed the close link between food and memory was Marcel Proust. In the first volume, *Swann's*

Way (1913), of the seven-volume autobiographical account *Remembrance of Things Past* (1913–1927), he is transported back to his childhood days by a bite of a madeleine dipped in tea:

> I raised to my lips a spoonful of . . . tea in which I had soaked a morsel of . . . cake. No sooner had the warm liquid, and the crumbs with it, touched my palate than a shudder ran through my whole body, and I stopped, intent upon the extraordinary changes that were taking place. An exquisite pleasure had invaded my senses. . . . I was conscious that it was connected with the taste of tea and cake, but that it infinitely transcended those savours. (7)

The bite of the small cake led Proust think of his childhood, and then what followed was an epic stream-of-consciousness account of his life. It is a book not just about Proust but also about the passage of time. For him, it was impossible to separate the taste of food from one's experiences. In a similar fashion, the Ladies used food to conjure memories of the past, reminding people that food is not only about nutrition; it is also an intimate connection to our individual and collective human past. For them, food served as a bridge to past experiences that deserved to be remembered, so it is not surprising that their television program was filled with accounts of their younger lives and historical accounts of earlier times. They wanted us to remember that one of the joys of food is that it helps us to connect to the past.

Was the Duchess of Windsor Right? Fat Ladies Fight Back

The Ladies rebelled against how women and their appetites are stereotyped in mass culture. In American society, it is a moral sin for a woman to have a generous appetite. Men are expected to have large appetites because this confirms their masculinity. It is also a widespread cultural assumption, however, that such gargantuan meals are reserved for men. Women are expected to excuse themselves when it comes to eating huge "man-sized" meals. No matter how hungry a woman is, she is supposed to shun such feasting in favor of dainty and more "feminine" fare, such as a salad or a piece of quiche. A woman is expected to eat lightly; this assumption is especially believed to be strong if she is on a date with a man. If she eats heartily or, even worse, polishes off more food than he does, their relationship might be doomed, at least according to a widely held stereotype. Women are supposed to hide their hearty appetites. In a society where women's eating is constantly under scrutiny, one of the tragic end results is anorexia and bulimia. Fighting the stereotype that women should not eat heavily, the Ladies showed that it was acceptable to eat generously. They prepared big meals and did not fear that they seemed "unladylike." They talked openly about the pleasure of eating and delighted in it, subverting a society where such eating for women is taboo.

Not only did the Ladies eat hearty meals, they also ate ones that were rich and high in calories. The women showed no fear of cream, butter, bacon, and other fattening or high-cholesterol foods but, instead, found great pleasure in them. It was a rare meal that did not include such ingredients. Modern culture condemns such ingredients as unhealthy and shuns them in favor of less fattening ingredients. The Ladies suggested that part of life's pleasure was to delight in rich and high-calorie cooking, despite what nutrition counselors might suggest. The British women scoffed at a culture where the pleasure of eating has been forgotten in favor of good nutrition.

In addition, the Ladies demonstrated that it is fine to be fat and still enjoy life. American society is obsessed with being slender, fit, beautiful, and young. This is especially true for women, who are taught at an early age that the only desirable body is slender and young. This results in a society in which women labor endlessly to be fit and thin or feel guilty if they are not. The obsession only worsens because sleek young females overwhelmingly dominate the popular media. Fat women have literally vanished from television shows, movies, and other media genres, unless added to provide comic relief or depicted losing that weight. The media create an unrealistic and impossible image of women's bodies as all being fit, toned, and young; obviously, this is a fantasy that has little connection with a society where a large number of women (and men) are obese or at least overweight, but such heavy women rarely appear on screen. This absence creates the idea that the only acceptable female body must be toned and slender, which many women cannot achieve no matter how frequently they visit the gym. But the Fat Ladies were not apprehensive about their bodies and still enjoyed life. The Ladies suggested that women should stop agonizing about a few extra pounds, a radical notion in a society obsessed with losing weight.

Finally, the Ladies used their culinary shows and books to question more than the way society perceives women's bodies. The two also critiqued a whole food culture that has increasingly grown homogeneous and bland as large supermarkets and multinational corporations have taken over supplying foods. The Ladies showed the importance of preserving earlier food traditions in order to preserve humanity's cultural past. In a world dominated by fast food chains and massive supermarkets, the women demonstrated that the real shame is that such corporations, which are primarily concerned with the bottom line, have taken over. The Ladies urged their audience to fight large food companies by visiting small suppliers, including local butchers, fishmongers, dairies, and farmers. Such small suppliers, the Ladies suggested, actually provide far healthier foods than those that are available in large stores. Ultimately, the women sought to change people's thoughts about eating and help make them aware that it is impossible to separate food from those who supply it, a message very similar to what 1970s natural foods writers believed. Both tried to encourage people to question their diets and recognize that large-scale agribusiness did not always have the consumers' best interests in mind.

Notes

Introduction: Recipes for Revolution

1. Other works that focus specifically on women and cookbooks include Bower, Fordyce, and Zafar.
2. For studies of women and food culture, see Bentley, Haber, Meyers, and Shapiro, *Perfection*.
3. She also discusses that recipes need a reason to exist and exist as one smaller element of a larger discourse. "A recipe is . . . an embedded discourse, and like other embedded discourses, it can have a variety of relationships with its frame or its bed" (Leonardi 340). Both cookbooks and their recipes are part of a larger discourse community about women, cooking, and gender roles.
4. She continues, "There is much to be learned from reading a cookbook besides how to prepare food. . . . Leafing through a cookbook is like peering through a kitchen window. The cookbook, like the diary and journal, evokes a universe inhabited by women both in harmony and in tension with their families, their communities and the larger social world" (Theophano 6). Whether cookbooks, diaries, or journals, such forms of writing offer a unique view into women's lives.
5. General works on food culture in the United States include Hooker, Gabaccia, and Levenstein, *Paradox* and *Revolution*.
6. See Lustig, McClain, M. F. Porter, and Wynette.
7. Examples include First Congregational Unitarian Church, Ladies' Aid Society, and Muddy Pond Mennonite Community.
8. See *Granny's Cookbook*, *Hispanic Recipe Book*, Tausend, and Urdaneta.
9. A few are Grossinger, Kasdan, Katz, Leonard, Nash, and Nathan.
10. Similarly, Laura Schenone observes, "Cookbooks gave many women their first public voice. . . . Through cookbooks, women would help define the values of the growing nation" (107). She points out that cookbooks, although intimately intertwined with life in the private sphere, also had a public role, giving women a place to be heard outside the home.

11. Not all of these feminine genres were standard written ones. For example, women also used patchwork quilts and cross-stitch to express themselves, finding they had to use whatever forms of expression were most available to voice their thoughts.

12. Examples include Christina Deyo, Bobby Flay, Emeril Lagasse, Rachael Ray, Rocco DiSpirito, and Wolfgang Puck.

13. A number of recent scholars have written about culinary culture and women from different races, ethnicities, or class backgrounds. See A. Avakian, Counihan and Esterik, Heldke, and Witt.

1   "34,000,000,000 Work-Hours" Saved: Convenience Foods and Mom's Home Cooking

1. "No Relief" 43.

2. One 1960s article noted, "Quick-serve food products intended to lighten the housewife's kitchen tasks are pouring onto the market in a rush. New ones show up almost daily at stores and supermarkets" ("Better Days" 118). Despite the fact that the 1960s was an era in which some women began to experiment with natural foods, countless other women continued to depend primarily on convenience foods. Large manufacturers met this need with a plethora of new products.

3. Mary Drake McFeely describes a typical middle-class refrigerator as filled with convenience foods, including "onion soup dip, three bean salad, tuna-noodle casserole, frozen spinach 'creamed' with canned mushroom soup, fanciful structures based on Jell-O, cream pies made with packaged graham cracker crust and pudding mix and topped with Reddi-Whip" (98). From appetizer to dessert, a whole meal of convenience foods could be easily prepared. No longer did a woman need to worry if company was coming; she could whip together an elaborate meal in a short amount of time. Convenience foods transformed the entire cooking process.

4. For articles that discuss the shift toward using more convenience foods, see "Frozen" and Nagle.

5. For more cooking literature that suggested that marvelous meals could be produced in minutes with convenience foods, see "From the Larder," "Good Things," "How to Be," "New Foods," "Treat Yourself," and Watts.

6. Among the articles that argued that convenience foods were superior to homemade ones were "Spend & Save" and Weston.

7. For scholarship that focuses on the relationship between women and convenience foods, see Marling 202–240.

8. Other cookbooks from this period that focused on convenience foods include General Foods and *The Guide*.

9. The mass media were enthusiastic when describing the pathbreaking nature of authors who wrote about convenience foods. In her introduction to Cannon's *The Frozen Foods Cookbook*, Helen E. Ridley wrote, "One of the valuable contributions that Poppy Cannon has made during her distinguished career has been to study and analyze the finest cooking all over the world, refining and simplifying the techniques so that women with 'educated palates' can prepare them in their own homes" (viii). Not everyone was equally enthusiastic, however. For example, Cannon's cooking segments on NBC's *Home* show horrified James Beard. He lamented, "Cannon is [a] food person, and she did a vichyssoise with frozen mashed potatoes, a leek sautéed in butter, and a can of cream of chicken soup from Campbell's" (qtd. in Shapiro 4). This stood in contrast to his authentic version made with cream and homemade chicken stock. Cannon recognized that countless women did not possess the time or desire to prepare his recipe, no matter how delectable, and this was acceptable. A businesswoman did not have to fret that her soup lacked Beard's touch because she was busy with work and family responsibilities. She owed it to herself, Cannon believed, to take any possible kitchen shortcuts.

10. An assistant professor of Foods and Nutrition at Michigan State College in 1951, Mary Morr reached a similar conclusion in the article she published in the *Journal of Home Economics*, "Food Mixes and Frozen Foods." Another study by a home economist about the efficiency and cost of convenience foods is Asp.

11. This fear of modernism was not new in the United States, where it has cropped up repeatedly over the decades. For example, in the 1920s, 1930s, and 1940s, modern design was used in fallen-women films to show that the women were immoral. Donald Albrecht writes, "Modern design came to be associated with forces that were threatening domestic security" (111). See Lea Jacobs 52–56. Americans have always had an uneasy relationship with modernism.

12. Numerous cooking articles focused on the delights of instant potatoes and other packaged potato products. See "Make It," "Potato Favorites," and "Work Wonders."

13. For an article that discusses how convenience foods allowed inexperienced cooks to prepare gourmet dishes, see "Here Is Baker's Magic."

14. *Easy Ways to Delicious Meals* included soup recipes for Mexican chicken gumbo soup, gazpacho, quick borscht, and beef broth Cantonese. For a main course, the cookbook included recipes such as Polynesian ham bake (cooked ham bits, condensed beef broth, and chow mein noodles [44]), mock sukiyaki (71),

chicken Italiano (75), and Chinese barbecued ribs (Campbell 80). These recipes were not that unusual, but they did represent a move away from blander Anglo-American dishes.

15. McCarthy 3.

16. A number of articles focused on the speed and efficiency of convenience foods. See "Whole Family."

17. A 1965 article from *McCall's* proclaimed, "Want to be a great cook? It's a breeze with today's wonderful 'convenience' foods, convenient in a double sense since they're easily available at your supermarket, and they can be prepared with a minimum of time" ("Instant" 76). In previous centuries, the only way that a woman became a great cook was through countless hours of hard work and practice. Now she could obtain that label with less labor and have time for other pursuits. What was not challenged in this article was that women would still perform the cooking with little or no help from men.

2   "Unnatural, Unclean, and Filthy": Chinese-American Cooking Literature Confronting Racism in the 1950s

1. Horace Greeley qtd. in Gyory 17.

2. For more information on the popularity of Chinese food in the 1950s, see Claiborne.

3. Other cooking literature that focused on cooking Chinese food included Cheng, "Cooking in a Chinese Wak [sic]," "Chinese Cooking," "Foods"; Kinard, "One Dish," "Raviolis," J. Wong and "You Cook."

4. Non-Chinese women also wrote cooking literature that focused on Chinese and Chinese-American food. They wrote for different reasons, as Theophano observes: "Nonnative women, as did many others, . . . used what was close at hand as a way of crossing borders or patrolling them" (153). Non-Chinese women might have wished to write about such foods to increase cultural understanding. In other cases, they might have desired to police white society's boundaries by describing the oddities of Chinese cuisine and changing recipes to represent American taste preferences. Although white women's cooking literature played a role in spreading Chinese foods, this chapter focuses on Chinese and Chinese-American women, seeking to understand how cookbooks offered them a place to describe their experiences.

5. In the 1950s, the interest in Asian foods went beyond the kitchen. For an article that discusses the influence of Asian tastes in clothing and food, see "A New

Simplicity." This interest, however, was limited by the general paranoia provoked by the Communist scare.

6. Other white stars included Marilyn Monroe, Marlon Brando, Rock Hudson, Frank Sinatra, Cary Grant, Audrey Hepburn, and Paul Newman.

7. Examples of such shows include *The Mickey Mouse Club, The Honeymooners, Donna Reed, Ozzie and Harriet*, and *Father Knows Best*. This is just the list's beginning.

8. The most famous of these villains was Fu Manchu. Sammee Tong played the butler on the television show *Bachelor Father*, while Victor Sen Yung was the cook on *Bonanza*.

9. Other 1950s Chinese cookbooks by Chinese and non-Chinese authors include Caleva, Son Chan, Chow, Donovan, Francetta, Hong, Jackson, *Oriental*, and Richards and Richards. Men, mostly restaurant owners or chefs, wrote some of these cookbooks. Since the 1800s, many Chinese males have entered the cooking profession because it was one of the few employment opportunities that were open to them. Thus, both male and female authors were involved with changing how their readers thought about Chinese culture and Chinese people. This chapter, however, limits its focus to women, exploring how they utilized cooking literature in subversive ways.

10. This acceptance had limits. The sauce was often changed to make it appeal to white American tastes, so garlic was removed entirely (Levenstein 30).

11. J. A. G. Roberts in his book *China to Chinatown: Chinese Food in the West* (2002) writes, "The spread of Chinese food through the Western world has occurred not only through the opening of Chinese restaurants and takeaways but also through attempts by Westerners to cook Chinese food for themselves. These attempts have been facilitated by the publication of recipe books" (187). Around the world, Chinese cooking literature has played a part in the globalization of Chinese food.

12. Qtd. in Gyory 17.

13. More than a thousand Chinese died (Iris Chang 59, 64). For additional information on the conditions that workers faced, see Sucheng Chan and Pan.

14. Similarly, writer Bayard Taylor described the Chinese as "the most debased people on the face of the earth" (qtd. in Gyory 17). Hinton Rowan Helper remarked that they were "counterfeit human beings" (qtd. in Gyory 18). In 1862, Dr. Arthur Stout suggested that the Chinese posed a health threat to the United States (qtd. in Iris Chang 123). In the 1870s, newspaper writer John Swinton wrote, "all anthropologists and ethnologists are agreed . . . [that the] Mongolian blood is a depraved and debased blood. The Mongolian type of humanity is an inferior type . . . " (qtd. in Tchen 189). These commentators and others thought that the Chinese were scarcely human, so they did not need the same protection under American law. Not only did whites judge the Chinese to be morally depraved, but they were also considered unfair workplace

competition. In 1902, an American Federation of Labor pamphlet described the Chinese as "heathen competition" (qtd. in Wong and Chan 8).

15. Another senator who shared Blaine's views about exclusion was John P. Jones of Nevada. In 1882, he observed, "Can a current of barbarians be permitted to flow into this country without affecting its white people for the worse?" (qtd. in Wu 129).

16. This was one of the many instances when white Americans in the nineteenth and twentieth centuries used the Chinese diet as a way to justify discrimination, including why Chinese could not live in the United States. It is important to remember this background when thinking about 1950s Chinese and Chinese-American cooking literature; more was at issue than just changing white food preferences.

17. President Franklin D. Roosevelt eventually repealed the law in 1943 as an act of friendship to our war ally. The number of immigrants was only raised to 105 every year, however, not enough to change America's demographics drastically (E. Lee 245).

18. For more on the Chinese-American experience during World War II, see Takaki.

19. E. Lee 29.

20. The gender imbalance was significant. In 1890, there were 2,678 Chinese men for every single woman. It took decades for this balance to shift (Yung 293).

21. To cater to wary whites, some Chinese restaurant owners in the mining districts actually went so far as to operate English kitchens that served roast beef, chocolate cake, and other Anglo-American foods (Denker 96).

22. Similarly, Alice Miller Mitchell dedicated her book *Oriental Cookbook* (1950) to "the 'breaking of bread' between the East and the West" (n.p.). This was a common philosophy in Chinese cooking literature, including that written by women (and men) not of Chinese descent.

23. Male authors of cookbooks also showed an interest in teaching about culture and history. For instance, Calvin Lee's *Chinese Cooking for American Kitchens* (1959) included information about Chinese philosophy, history, and art.

24. Roberts 147.

25. La Choy Food Products' chow mein and chop suey were an established part of the American food scene, its cans of Americanized products cropping up on tables across the United States. A La Choy company cookbook, *The Art and Secrets of Chinese Cookery* (1958), included recipes such as tuna chop suey and hamburger chop suey (10, 19). Although not authentic, the recipes at least exposed white Americans to the idea that Chinese foods were not as unusual as they might have assumed.

   More than expanding white America's culinary food boundaries too greatly, La Choy Food Products seemed concerned about demonstrating to nervous whites that Chinese food products were wholesome and sanitary. The company's cookbook reassured readers by showing an aerial view of La Choy Food Products in Archbold, Ohio, with the caption: "More than six acres of floor area are equipped with the most modern facilities for cooking, blending, and packing La Choy products. Scrupulously clean, you can be sure ingredients are carefully selected to safeguard quality . . . " (*The Art* 31). The stereotype that Chinese food was "dirty" or contaminated was a widely believed whites, a fear closely linked to the racist notion that the Chinese people were also unsanitary.

26. For an article that focused specifically on chop suey's gastronomic delights, see "Cook's Heaven."

27. White cooking authors in the 1950s also focused on Chinese foods that were fairly tame, suited to the American appetite. For example, McCully in her *McCall's* article discussed Americanized staples such as egg rolls, sweet-and-sour shrimp, egg foo yong, and Chinese spareribs (40).

28. Male authors writing about Chinese food also addressed this stereotype. In his book, *Cooking the Chinese Way* (1955), Kenneth Lo observed, "To the uninitiated Westerner, Chinese cooking appears, like the 'Chinese puzzle,' something best left to the Chinese" (4). But this was only the first reaction before the Westerner tackled the challenge, discovered the merits of Chinese cooking, and was "richly rewarded" (7). Similarly, Frank Oliver in his book, *Chinese Cooking* (1955), wrote, "Many people consider Chinese food too exotic to be attempted in the ordinary household kitchen but nothing could be further from the truth" (10). This image of Chinese cuisine and other Asian cuisines as too mysterious is a long-standing image about Asian people, also. "The mysterious East" has been a stereotype that has distanced Asian Americans because it has supported the racist ideology that their ways are too unusual for whites to understand.

29. Research on "exotic" food includes Long.

30. "Exotic" is a troubling word because it suggests that a culture is not "normal." Heldke observes foreign dishes are exotic, but from whose perspective? Middle-class Euro-Americans, although this is unstated (19). "Exotic" is used to define cuisines and peoples. Thus, whites consider Indian or Japanese food to be more "exotic" than Italian or Irish. The way they define "exotic" depends on how they view a culture.

31. In the suburbs, Chinese also faced racism. Whites feared that minority families would hurt property values, so some Realtors refused to show or sell them houses. When the future Nobel Prize winner C. N. Yang attempted to buy a house in Princeton, New Jersey, a seller refused his down payment (Iris Chang 452).

32. For more information about these earlier Chinese and Chinese-American cookbooks, see Inness, *Dinner*, 88–108.

3   "All Those Leftovers Are Hard on the Family's Morale": Rebellion in Peg Bracken's *The I Hate to Cook Book*

1. Bracken 32.
2. Today, many Americans still assume that the shared family dinner helps build unity. This is such a strong belief that some families insist that all members share this meal, but breakfast and lunch lack the same significance.
3. For more information about Bracken's life and her writing career, read her autobiography, *A Window over the Sink*. Also, see Hoffman.
4. Other research on women's changing household responsibilities includes Berk, Boydston, Matthews, Ogden, Phyllis Palmer, Sprankle, Strasser, and Wandersee. McHugh provides a thoughtful study of the housewife's changing image in films.
5. Friedan 60.
6. Friedan noted that designers were intent on making the home appear as appealing as possible to the women who were confined there for many hours of their lives. The kitchen gained new significance: "Interior decorators were designing kitchens with mosaic murals and original paintings, for kitchens were once again the center of women's lives" (13). With America going on a buying spree after the war ended, the kitchen was not the only room that changed to make it more attractive for females. The living room was full of modern furniture. The family room contained a brand-new television set. Nevertheless, what had not changed was who performed the cooking.
7. The cooking mystique is not relegated to the 1950s. It continues today in our supposedly more liberated era when women are free to choose whether or not they wish to cook. But still the cooking mystique lingers and influences women, who assume that they should be the ones who cook for their families, and in many American homes, Mom, not Dad, performs the bulk of cooking-related tasks because they are considered to be women's responsibility. The cooking mystique remains tenacious.
8. For more information on the cooking mystique, see Inness, *Dinner Roles*.
9. For other reviews, see Benet and Ickeringill. Additional information about the book's success in Great Britain can be found in Humble.
10. One writer for the *Oregonian* in 1999 observed, "in the 60s, when gourmet cookbooks and Julia Child were exciting many and terrifying others with their techniques and ingredients lists, Bracken was a friendly and funny voice in the haute cuisine jungle. . . . Canned soup? You betcha" (Perry L18). In an era when many women assumed that being good mothers and wives meant laboring

over ever more ambitious meals, Bracken said that it was acceptable not to keep up with Child and similar gourmet chefs.

11. Bracken also observed, "If anyone gives you a shiny new cooking utensil for Christmas, you're as thrilled as a janitor with a new bucket of cleaning solvent" (x). For the woman who hated to cook, no new cooking utensil could ease her chore. If anything, her job was made harder because she had to figure out how to use the new tool and act as though she was excited to get it and did not just want to ship it to Goodwill as soon as possible.

12. Many articles and books focus on the connection between mothers and the love that they show through home cooking. See Meyer. This stereotype also crosses national boundaries. Kashmira Tumbol Baldauf discusses her Indian mother's curry as a sign of maternal devotion (14). A courier service between Latin America and New York City conveys, among other items, mothers' home-cooked food (Elliott A1). Jenny Kwak writes about how her Korean mother demonstrated her love for her family by cooking traditional Korean meals (119). The connection between love and mother's cooking passes across cultural, ethnic, racial, and economic boundaries. The connection between dad's cooking and love rarely appears and is seldom discussed.

13. Mom's cooking and its supposed connection to love is part of the larger iconography that surrounds the American kitchen. It, not the living room or dining room, is the "heart" of the home. One reason for this is that the kitchen has always been associated with warmth. When people cooked over an open hearth or a wood-fired iron stove, the kitchen was often the one room that was warm and comforting, so people congregated there. At the center of this space were mother and her cooking, which were central to the family's well-being. Bracken rebelled against the kitchen being considered women's "natural" domain. For more information about the significance of the American kitchen and its design, see Lupton. For a more general discussion of home design, see Rothschild and Cheng.

14. Contemporary cookbooks also emphasize the connection between mother's love and cooking. See Lutisha Smith and Heatter. Both books discuss the authors' mothers and their love for cooking.

15. Sylvia Plath in her novel, *The Bell Jar*, described a similar experience. The main character goes insane because she is not able to conform to narrow expectations in the 1950s for how women should behave. Whether for Friedan, Bracken, or Plath, madness lurked in women's lives because of society's tight restrictions and expectations.

16. Bracken, *Appendix* 106.

17. For books that focus on how food can be used to get a man and keep him, see Brooks and Bosker, Lapanja, and Malouf and Gumbinner. These books and others stress that any woman wishing to appeal to a man must consider his taste preferences. Today, the emphasis is still on how food can attract a male.

18. Bracken 90.

4 "Boredom Is Quite Out of the Picture": Women's Natural Foods Cookbooks and Social Change

1. Robertson 45.
2. For more information about Graham's theories, see Nissenbaum and Sokolow.
3. Also, see Johnson and Lenica and Sauvy.
4. Bob Dylan.
5. Food scholar Catherine Manton writes, "The individual food consumer can actively do something to help resolve huge, global issues such as world hunger, global environmental pollution, and food supply contamination" (10). Since individuals could have a direct impact on a variety of social ills, this made the natural foods movement appealing to millions of women (and men).
6. Many large food companies quickly began to produce "natural" foods because they represented big money makers. Dannon Yogurt claimed it contained no chemical additives. Borden's tried producing organic fruit juice (Levenstein, *Revolution* 198). In 1972, Pepperidge Farm started selling healthier breads with no additives (Frum 176). Companies recognized that labels such as "natural" or "organic" could sell anything from cat food to baby formula at premium prices, as consumers were increasingly dubious about the nutritional value of the foods that they bought. They needed reassurance, and manufacturers recognized that such terms offered that, although the companies remained vague about what such terms actually meant.
7. Other 1970s books and articles that focused on the popularity of natural foods include Ewald, Goldstein, Hewitt and "Nature's Table" and "Recipes"; Sokolov, "The Food" and "Learning"; and Wiener. For an article on the high prices of natural foods, see Colamosca.
8. Even some family pets were impacted by the natural food craze. When I was a child in the 1970s, my cat had brewer's yeast or wheat germ sprinkled on her food, and my family was not alone in changing pets' diets. Joan Harper wrote in her *The Healthy Cat and Dog Cook Book* (1975) that cats and dogs would be healthier on a more natural diet and suggested feeding animals recipes such as soy loaf, soy patties, carob cakes, bean burgers, and lentil loaf. If people desired to change their lives, they had to change their pets' diets as well.
9. Additional articles from *Seventeen* that discussed natural foods' pleasures include "Nature's Table: Bulgur" and "Nature's Table: Seeds."
10. In recent decades, women continue to operate small and large natural foods businesses. One of the co-founders of the nationally distributed Amy's Kitchen foods was Rachel Berliner, who helped start the business in 1988.

Allison Reisner Hooper is co-owner of another natural foods business, a cheese company, Vermont Butter and Cheese, which she founded in 1984 (Julian, "Smile" C1). For many years, Ellen Straus was in charge of the Straus Family Dairy, in 1992 the first dairy west of the Mississippi to become entirely organic (Fimrite A21). Diana Flynn is the owner of Thankful Earth Organic Farm in Massachusetts, which she took over in the mid-1990s (Julian, "Dreams" E1). Barbara Jaffe was a co-founder of Newmarket Foods, which produced natural ice cream toppings, in the 1990s (Bianchi 46). Since the 1980s, Leslie McEachern has owned the vegan and organic restaurant Angelica Kitchen in New York City; since 1993, Joy Pierson has been a co-owner of the vegetarian Candle Café, also in New York City. Many more names could be added to this list.

11. Other natural cookbooks authored by women include Hewitt, *The New York Times Natural Foods Cookbook*; Judd, Katzen, and McCracken.

12. Articles that discussed the potential health risk of natural foods include "Facts"; Schultz; Snider; "We've Been Asked"; and "What's So Great."

13. Two other commentators wrote, "For many years the so-called health food store held a mystique alien to most Americans. Now, all over the country, natural food stores are springing up full of products. . . . We are very optimistic" (Cadwallader and Ohr xix).

14. For articles by 1970s nutritionists who had ambivalent reactions to the hippie culture and its eating habits, particularly vegetarianism, see Dwyer et al. and Erhard.

15. Additional reviews of *Diet* include Bush and Rev. of *Diet*.

16. Many writers tried to jazz up natural foods' plain image. One author noted, "Health foods can be sensuous, spartan, exotic—anything your mood requires. To be nutritious is far from synonymous with being dull" (M. Miller 148). This writer and others challenged the idea that natural foods were always tasteless.

17. For additional reviews of *Laurel's Kitchen* when it was originally published, see Barbara Jacobs and Rev. of *Laurel's Kitchen*. For more information about the book's success, see Steinle.

18. Many authors believed in the importance of good nutrition. Cookbook authors Judith Goeltz and Patricia Lazenby wrote in 1975, "We suppose people just aren't convinced of the seriousness of diet, and that is easy to understand. . . . If we can help a few of our readers take the first step toward healthier eating and better nutrition, we will consider our efforts rewarded" (21). The emphasis in this cookbook and others was not on making money but on spreading a new diet that promised to transform people's lives.

19. Similarly, Sharon Cadwallader and Judi Ohr wrote in their *Whole Earth Cook Book*, "None of our recipes are complicated, as we want to turn you on to the relaxation in simple, natural cooking. The country kitchen is a traditional gathering place. Let this style pull you into the fun of cooking" (xix).

For Cadwallader, Ohr, and others, the kitchen was supposed to become the revitalized center for the new home, based on all-natural foods.

20. In her book, *Natural Cooking* (1971), Barbara Farr praised bread and other simple foods: "A steaming bowl of soup, a ripe tomato still warm from the heat of the sun, and a loaf of crusty whole-grain bread; all of these are natural foods. On the other hand, a TV dinner is unnatural in its concept, unsatisfying in its flavor and unbeautiful to behold!" (4). Such simple foods represented a food movement that rebelled against the mainstream food system that was based on overly processed and artificial ingredients and flavors.

21. Belasco 27.

22. Our culture is fascinated with healthy eating. Sallie Tisdale writes, "A minority of Americans eat healthy food . . . but socioculturally this is the leading image on consumption and success" (158). No matter whether one turns to television, films, popular magazines, or advertisements, the image of people eating healthy, nutritious food dominates. As Tisdale points out, this image is closely connected with an image of success. American mainstream culture promotes that both men and women should appear healthy and in shape, but millions of people have not achieved this. Thus, they rush to the grocery store to purchase whatever natural and healthy foods are available, since they offer the promise of achieving that image. They have become status markers, and shopping at many of the larger natural foods stores, at least in some cases, has become a display of one's high-class status. Just browse around one of the big natural health food chains (Whole Foods Market, for instance). These stores present expensive, artistically prepared foods that are far beyond the price range of many lower- or middle-class pocketbooks.

5 "More American than Apple Pie": Modern African-American Cookbooks Fighting White Stereotypes

1. Zanne Zakroof qtd. in Sanchez-Klein 1E.

2. Research on African-American cookbooks includes Prettyman, Witt, and Zafar.

3. Other contemporary African-American cookbooks written by women include *The Black Gourmet*, Butler, Grosvenor, and Marsh.

   An African-American cookbook writer who was concerned about passing on black cultural history was Lena Richard. In New Orleans, she was regarded as one of the city's great cooks. A chef, restaurant owner, and caterer, she decided to publish cookbook in 1939 to share her recipes with more people. *New Orleans Cook Book* (1940) is widely regarded by experts as a Creole classic. In the book,

Richard was especially concerned about including African-American recipes that she had first heard orally. She also had a popular televised cooking show on WDSU, making her among the earliest black women to star in such a show.

4. As Rafia Zafar writes about black women's cookbooks, they engage with the "linked issues of black stereotyping and class" and take an active role in rewriting them (450). For blacks and other minority groups, cookbooks become an arena to question and challenge racist, sexist, and classist stereotypes.

5. Mammies and other house servants played a subversive role, being "the primary agents for the cultural fusion of Africa and Europe and of diverse white and black experiences in the plantation community" (Genovese 365). Whether whites desired it or not, they were brought into closer contact with African beliefs and traditions by their domestic servants.

6. Ivy Schweitzer writes about this opposition, "The proximity of the mammy to affluent Southern women helped construct their relationship as antithetical and mutually constitutive" (125). Such closeness could have made black and white women appear too similar. That would have brought up disturbing issues about why black women were enslaved and did not receive the same genteel treatment from Southern men that white women did. To fight this, whites created a stereotype of black women being strong, large, and dominant, more like men than women. For plantation owners, this image served as justification for working female field slaves in the same way as males.

7. See Eppes, Ripley, and Smedes.

8. Aunt Jemima products were produced throughout the twentieth century. They included salt and pepper shakers, cookie jars, and syrup pitchers (M. Harris 88). Aunt Jemima was also imprinted on flour scoops, pancake spatulas, mixing bowls, and toy stoves (Goings 28). The depictions served to suggest that, even though slavery was gone, the consumer still had a figurative slave in the kitchen.

9. In addition, McDaniel played loyal mammy roles in *The Mad Miss Manton* (1938), and *Blonde Venus* (1932).

10. She also appeared outside the kitchen. Sewing kits, string dispensers, wall sconces, and sheet music featured mammy (P. Turner 51).

11. Black cookbooks emphasize the significance of passing down recipes and historical facts so such history will not be lost, which is vital because as Dorothy I. Height writes in *The Black Family Reunion Cookbook* (1991), "You are embarking on a process that goes beyond the preparation of food. You are partaking in centuries of history, tradition, and culture. You are continuing an important legacy that is central to the fabric of African-American life" (National iii). In her book *Ideas for Entertaining from the African-American Kitchen* (1997), Angela Shelf Medearis notes, "What is not recorded is not preserved, and what is not preserved is lost forever. . . . I am trying to do my part to preserve, share, and enlighten others about the wonderful history behind African-American

celebrations and recipes" (1). Similarly, cookbook author Kathy Starr observes, "This is the first time the recipes have been written down. My grandmother and I have never used a cookbook. . . . We cook a lot by intuition—like playing the piano by ear. I have tried to put that intuition into words . . . " (xiv). These cookbooks and others emphasize that black history needs to be remembered to preserve African Americans' cultural identity.

12. For cookbooks that focus on African influences on cooking in *all* the Americas, see Cusick and Shange.

13. Similarly, in her cookbook, *A Date with a Dish: A Cook Book of American Negro Recipes* (1948), Freda De Knight wrote, "There are no set rules for dishes created by most Negroes. They just seem to 'have a way' of taking a plain, ordinary, everyday dish and improving it into a creation that is a gourmet's delight" (xiv). Sometimes they had no other choice because "plain, ordinary" foods were the only ones to which they had access.

14. The cookbook also includes a glossary of African-American foods, including ashcake, fritters, gumbo, hoecake, hopping John, pot likker, and red-eye gravy (200). This suggests the importance of new generations of blacks learning about these traditional foods, even if they might be able to afford other foods, since such traditional recipes are essential for keeping black culture alive.

15. In her influential article, "Deciphering a Meal" (1975), anthropologist Mary Douglas discusses the meaning of meals. "Each meal is a structured social event which structures others in its own image. . . . The cognitive energy which demands that a meal look like a meal . . . distinguishes order, bounds it, and separates it from disorder" (44). She describes some of the reasons why my students would not eat Indian food; they rebelled against a meal that did not look like they assumed it should and wanted something that was "ordered" in a familiar way. Their views, however, were also racist. They assumed that foods from different race and ethnic groups would be unappealing or not edible.

16. Whether watermelon or steak, individual foods are linked with society. Archaeologist Mark Warner observes, "Foods undeniably evoke culture; think of chicken noodle soup or a hot dog at a baseball game" (51–52). As he suggests, foods always have a cultural context. It is impossible to imagine a food without also thinking about the culture that created it. Thus, chicken noodle soup conjures up different images than those conjured up by a plate of fried chicken.

17. Although this is a flexible hierarchy—for example, Italian food can be lower on the hierarchy if one is thinking of spaghetti from a can or a take-out pizza—it is rigid in some ways. French food has more prestige than African-American food. Such stereotypes are dangerous because they easily move from the foods to the people themselves.

18. For those who criticized Zoeller's comments, see Sandomir, and Simons and Mallory.

19. A number of scholars have written about the historical development of soul food, including Poe. For earlier cookbooks that focused on soul food, see Bowser and Eckstein and Princess Pamela.

20. Soul food builds a bridge between African Americans and Africans around the globe. "Soul food unites African Americans not only with their people's history, but with contemporary Black brothers and sisters around the world" (Mendes 85).

21. For more information on the black diet today, see Bullock, Chatterjee, Culbertson, and Tucker. Factors other than poor nutrition influence blacks' earlier death rate compared to whites. For example, Sir Michael Marmot, an epidemiologist, studies how social status influences poor health for those with low rank (qtd. in Cohen B9). Most scientists, however, agree that poor nutrition has a devastating impact on African-American health. It is a complex problem with no easy solution. Physician Noel W. Solomons observes, "The lack of control over lifestyle, diet, and social circumstances may be entrenched factors [in black culture] that both explain the epidemic and militate against a facile solution" (318). He points out that these health problems are not only a concern for African Americans but also for other blacks that the African Diaspora distributed in the Caribbean and South Africa (314). All of these groups share similar health and nutrition concerns, although these are influenced by the different cultural backgrounds.

22. Even earlier books contained recipes influenced by different cultural traditions, including one of the first cookbooks by an African-American woman, Abby Fisher's *What Mrs. Fisher Knows about Old Southern Cooking, Soups, Pickles, Preserves, etc.* (1881). This book included traditional southern recipes for Maryland beaten biscuits and hoecake. It also had a recipe for Sally Lund bread, which originated in England, and other recipes from different cultural backgrounds. Fisher's book was published with the help of San Francisco and Oakland benefactors; it was a logical extension from her pickles and preserves business (Longone 98). The first black woman–authored cookbook was Melinda Russell's *A Domestic Cook Book: Containing a Careful Selection of Useful Receipts for the Kitchen* (1866), although Fisher's is better known.

6 "You Can't Get Trashier": White Trash Cookbooks and Social Class

1. Mickler, *White Trash* 29.

2. He continued, "Poor whites in this country . . . are often made fun of and referred to as 'welfare cheats.' . . . Unlike blacks and other racial minorities,

poor and mostly rural whites have few defenders. . . . To be white and poor is unforgivable" (Van Brunt 38).

3. For works that discuss the popularity of white trash, see Friend, Cohen and Rubiner, Spindler, and Wilson.

4. Disgust is mixed with other emotions. There is a "potent mixture of disgust and desire produced by the transgression of bodily decorum" (Arthurs 140). This is true not only of body decorum but also other ways in which poor whites violate upper- and middle-class norms. The American mainstream's disgust about white trash and their lives is mixed with desire because white trash are not confined by society in the same way as people higher on the social ladder are.

5. An example she provides of a television show that uses humor to make light of the reality of poverty is *Roseanne*. McDonald observes, it "reinforces white trash as humorous, allowing viewers to witness, without guilt, the social and economic conditions that create that reality" (17). What she does not fully address is how humor can serve a subversive purpose, showing a darker reality under the jokes. In addition, in popular culture, white trash is used to express self-identity (Hartigan 314). Such an approach rebels against centuries of mainstream society informing white trash that they should not admit to their backgrounds.

6. For studies of whiteness, see Bouson, Hill, and Talbot. Also, see the essays in Delgado and Stefancic's anthology.

7. Cultural historian Jamie Winders notes, "Many analyses of whiteness assume *a priori* that a white identity intimates unproblematic claims to white privilege. . . . Simply being white does not automatically bring social, economic, or any other kind of privilege" (46). White trash highlights that whiteness is not always a privileged identity associated with high social status and economic success.

8. Sessions 292.

9. Literary historian Shields McIlwaine adds "woolhat, dirt-eater, or tacky" as terms for poor whites (241). Whatever they were referred to as, poor southern whites were described early in America's history. In 1728, William Byrd II led an expedition to survey the boundary line between Virginia and North Carolina. When he wrote about his experiences, he described the "lubbers" as "wretches," who were "lazy, dirty, vulgar, ignorant, promiscuous, and deceitful" (qtd. in Kathleen McDonald 16). Writing for *The Chicago Tribune* and *Boston Advertiser* in 1865 as he traveled through the South, Sidney Andrews described North Carolina "clay-eaters" as lower on the "scale of human existence" than slaves; the whites "reached a yet lower depth of squalid and beastly wretchedness" (qtd. in Winders 56). From such early roots sprung today's southern redneck stereotype.

10. Research on the South's poor whites includes Ash, Bolton, Flynt, and McWhiney.

11. Information on the hillbilly stereotype is found in Williamson.

12. For more information on the original eugenics studies that labeled white trash and other poor whites as genetically inferior, see Larson and Rafter.
13. Additional information about Southern cooking and its traditions is found in Egerton.
14. Mickler's cookbook led to others. "The imitators spawn[ed] like crawfish in June. The TV people arrive[d] in Rolling Fork, Mississippi. The op-ed writers opine[d] that Mr. Mickler . . . launched a revolution in American cuisine" ("Puttin' " 73). After the success of Mickler's book, white trash cooking suddenly became very popular.
15. *Cookbook* xii.
16. One reason for the trailer park community's passion for BBQ and other high-caloric foods is that the poor and the working classes have different ideas about the shape of bodies than do other classes. In his influential book, *Distinction: A Social Critique of the Judgment of Taste* (1979), sociologist Pierre Bourdieu writes, "The working classes are more attentive to the strength of the [male] body than its shape" (190). He continues: "Tastes in food . . . depend on the idea each class has of the body and of the effects of food on the body, that is, its strength, health, and beauty" (190). Although he is discussing French society, his words are also applicable to Boxcar's trailer-park community, where the strength and durability of male and female bodies are more important than their beauty.
17. Jill Conner Browne condemns Betty Crocker's cookbook: "If you are still wondering where we as women got some of the insane ideas we have struggled with and against for the last fifty years . . . look no further than Betty Crocker" (4). Browne suggests that any woman should burn a copy of Crocker's book as a good form of therapy (7). In this white trash world, women are not bound by Betty's middle-class culinary ideals.

7 "Dining on Grass and Shrubs": Making Vegan Food Sexy

1. Barnard and Kramer 11.
2. Our negative cultural image of vegans was strengthened when newspapers and magazines in 2004 reported on a vegan couple, Ralphael and Alexandria Spindell, who kidnapped their infant son from his grandmother. She was caring for him after a physician had found him to be malnourished, so he was removed from the parents' custody. If arrested, the father vowed to kill his child and himself (Perez A30). This story raised the common stereotype that a vegan diet cannot be healthy for anyone, especially a child or teen. Such stories about extremists,

which the media emphasize, strengthen popular perceptions that vegans are irrational and potentially dangerous.

3. Additional information about the potential health benefits of vegan and vegetarian diets is found in Fallon and Friedrich, Melina and Davis, "Respectable," Robbins, and Varner.

4. Among the left-wing groups that the media criticize is PETA, a group whose members are disparaged more harshly than vegans. Both are depicted as radical extremists, but PETA is shown as a group of zealots so obsessed by animal rights that they are willing to do anything to protect animals, including blowing up buildings and destroying scientific laboratories. The media's portrayal of vegans and PETA activists makes many Americans not take the movements or their beliefs seriously.

5. Some PETA activists carried this one step further. A couple participated in the "live make-out tour" in which they set up an air-mattress and made out for an hour, suggesting that vegans are better lovers, possessing more endurance and sexual vigor (Doucette 3). For another perspective of this tour, see Carere.

6. Tanya Barnard and Sarah Kramer's books are Canadian, but I included them because they have been very popular in the United States.

7. Other British or U.S. vegan cookbooks written by women include Batt, Berkoff, Dieterly, Elliot, Freed, Gartenstein, Klein, Majzlik, and Wasserman.

8. Pope 6.

9. Much of the information about the spread of vegetarianism in Great Britain came from the Vegan Society's official website ("Vegan Society").

10. In 1877, the London Food Reform Society was founded by Dr. T. R. Allinson; this organization later became The London Vegetarian Society in 1888, leaving Britain with two thriving vegetarian societies.

11. A man did not even need to be a good hunter to provide for himself and his family because game was so plentiful that the most incompetent provider did not have to fear. Among the most prolific of the birds was the passenger pigeon. Over nine billion existed at their peak, so any man could net or shoot hundreds in a single day. The last passenger pigeon died in 1914 in the Cincinnati Zoo (Root and de Rochemont 69–70).

12. For European visitors in earlier centuries, a common complaint was that Americans consumed too much meat, mainly salt pork (Root and de Rochemont 125). Charles Dickens describes a gargantuan dinner on a Pennsylvania canal boat in his novel *Martin Chuzzlewit*, composed of "bread, butter, salmon, shad, liver, steak, potatoes, pickles, ham, chops, black-puddings, and sausage." Breakfast and lunch are identical (qtd. in Root and de Rochemont 124). Although the author was being humorous, there was some truth in his portrait of a society where meat was perceived as any meal's focal point. It might not have been carefully cooked, but it was available in seemingly inexhaustible amounts, as Dickens highlighted.

13. Additional research on the history of vegetarianism and veganism includes Barkas and Gregerson.
14. The information in this paragraph about veganism in the United States came from the American Vegan Society's website ("American Vegan").
15. This hip image is apparent in other areas, including fashion. *Newsweek* writer Julie Scelfo wrote in 2004, "Just because they don't use animal products doesn't mean that vegans can't be stylish. . . . Today's creature-friendly designers are making such chic accessories, even carnivores crave them" (68). She describes vegan shoes, handbags, wallets, and belts. Clearly, veganism has become more mainstream when even such a popular magazine has a positive review of vegan fashions.
16. For additional information on the growing number of vegetarians and vegans, see Armstrong, Fulbright, Z. Smith, and "Will." For an article on how vegans learn how to become vegans, see B. McDonald.
17. For more information about the popularity of veganism and vegetarianism with teenagers, see Suzanne Brown and Samuels.
18. R. Robertson xiv.
19. She describes fusilli with roasted asparagus, sun-dried tomatoes, and pine nuts: "The smoky flavor of sun-dried tomatoes teams up with roasted asparagus and pine nuts . . . for a wonderful combination of textures and flavors" (240). In her book, a recipe for Tuscan white bean and fennel stew with orange and rosemary appears with a brief lesson on history: "Tuscany is known for its olive oil, wine, and sun-ripened produce. . . . This stew incorporates many of these ingredients in a salute to the Tuscan countryside." (304). Such language that combines brief cultural or historical lessons with lush and evocative descriptions of food is prevalent in gourmet magazines, as well.
20. For other articles about the growing popularity of vegan food both at restaurants and at home, see Bauer, Drake, Greeley, Novak, McBee, and "Vegan."
21. Not every vegan cookbook author is a vegan or insists that everyone must be one. Susann Geiskopf-Hadler and Mindy Toomay observe, "Our purpose . . . is not to preach the virtues of veganism. No single eating plan is right for everyone" (xi). Similarly, Leslie McEachern writes, "Personally, I'm not ethically opposed to eating animal protein. However, I believe in using it prudently and with respect" (53). Today, veganism has become a more flexible and multifaceted philosophy for some, although many insist that the only "right" lifestyle is vegan. Both vegetarianism and veganism have become more complex food movements as their followers have grown in number.
22. For works that discuss the ethics of being vegan or vegetarian, see Clements, Fox, Garofoli, Marcus, McGrath, Moran, and Zamir.
23. She continues, "One of the finest rewards of running Angelica Kitchen is the ability to take a stand about specific issues. It has given me the opportunity to vote with the restaurant's dollars for the kinds of political, social, and economic

changes the staff and I believe are important" (McEachern 12). She shows how
local vegan activism can lead to greater world change.

24. Stepaniak writes, "Veganism is not merely passive resistance. It compels
    practitioners to find alternatives to commodities typically made from animal
    products . . . and to make deliberate and dynamic choices about each and every
    activity in their lives" (*The Vegan* 29). Vegan choices are not just about animal
    welfare but also about changing the world through making ethical choices
    about how one leads one's life.

25. For more information on vegan food on campus, see Oliveri.

8   Thin Is Not In: Two Fat Ladies and Gender Stereotypes on the Food Network

1. Information about the growing girth of America can be found in Critser.

2. Gilman qtd. in Dinitia Smith 7.

3. For studies that focus on America's obsession with thinness, see Braziel and
   Lebesco, Hesse-Biber, Schwartz, and Stearns.

4. Works that discuss weight as a social issue include Bordo, Malson, Sobal and
   Maurer, and Wolf.

5. American society has not always assumed that the most beautiful woman was
   slender. In the nineteenth and early twentieth centuries, thinness was perceived
   as a sign of illness since it was associated with tuberculosis (Grogan 9). Idealizing
   slim women began in the 1920s when the flapper look was popular (Grogan 14).
   Although it was difficult for many women to obtain the curveless, boyish bodies
   demanded by this style, it did not stop them from trying by dieting and binding
   their breasts. This fashion trend, however, did not last as the rigors of the
   Depression and World War II brought more well-curved forms into the media
   limelight. In the 1950s, the image was even more voluptuous as Marilyn Monroe
   dominated, and women went from binding their breasts to padding them to
   have her figure. When ultra-thin Twiggy took center stage in the 1960s,
   Monroe's appeal diminished. From the 1960s to the present, the female ideal has
   been for someone who is slender, although, increasingly, she also has to be fit.

6. Not all women in the popular media are thin. On television, African-American,
   Latino, or working-class women are commonly depicted as fat or heavyset, but
   they are typically not taken as seriously as thin white women.

7. Another location for the disappearing fat lady is high-fashion stores, such as
   Abercrombie & Fitch, where the shelves are crowded with women's clothing in
   sizes zero, two, and four. Larger sizes, such as a fourteen or sixteen, are simply
   not available. Like television shows and magazines, Abercrombie & Fitch and
   other similar stores make fat women (or even mildly plump ones) vanish.

8. Since losing weight obsesses our society, we have transmogrified fat into something evil. It must be eternally fought or it will sneak back, a story that the media focus on repeatedly. For example, Oprah's battle with losing weight and regaining it was a classic battle of good (Oprah) against evil (fatness). Similarly, whenever a female star gains a few extra pounds, photographs of her barely clad middle appear everywhere in the popular media, and stories proclaim, "Should Britney Spears have worn this outfit despite her chunky form?" Even the slightest slip by female stars is highlighted. The media never suggest that a woman should just live with her acquired pounds; instead, fat is always something to be battled as the ultimate sign that she has let herself go.

9. For more information about the popularity of *The Iron Chef*, see Lafayette.

10. There are other reasons that food television shows have grown popular. They offer a dream of remaking ourselves into "better selves. It may be the fantasy of transformation, the knowledge that we might or could makeover the self, that is itself pleasurable" (Ashley et al. 184).

11. For articles that focus on the Food Network's development, see Crist and Granatstein. Additional information about superstar chefs is found in Aikman.

12. Articles that discuss the show's wild popularity include Manly and Margolis.

13. Similarly, another writer mentioned that the Ladies were successful because they "joyfully salted their recipes with political incorrectness" (Audrey Woods A9).

   Not everyone was equally ebullient about the show and its stars. One journalist observed, "While the glitz and silliness of shows like 'Iron Chef' and 'Two Fat Ladies' may have alienated serious cooks, they have brought more viewers to the network" (Slatalla F1). What this commentator ignores, however, is that the Ladies' show was not primarily about how to cook fine food; it was about the women and their friendship.

14. The Fat Ladies found it equally surprising that they were stars. "In a culture that usually confers stardom on the young and thin, both find it a bit odd to have found celebrity at their age" (Mack E5).

15. "Have" F3.

16. Similarly, *The Two Fat Ladies Ride Again* includes many meat and game dishes: duck terrine, Welsh lamb pie, Cornish pasties, herrings in oatmeal and mustard with bacon, and ham 'n' haddie.

17. The Ladies used local ingredients in a number of other episodes. In one, they prepared a splendid tea for a cricket club. Before making Queen Alexandra's sandwiches, gentleman's savory shortcrust, and fresh fruit tartlets, they visited a local farm and picked their own strawberries and raspberries. In another episode, the Ladies joined a Boy Scout troop in Northumberland and prepared a meal of shooter's sandwich, frittata, onion soup with Stilton, spiced eggs, and grilled trout. The Ladies caught their fish and gathered fresh mushrooms.

Works Cited

Adams, Carol J. *The Sexual Politics of Meat: A Feminist-Vegetarian Critical Theory.* New York: Continuum, 1990.

Agren, David. " 'Lips that Touch Meat Sauce Will Never Touch Mine': Are Meat Eaters a Bust in Bed?" *Ottawa Citizen* August 7, 2004: 15.

Aikman, Becky. "Recipes for Success; Hot Chefs, Cookin' Empires." *Newsday* August 2, 2004: A32.

Albrecht, Donald. *Designing Dreams: Modern Architecture in the Movies.* New York: Harper & Row, 1986.

Alcott, William A. *Vegetable Diet: As Sanctioned by Medical Men, and by Experience in All Ages.* Boston: Marsh, Capen, and Lyon, 1838.

Allison, Dorothy. *Bastard Out of Carolina.* New York: Plume-Penguin, 1992.

"The American Vegan Society." September 1, 2004. <http://www.americanvegan/org.>

"America's First Certified Organic Restaurant." July 23, 2003. http://www.noras.com.

Anderson, Susan Heller. "Ernest Matthew Mickler, 48, Dies." *New York Times* November 18, 1988: 8.

Angier, Natalie. "Who Is Fat? It Depends on Culture." *New York Times* November 7, 2000: F1.

Armstrong, Neil. "In the Raw." *Times* (London) July 24, 2004: 91.

The Art and Secrets of Chinese Cookery. Archbold, Ohio: La Choy Food Products, 1958.

Arthurs, Jane. "Revolting Bodies: The Body in Comic Performance." *Women's Bodies: Discipline and Transgression.* Ed. Jane Arthurs and Jean Grimshaw. London: Cassell, 1999. 137–164.

Arthurs, Jane, and Jean Grimshaw, eds. *Women's Bodies: Discipline and Transgression.* London: Cassell, 1999.

Ash, Stephen V. "Poor Whites in the Occupied South, 1861–1865." *Journal of Southern History* 57.1 (1991): 39–62.

Ashley, Bob, Joanne Hollows, Steve Jones, and Ben Taylor. *Food and Cultural Studies.* New York: Routledge, 2004.

Asp, Elaine, Isabel Noble, and Faith Clarth. "Pilot Study of Money and Time Spent in Preparing Baked Products from Individual and Premixed Ingredients." *Journal of Home Economics* 49.9 (1957): 717–719.

Atchison, Jeani-Rose. *Everyday Vegan: 300 Recipes for Healthful Eating*. Berkeley: North Atlantic Books, 2002.

Atwater, Maxine H. *Natural Foods Cookbook*. Concord, NH: Nitty Gritty Productions, 1972.

Avakian, Arlene Voski, ed. *Through the Kitchen Window: Women Explore the Intimate Meanings of Food and Cooking*. Boston: Beacon, 1997.

Avakian, Monique. *Atlas of Asian-American History*. New York: Facts on File, 2002.

Baca, Maria Elena. "More Teens Turn Away from Meat, Become Vegetarians." *Star Tribune* October 1, 2003: 1E.

Bailey, Phoebe. *An African-American Cookbook: Traditional and Other Recipes*. Intercourse, PA: Good Books, 2002.

Baldauf, Kashmira Tumbol. "When 'Comfort Food' Is Mom's Curry." *Christian Science Monitor* October 19, 1995: 14.

Banks-Payne, Ruby. *Ruby's Low-Fat Soul Food Cookbook*. Chicago: Contemporary Books, 1996.

Barkas, Janet. *The Vegetable Passion*. New York: Scribner's, 1975.

Barnard, Tanya, and Sarah Kramer. *How It All Vegan! Irresistible Recipes for an Animal-Free Diet*. Vancouver, CA: Arsenal Pulp Press, 1999.

————. *The Garden of Vegan: How It All Vegan Again*. Vancouver, CA: Arsenal Pulp Press, 2003.

Basiotis, Peter, Mark Lino, and Rajen S. Anand. "Report Card on the Diet Quality of African Americans." *Family Economics and Nutrition Review* 11.3 (1998): 61–63.

Batt, Eva. *Vegan Cooking: Recipes for Beginners*. London: Thorsons, 2002.

Bauer, Michael. "New Millennium, Same Concept." *San Francisco Chronicle Magazine* May 11, 2003: 60.

Beilly, Rosalyn. *The No Time to Cook Book*. New York: New American Library, 1969.

Belasco, Warren. *Appetite for Change: How the Counterculture Took on the Food Industry, 1966–1988*. New York: Pantheon Books, 1989.

Benet, Jane. "Some Seasonal Titles on the Art of Cooking (and Eating)." Rev. of *The I Hate to Cook Book*, by Peg Bracken. *San Francisco Chronicle* November 7, 1960: 7.

Bentley, Amy. *Eating for Victory: Food Rationing and the Politics of Domesticity*. Urbana: University of Illinois Press, 1998.

Beoku-Betts, Josephine A. "We Got Our Way of Cooking Things: Women, Food, and Preservation of Cultural Identity among the Gullah." *Gender and Society* 9.5 (1995): 535–555.

Berk, Sarah Fenstermaker. *The Gender Factory: The Apportionment of Work in American Households*. New York: Plenum, 1985.

Berkoff, Nancy. *Vegan in Volume: Vegan Quantity Recipes for Every Occasion*. Baltimore: Vegetarian Resource Group, 2000.

"Better Days for Housewives as Food Industry Changes; Convenience Foods." *U.S. News & World Report* March 22, 1965: 118–120.

Better Homes and Gardens. *Meals in Minutes*. Des Moines: Meredith, 1963.

Bianchi, Alessandra. "How Sweet It Is." *New Business* August 1993: 46.

The Black Gourmet Cookbook: A Unique Collection of Easy-to-Prepare, Appetizing, Black American, Creole, Caribbean, and African Cuisine. Westland, MI: Mademoiselles Noires, 1987.

Bledsoe, Erik. "The Rise of Southern Redneck and White Trash Writers." *Southern Cultures* 6.1 (Spring 2000): 68–90.

Bogle, Donald. *Toms, Coons, Mulattoes, Mammies, and Bucks: An Interpretive History of Blacks in American Films*. New York: Viking, 1994.

Bolton, Charles C. *Poor Whites of the Antebellum South: Tenants and Laborers in Central North Carolina and Northeast Mississippi*. Durham, NC: Duke University Press, 1994.

Bordo, Susan. *Unbearable Weight: Feminism, Western Culture, and the Body*. Berkeley: University of California Press, 1995.

Borgstrom, Georg. *Too Many: A Study of Earth's Biological Limits*. New York: Macmillan, 1969.

Bourdieu, Pierre. *Distinction: A Social Critique of the Judgment of Taste*. 1979. Cambridge, MA: Harvard University Press, 1984.

Bouson, J. Brooks. " 'You Nothing But Trash': White Trash Shame in Dorothy Allison's *Bastard Out of Carolina*." *Southern Literary Journal* 34.1 (2001): 101–123.

Bower, Anne L., ed. *Recipes for Reading: Community Cookbooks, Stories, Histories*. Amherst: University of Massachusetts Press, 1997.

Bowser, Pearl, and Joan Eckstein. *A Pinch of Soul*. New York: Avon, 1970.

Boxcar, Ruby Ann. *Ruby Ann's Down Home Trailer Park Cookbook*. New York: Citadel, 2002.

———. *Ruby Ann's Down Home Trailer Park Holiday Cookbook*. New York: Citadel, 2002.

———. *Ruby Ann's Down Home Trailer Park BBQin' Cookbook*. New York: Citadel, 2003.

Boydston, Jeanne. *Home and Work: Housework, Wages, and the Ideology of Labor in the Early Republic*. New York: Oxford University Press, 1990.

Bracken, Peg. *The I Hate to Housekeep Book*. New York: Harcourt, Brace & World, 1958.

———. *The I Hate to Cook Book*. New York: Fawcett, 1960.

———. *Peg Bracken's Appendix to The I Hate to Cook Book*. New York: Harcourt, 1966.

———. *I Didn't Come Here to Argue*. New York: Harcourt, 1969.

———. *A Window over the Sink: A Mainly Affectionate Memoir*. New York: Harcourt Brace Jovanovich, 1981.

Braziel, Jana Evans, and Kathleen Lebesco, eds. *Bodies Out of Bounds: Fatness and Transgression*. Berkeley: University of California Press, 2001.

Brooks, Karen, and Gideon Bosker. *Dude Food: Recipes for the Modern Guy*. Berkeley: Chronicle Books, 2000.

Brotherton, Martha Harvey. *Vegetable Cookery: With an Introduction Recommending Abstinence from Animal Food and Intoxicating Liquors*. London: Wilson, 1829.

Brown, Rich. "Food Net Boasts Crowded Table, Small Ad Servings." *Broadcasting & Cable* 123.47 (November 22, 1993): 27.

Brown, Suzanne S. "When Teens Veg Out: A Guide for Parents When Their Kids Go Meatless." *Denver Post* March 24, 2004: F-01.

Browne, Jill Conner. *The Sweet Potato Queens' Big-Ass Cookbook (and Financial Planner)*. New York: Three Rivers, 2003.

Buck, Pearl. *The Good Earth*. New York: John Day, 1931.

Bullock, Lorinda. "The Explosive Health Crisis that No One Talks About." *Ebony* December 2001: 136.

Burke, Julie. "The Veggie Way." *Buffalo News* October 16, 2002: N6.

Burr, Hattie A., ed. *The Woman's Suffrage Cook Book*. Boston: C. H. Simonds, Printers, 1886.

Bush, Monroe. "The Protein Problem." Rev. of *Diet for a Small Planet*, by Frances Moore Lappé. *American Forests* 78 (May 1972): 42–43.

Butler, Cleora. *Cleora's Kitchens: The Memoir of a Cook and Eight Decades of Great American Food*. Tulsa, OK: Council Oak Books, 1985.

Cadwallader, Sharon, and Judi Ohr. *Whole Earth Cook Book*. Boston: Houghton Mifflin, 1972.

Caleva, Harry. *Chinese Cookbook for Quantity Service; Authentic Professional Recipes*. New York: Ahrens, 1958.

Campbell Soup Company. *Easy Ways to Delicious Meals: 465 Quick-to Fix Recipes Using Campbell's Convenience Foods*. Camden, NJ: Campbell Soup Company, 1968.

Cannon, Poppy. "Dear Food Industry—I Love You." *House Beautiful* January 1955: 74+.

————. *The Frozen-Foods Cookbook*. New York: Crowell, 1964.

Carere, Suzanne. "Vegetarians Think They Live Healthier." *Toronto Sun* April 17, 2004: 65.

Carroll, Jon. "Daily Datebook." *San Francisco Chronicle* August 10, 2004: D10.

Carruth, R. "Race Degeneration: What Can We Do to Check It?" *New Orleans Medical and Surgical Journal* 72 (1919): 183–190.

Chan, Sou. *The House of Chan Cookbook*. Garden City, NY: Doubleday, 1952.

Chan, Sucheng. *Asian Americans: An Interpretative History*. New York: Twayne Publishers, 1991.

Chang, Iris. *The Chinese in America: A Narrative History*. New York: Viking, 2003.

Chang, Isabelle C. *What's Cooking at Chang's: The Key to Cooking Chinese.* New York: Liveright, 1959.

Chatterjee, Camille. "Salvation for Unhealthy Diets." *Psychology Today* 33.11 (2000): 18.

Chen, Shehong. *Being Chinese, Becoming Chinese American.* Urbana: University of Illinois Press, 2002.

Cheng, F. T. "Try the Beautiful Simplicity of Chinese Cooking." *House Beautiful* March 1959: 112+.

"Chinese Cooking: Dishes Are Exotic, the Recipes Simple." *Life* December 15, 1952: 64+.

Chow, Dolly. *Chow! Secrets of Chinese Cooking with Selected Recipes.* Rutland, VT: Charles E. Tuttle, 1953.

Choy, Philip P., Lorraine Dong, and Marlon K. Hom. *The Coming Man: 19th Century American Perceptions of the Chinese.* Seattle: University of Washington Press, 1995.

Claiborne, Craig. "Food: Chinese Cuisine." *New York Times* June 14, 1958: 25.

Clements, Kath. *Why Vegan: The Ethics of Eating and the Need for Change.* London: Heretic Books, 1995.

Cohen, Patricia. "Forget Lonely: Life Is Healthy at the Top." *New York Times* May 15, 2004: B9+.

Cohen, Rich, and Michael Rubiner. "Hot Subculture." *Rolling Stone* May 19, 1994: 682.

Colamosca, Anne. "Health Foods Prosper Despite High Prices." *New York Times* November 17, 1974: 205.

Coleman, Calmetta Y. "Teen Vegans' Diet Rules Bring Parents to Boiling Point." *Wall Street Journal* July 18, 1995: B1.

Coltrane, Scott. *Family Man: Fatherhood, Housework, and Gender Equity.* New York: Oxford University Press, 1996.

"Convenience Foods Make Meal Planning Easier, Lighten Work, Save Time." *Redbook* January 1968: 74+.

"Cooking a Chinese Festival Dinner." *Sunset* February 1955: 112+.

"Cooking in a Chinese Wok." *Sunset* June 1955: 164–165.

"Cook's Heaven: Chop Suey." *Good Housekeeping* February 1952: 22–23.

Coontz, Stephanie. *The Way We Never Were: American Families and the Nostalgia Trap.* New York: Basic Books, 1992.

Counihan, Carole, and Penny Van Esterik, eds. *Food and Culture: A Reader.* New York: Routledge, 1997.

Crea, Joe. "African-American Cooking Replete with Flavor." *Times-Picayune* February 26, 1993: L27.

Crist, Judith. "The Joy of Looking." *Gourmet* June 1, 2000: 98+.

Critser, Greg. *Fat Land: How Americans Became the Fattest People in the World*. New York: Houghton Mifflin, 2003.

Crocker, Betty. *How to Have the Most Fun with Cake Mixes*. Minneapolis: General Mills, 1950.

Croft, Karen B. *The Good for Me Cookbook*. San Francisco: R & E Research Associates, 1971.

Culbertson, Amy. "Putting Heart Health in Soul Food." *Milwaukee Journal Sentinel* March 21, 2004: 5N.

Cusick, Heidi Haughy. *Soul and Spice: African Cooking in the Americas*. San Francisco: Chronicle Books, 1995.

Danielson, Florence H., and Charles B. Davenport. "The Hill Folk: A Report on a Rural Community of Hereditary Defectives." *White Trash: The Eugenic Family Studies, 1877 to 1919*. Ed. Nicole Hahn Rafter. Boston: Northeastern, 1988. 81–163.

Darden, Norma Jean, and Carole Darden. *Spoonbread and Strawberry Wine: Recipes and Reminiscences of a Family*. 1978. New York: Doubleday, 1994.

Davis, Adelle. *Let's Cook It Right*. New York: Harcourt Brace, 1947.

————. *Let's Eat Right to Keep Fit*. New York: Harcourt Brace, 1954.

Deck, Alice A. " 'Now Then—Who Said Biscuits?' The Black Woman Cook as Fetish in American Advertising, 1905–1953." *Kitchen Culture in America: Popular Representations of Food, Gender, and Race*. Ed. Sherrie A. Inness. Philadelphia: University of Pennsylvania Press, 2001. 69–94.

Delgado, Richard, and Jean Stefancic, eds. *Critical Race Studies: Looking Beyond the Mirror*. Philadelphia: Temple University Press, 1997.

Denker, Joel. *The World on a Plate: A Tour Through the History of America's Ethnic Cuisines*. Boulder, CO: Westview, 2003.

Dieterly, Lois. *Sinfully Vegan: 140 Decadent Desserts to Satisfy Every Vegan's Sweet Tooth*. New York: Marlowe & Co., 2003.

Donovan, Maria Kozslik. *The Far Eastern Epicure: A Culinary Journey to the Far East with Original Recipes and Drawings*. Garden City, NY: Doubleday, 1958.

Doucette, Chris. "They're Sexual Beans; No Meat Makes You Better Lover, Say PETA Partners." *Toronto Sun* April 15, 2004: 3.

Douglas, Mary. "Deciphering a Meal." *Food and Culture: A Reader*. Ed. Carol Counihan and Penny Van Esterik. New York: Routledge, 1997. 36–54.

Drake, Laurie. "Raw Sophistication: The Great Cooks Discover Noncooking." *New York Times* April 11, 2001: F1.

DuBois, Rita. "Convenience Cookery." *American Home* November 1968: 114–115.

DuSablon, Mary Anna. *America's Collectible Cookbooks: The History, the Politics, the Recipes*. Athens: Ohio University Press, 1994.

Dutton, June. *The Peanuts Cookbook*. New York: Scholastic Book Services, 1970.

Dwyer, Johanna, et al. "The New Vegetarians." *Journal of the American Dietetic Association* 62 (1973): 508–514.

"Earthologies: New Focus on Food, with Recipes." *Seventeen* May 1971: 152+.

Eby, Doris, and Helen Kowtaluk. "What's Cooking?" *Better Homes and Gardens* October 1968: 68–77.

Egerton, John. *Southern Food: At Home, on the Road, in History.* New York: Knopf, 1987.

Ehrlich, Paul. *The Population Bomb.* New York: Ballantine Books, 1968.

Elliot, Rose. *Vegan Feasts.* London: Thorsons, 2000.

Elliott, Andrea. "For Mom's Cooking, 2,200 Miles Isn't Too Far." *New York Times* August 11, 2003: A1.

Endrijonas, Erika. "Processed Foods from Scratch: Cooking for a Family in the 1950s." *Kitchen Culture in America: Popular Representations of Food, Gender, and Race.* Ed. Sherrie A. Inness. Philadelphia: University of Pennsylvania Press, 2001. 157–173.

Engs, Ruth Clifford. *Clean Living Movements: American Cycles of Health Reform.* Westport, CT: Praeger, 2001.

Eppes, Mrs. Nicholas Ware. *The Negro of the Old South.* Chicago: Joseph G. Branch, 1925.

Erhard, Darla. "Nutrition Education for the 'Now' Generation." *Journal of Nutrition Education* 2 (1971): 135–139.

Ewald, Ellen Buchman. *Recipes for a Small Planet.* New York: Ballantine, 1973.

"The Fabulous Market for Food." *Fortune* October 1953: 135+.

"Facts about Those So-called Health Foods." *Good Housekeeping* March 1972: 175–177.

Fallon, Sally, and Bruce Friedrich. "Is Veganism a Better Way of Life?" *Ecologist* 31.8 (2001): 20–24.

Farr, Barbara. *Natural Cooking.* Greensboro, NC: Potpourri, 1971.

Fearon, Ethelind. *The Reluctant Cook.* London: Herbert Jenkins, 1953.

Feng, Doreen Yen Hung. *The Joy of Chinese Cookery.* New York: Grosset & Dunlap, 1954.

Fernandez-Armesto, Felipe. *Near a Thousand Tables: A History of Food.* New York: Free, 2002.

Fimrite, Peter. "Ellen Straus—Dairywoman and Environmentalist." *San Francisco Chronicle* December 3, 2002: A21.

First Congregational Unitarian Church, Cincinnati. *Helps to Good Living.* Cincinnati: Ebert and Richardson, 1902.

Fisher, Abby. *What Mrs. Fisher Knows about Old Southern Cooking, Soups, Pickles, Preserves, etc.* San Francisco: Women's Co-operative Printing Office, 1881.

Flexner, Marion W. *Cocktail-Supper Cookbook.* New York: Bramhall House, 1955.

Florio, Donna. "She's Still Cooking: Author Peg Bracken at 80." *Washington Post* December 2, 1998: E1.

Flynt, J. Wayne. *Dixie's Forgotten People: The South's Poor Whites.* Bloomington: Indiana University Press, 1979.

"Foods with a Foreign Flavor." *Good Housekeeping* April 1959: 10–11.

Fordyce, Eleanor T. "Cookbooks of the 1800s." *Dining in America 1850–1900.* Ed. Kathryn Grover. Amherst: University of Massachusetts Press, 1987. 85–113.

Foster, Gary S., and Richard L. Hummel. "Wham, Bam, Thank You, Sam: Critical Dimensions of the Persistence of Hillbilly Caricatures." *Sociological Spectrum* 17.2 (1997): 157–176.

Fox, Michael Allen. *Deep Vegetarianism.* Philadelphia: Temple University Press, 1999.

Francetta, M. *The Art of Chinese Cooking.* Rutland, VT: Charles E. Tuttle, 1956.

Freed, Hermine. *Eating in Eden: A Gourmet Vegan Cookbook.* Portland, OR: Rudra Press, 1998.

Friedan, Betty. *The Feminine Mystique.* 1963. New York: Dell, 1977.

Friend, Tad. "The White Trashing of America." *New York* August 22, 1994: 22–31.

"From the Larder or Freezer." *American Home* March 1967: 102+.

"Frozen Food Industry Convenes Here, Sights Set on Still Further Huge Growth." *New York Times* February 21, 1954: F1+.

Frum, David. *How We Got Here: The 70s: The Decade that Brought You Modern Life (For Better or Worse).* New York: Basic Books, 2000.

Fulbright, Leslie. "Something's Cookin'; Hip-hop Healthy; More Black Artists Sing Praises of Going Vegan." *Seattle Times* July 15, 2004: 1.

Funkhouser, W. L. "Human Rubbish." *Journal of the Medical Association of Georgia* 26 (1937): 197+.

Gabaccia, Donna R. *We Are What We Eat: Ethnic Food and the Making of Americans.* Cambridge, MA: Harvard University Press, 1998.

Garofoli, Joe. "The Believers: What Does It Mean to Eschew All Animal Products?" *San Francisco Chronicle Magazine* February 8, 2004: 8.

Gartenstein, Devra. *The Accidental Vegan.* Freedom, CA: Crossing Press, 2000.

Gaskins, Ruth L. *Every Good Negro Cook Starts with Two Basic Ingredients: A Good Heart and a Light Hand.* New York: Simon & Schuster, 1968.

Geiskopf-Hadler, Susann, and Mindy Toomay. *The Complete Vegan Cookbook: Over 200 Tantalizing Recipes.* Rocklin, CA: Prima Lifestyles, 2001.

General Foods Corporation. *General Foods Kitchens Frozen Foods Cookbook: Modern Living with Frozen Foods.* New York: Random House, 1961.

Genovese, Eugene D. *Roll Jordan, Roll: The World the Slaves Made.* New York: Vintage, 1976.

George, Kathryn Paxton. *Animal, Vegetable, or Woman? A Feminist Critique of Ethical Vegetarianism.* Albany: State University of New York Press, 2000.

Gitelson, Joshua. "Populux: The Suburban Cuisine of the 1950s." *Journal of American Culture* 15.3 (1992): 73–78.

Gittelson, Natalie. "The $2 Billion Health Food . . . Fraud?" *Harper's Bazaar* November 1972: 32.

Goeltz, Judith, and Patricia Lazenby. *Thanks, I Needed That: The Beginner's Natural Food Cookbook*. Salt Lake City, UT: Hawkes, 1975.

Goings, Kenneth W. *Aunt Jemima and Uncle Mose: Black Collectibles and American Stereotyping*. Bloomington: Indiana University Press, 1994.

Goldberg, Jonah. "Soy Vey! My Agonizing Days as a Vegan." *National Review* February 10, 2003: 36–37.

Goldman, Anne. "'I Yam What I Yam': Cooking, Culture, and Colonialism." *De/Colonizing the Subject: The Politics of Gender in Women's Autobiography*. Ed. Sidonie Smith and Julia Watson. Minneapolis: University of Minnesota Press, 1992. 169–195.

Goldstein, Jerome. "Love and the Food You Eat." *Organic Garden and Farm* March 1977: 132+.

"Good Things that Come from Small Packages." *Redbook* June 1963: 70+.

Gordon, Elizabeth. "The Threat to the Next America." *House Beautiful* April 1953: 126+.

Granatstein, Lisa. "Family Affair." *Media Week* 13.35 (2003): 29–30.

Granny's Cookbook. Los Lunas, NM: n.p., 1970.

Greeley, Alexandra. "Millennium: Curtain's Up." *Vegetarian Times* August 2003: 38+.

Gregerson, Jon. *Vegetarianism: A History*. Fremont, CA: Jain Publishing, 1994.

Grimes, William. "Can't Stand the Heat?" *New York Times* April 23, 1998: TV5+.

Grogan, Sarah. *Body Image: Understanding Body Dissatisfaction in Men, Women, and Children*. London: Routledge, 1999.

Gross, Bernice J., and Kay Young Mackley. "Should the Homemaker Use Ready-made Mixes?" *Journal of Home Economics* 42 (June 1950): 451.

Grossinger, Jennie. *The Art of Jewish Cooking*. New York: Random House, 1958.

Grosvenor, Vertamae. *Vertamae Cooks in the Americas' Family Kitchen*. San Francisco: KQED Books, 1996.

The Guide to Convenience Foods: How to Use, Plan, Prepare, Present. Chicago: Patterson, 1968.

Gyory, Andrew. *Closing the Gate: Race, Politics, and the Chinese Exclusion Act*. Chapel Hill: University of North Carolina Press, 1998.

Haber, Barbara. *From Hardtack to Home Fries: An Uncommon History of American Cooks and Meals*. New York: Free Press, 2002.

Hamlin, Suzanne. "Television's 'Two Fat Ladies' Have Sung." *New York Times* February 25, 1998: F1+.

Harper, Joan. *The Healthy Cat and Dog Cook Book: Natural Recipes Using Nutritious, Economical Foods for Happier, Healthier, and More Beautiful Pets*. Chicago: Soodik, 1975.

Harris, Jean. "You Have 1001 Servants in Your Kitchen." *House Beautiful* March 1951: 74+.

Harris, Jessica B. *Iron Pots and Wooden Spoons: Africa's Gifts to New World Cooking.* New York: Atheneum, 1989.

————. *A Kwanzaa Keepsake: Celebrating the Holiday with New Traditions and Feasts.* New York: Simon & Schuster, 1995.

————. *The Welcome Table: African-American Heritage Cooking.* New York: Fireside, 1996.

Harris, Michael D. *Colored Pictures: Race and Visual Representation.* Chapel Hill: University of North Carolina Press, 2003.

Hartigan, John Jr. "Unpopular Culture: The Case of 'White Trash.'" *Cultural Studies* 11.2 (1997): 316–343.

Haspel, Barbara, and Tamar Haspel. "All in the Vegetarian Family." *Vegetarian Times* June 1997: 84–86.

"Have Motorbike, Will Cook." *New York Times* October 30, 1997: F3.

Hayden, Dolores. *Redesigning the American Dream: The Future of Housing, Work, and Family Life.* New York: Norton, 1984.

Heatter, Maida. *Maida Heatter's Book of Great Desserts.* Kansas City: Andrews McMeel Pub., 1999.

Heldke, Lisa. *Exotic Appetites: Ruminations of a Food Adventurer.* New York: Routledge, 2003.

Henderson, Fay K. *Vegan Recipes.* London: H. H. Greaves, 1946.

"Here Is Baker's Magic: Using a Packaged Roll Mix." *Sunset* January 1956: 56–57.

Hess, John L. "Food Lovers Don't Despair—There Is Life in the Wasteland." *New York Times* November 29, 1973: 52.

Hesse-Biber, Sharlene. *Am I Thin Enough Yet? The Cult of Thinness and the Commercialization of Identity.* New York: Oxford University Press, 1996.

Hewitt, Jean. *The New York Times Natural Foods Cookbook.* New York: Quadrangle, 1971.

————. "Teen-agers Choose the Meatless Diet." *New York Times* June 5, 1972: 39.

Hill, Mike, ed. *Whiteness: A Critical Reader.* New York: New York University Press, 1997.

Hispanic Recipe Book. Baltimore: U.S. Social Security Administration, 1985.

Hoffman, Marilyn. "Peg Bracken: A No-frills Approach to Home, Hearth, and Good Food." *Christian Science Monitor* September 23, 1981: 19.

Hong, Wallace Yee, and Charlotte Adams. *The Chinese Cook Book.* New York: Crown Publishers, 1952.

Hooker, Richard J. *Food and Drink in America: A History.* Indianapolis: Bobbs-Merrill, 1981.

"How to Be a Mealtime Artist with Food from a Package." *Better Homes and Gardens* August 1956: 66+.

Humble, Nicola. "A Touch of Boheme." *Times Literary Supplement* June 14, 1996: 16.

Hunter, Beatrice Trum. *The Natural Foods Primer: Help for the Bewildered Beginner.* New York: Simon & Schuster, 1972.

Ickeringill, Nan. "Food: The Range Haters." *New York Times* September 30, 1960: 18.

Inness, Sherrie A. *Dinner Roles: American Women and Culinary Culture.* Iowa City: University of Iowa Press, 2001.

Inness, Sherrie A., ed. *Pilaf, Pozole, and Pad Thai: American Women and Ethnic Food.* Amherst: University of Massachusetts Press, 2001.

"Instant Gourmet." *McCall's* May 1965: 76.

Jackson, Lenli. *100 Simple Chinese Recipes.* Brooklyn: K. P. Shick, 1958.

Jackson, Mary, and Lelia Wishart. *The Integrated Cookbook; or the Soul of Good Cooking.* Chicago: Johnson, 1971.

Jacobs, Barbara. Rev. of *Laurel's Kitchen: A Handbook for Vegetarian Cookery and Nutrition*, by Laurel Robertson, Carol Flinders, and Bronwyn Godfrey. *Booklist* May 1, 1977: 1324.

Jacobs, Lea. *The Wages of Sin: Censorship and the Fallen Woman Film, 1928–1942.* Berkeley: University of California Press, 1995.

Jennings, Linda Deziah, comp. *Washington Women's Cook Book.* Seattle: Washington Equal Suffrage Association, 1909.

Johnson, Kevin. "Cancer Claims 'Fat Lady.' " *USA Today* August 11, 1999: 2D.

Johnson, Stanley. *Life Without Birth: A Journey through the Third World in Search of the Population Explosion.* London: Heineman, 1970.

Johnston, Myrna. "Sleight-of-Hand Main Dishes." *Better Homes and Gardens* February 1961: 64+.

Jones, Anthony. "Healthy Living Supper Club, Oxford." *Guardian* August 28, 2004: 34.

Judd, Shilla A. *Tried and True Vegetarian Recipes: A First Vegetarian Cookbook.* Berkeley: Images, 1971.

Julian, Sheryl. "Dreams and Dirt." *Boston Globe* July 7, 1999: E1+.

———. "Smile and Say Vermont Butter and Cheese Co." *Boston Globe* August 8, 2001: C1.

Kaiser, Inez Yeargen. *Soul Food Cookery.* New York: Pitman, 1968.

Kasdan, Sara. *Love and Knishes: An Irrepressible Guide to Jewish Cooking.* New York: Vanguard, 1956.

Katz, Gail Weinshel. *Jewish Cooking.* New York: Weathervane Books, 1979.

Katzen, Mollie. *The Moosewood Cookbook: Recipes from Moosewood Restaurant in the Dewitt Mall, Ithaca, New York.* Ithaca, NY: Moosewood, 1974.

Keck, Edith Harwood. "To Mix or Not to Mix." *Practical Home Economics* 4 (February 1959): 46+.

Kern-Foxworth, Marilyn. *Aunt Jemima, Uncle Ben, and Rastus: Blacks in Advertising, Yesterday, Today, and Tomorrow.* Westport, CT: Greenwood, 1994.

Kinard, Epsie. "How to Broaden Your Cooking Repertoire." *House Beautiful* November 1959: 240+.

Kleber, Mrs. L. O. The *Suffrage Cook Book*. Pittsburgh: Equal Franchise Federation of Western Pennsylvania, 1915.

Klein, Donna. *The Mediterranean Vegan Kitchen: Meat-Free, Egg-Free, Dairy-Free Dishes from the Healthiest Place Under the Sun*. New York: HP Books, 2001.

Knight, Freda De. *A Date with a Dish: A Cook Book of American Negro Recipes*. New York: Hermitage, 1948.

Knox, Gerald M. "How Healthy Are 'Health' Foods?" *Better Homes and Gardens* June 1972: 30+.

Kornfeld, Myra. *The Voluptuous Vegan: More than 200 Sinfully Delicious Recipes for Meatless, Eggless, and Dairy-Free Meals*. New York: Clarkson Potter, 2000.

Kostir, Mary Storer. "The Family of Sam Sixty." *White Trash: The Eugenic Family Studies 1877–1919*. Ed. Nicole Hahn Rafter. Boston: Northeastern, 1988. 185–209.

Kwak, Jenny. *Dok Suni: Recipes from My Mother's Korean Kitchen*. New York: St. Martin's, 1998.

Ladies' Aid Society, Marion, Ohio. *Recipes, Tried and True*. Marion, OH: Press of Kelley Mount, 1894.

Lafayette, Jon. "Will Consumers Bite into This Promo?" *Television Week* 23.9 (2004): 2.

Lapanja, Margie. *Food Men Love: All-Time Favorite Recipes from Caesar Salad and Grilled Rib-Eye to Cinnamon Buns and Apple Pie*. York, ME: Conari, 2003.

Lappé, Frances Moore. *Diet for a Small Planet*. New York: Ballantine, 1971.

Lappé, Frances Moore, and Anna Lappé. *Hope's Edge: The Next Diet for a Small Planet*. New York: Putnam, 2002.

Larson, Edward J. *Sex, Race, and Science: Eugenics in the Deep South*. Baltimore: Johns Hopkins University Press, 1995.

Lee, Calvin. *Chinese Cooking for American Kitchens*. New York: Putnam, 1959.

Lee, Chang-Rae. "Coming Home Again." *New Yorker* October 16, 1995: 164+.

Lee, Dorothy Chuan. "Chinese Cooking: Adventure in Taste." *McCall's* November 1958: 52+.

Lee, Erika. *At America's Gates: Chinese Immigration During the Exclusion Era, 1882–1943*. Chapel Hill: University of North Carolina Press, 2003.

Lee, Jeremy. "Food and Drink: Old Smoothie." *Guardian* (London) November 21, 1998: 78.

Leneman, Leah. "No Animal Food: The Road to Veganism in Britain, 1909–1944." *Society and Animals* 7.3 (October 1999): 219–228.

Lenica, Jan, and Alfred Sauvy. *Population Explosion: Abundance or Famine*. New York: Dell, 1962.

Leonard, Leah W. *Jewish Cookery in Accordance with the Jewish Dietary Laws*. New York: Crown Publishers, 1949.

Leonardi, Susan J. "Recipes for Reading: Pasta Salad, Lobster à la Riseholme, and Key Lime Pie." *PMLA* 104 (1989): 340–347.

Levenstein, Harvey A. *Revolution at the Table: The Transformation of the American Diet.* New York: Oxford University Press, 1988.

———. *Paradox of Plenty: A Social History of Eating in Modern America.* New York: Oxford University Press, 1993.

Levitt, Eleanor. *The Wonderful World of Natural-Food Cookery.* Great Neck, NY: Hearthside, 1971.

Levy, Paul. "Something from the Oven: Lime Jell-O Marshmallow Cottage Cheese Surprise." Rev. of *Something from the Oven: Reinventing Dinner in 1950s America,* by Laura Shapiro. *New York Times Book Review* April 18, 2004: 16.

Ling, Mei-Mei. *Chop Suey: A Collection of Simple Chinese Recipes Adapted for the American Home.* Honolulu: South Sea Sales, 1953.

Littlejohn, Janice Rhoshalle. "Food Network Is Now a Daily Requirement." *USA Today* December 11, 2003: 5D.

Lo, Kenneth. *Cooking the Chinese Way.* New York: Arco Pub. Co., 1955.

Lon, Shen Mei, and Ruth Chier Rosen. *Ancestral Recipes of Shen Mei Lon.* New York: Richard Rosen Associates, 1954.

Long, Lucy M. "Culinary Tourism: A Folkloristic Perspective on Eating and Otherness." *Southern Folklore* 55.3 (1998): 181–204.

Longone, Jan. "Early Black-Authored Cookbooks." *Gastronomica* 1.1 (2001): 96–99.

Lupton, Ellen. *The Bathroom, the Kitchen, and the Aesthetics of Waste: A Process of Elimination.* Cambridge: MIT Visual Arts Center, 1992.

Lustig, Lillie S., ed. *The Southern Cookbook of Fine Old Recipes.* Reading, PA: Culinary Arts, 1969.

MacFadden, Bernarr. *Physical Culture Cookbook.* New York: MacFadden, 1929.

Mack, Tara. "Two Fat Ladies Stir Up Hugely Successful Show." *Gazette* (Montreal) April 26, 1999: E5.

Majzlik, Linda. *A Vegan Taste of Mexico.* Charlbury, England; Carpenter, 2002.

"Make It with Packaged Potatoes." *American Home* April 1964: 78.

Malouf, Jacqui, and Liz Gumbinner. *Booty Food: A Date by Date, Nibble by Nibble Course Guide to Cultivating Love and Passion through Food.* London: Bloomsbury, 2004.

Malson, Helen M. *The Thin Woman: Feminism, Post-Structuralism, and the Social Psychology of Anorexia Nervosa.* New York: Routledge, 1998.

Manly, Chris. "Two Ladies, Built for Comfort." *Daily Telegraph* (Sydney, Australia) September 16, 1998: F07.

Mano, D. Keith. "Health Food." *National Review* March 3, 1978: 291–292.

Manring, M. M. *Slave in a Box: The Strange Career of Aunt Jemima.* Charlottesville: University Press of Virginia, 1998.

Manton, Catherine. *Fed Up: Women and Food in America*. Westport, CT: Bergin & Garvey, 1999.

Marcus, Erik. *Vegan: The New Ethics of Eating*. Ithaca, NY: McBooks, 1998.

Margolis, Maxine L. *Mothers and Such: Views of American Women and Why They Changed*. Berkeley: University of California Press, 1984.

Margolis, Seth. "These Are Two Ladies Who Really Lunch." *New York Times* March 29, 1998: TV59.

Marling, Karal Ann. *As Seen on TV: The Visual Culture of Everyday Life in the 1950s*. Cambridge, MA: Harvard University Press, 1994.

Marsh, Carole S. *The Kitchen House: How Yesterday's Black Women Created Today's American Foods*. Decatur, GA: Gallopade Pub. Group, 1991.

Massachusetts Woman's Christian Temperance Union Cuisine. Boston: E. B. Stillings and Co., 1878.

Matthews, Glenna. *"Just a Housewife": The Rise and Fall of Domesticity in America*. New York: Oxford University Press, 1987.

May, Elaine Tyler. *Homeward Bound: American Families in the Cold War Era*. New York: Basic Books, 1988.

McBee, Julia. "Turning Tables: A Healthy Dose of Vegan Fare." *Atlanta Journal Constitution* July 8, 2004: 15P.

McCann, Paul. "One Fat Lady Shuns the Naked Chef." *Times* (London) August 24, 2000: 55.

McCarthy, Josephine. *Josie McCarthy's Favorite TV Recipes*. Englewood Cliffs, NJ: Prentice-Hall, 1958.

McClain, Charleen. *Southern Cookbook: Cooking with a Southern Accent*. Atlanta, GA: Tupper and Looe, 1952.

McCully, Helen. "Let's Cook Chinese Tonight." *McCall's* January 1954: 40+.

McCracken, Mary Lou. *The Deep South Natural Foods Cookbook*. Harrisburg, PA: Stackpole Books, 1975.

McDonald, Barbara. " 'Once You Know Something, You Can't Not Know It': An Empirical Look at Becoming Vegan." *Society and Animals* 8.1 (2001): 1–23.

McDonald, Kathleen. "Talking Trash, Talking Back: Resistance to Stereotypes in Dorothy Allison's *Bastard Out of Carolina*." *Women's Studies Quarterly* 26.1/2 (1998): 15–25.

McDowell, Edwin. "Popular Cookbook Celebrates Downstairs Fare." *New York Times* September 22, 1986: 11.

McEachern, Leslie. *The Angelica Home Kitchen: Recipes and Rabble Rousings from an Organic Vegan Restaurant*. Berkeley, CA: Ten Speed Press, 2003.

McFeely, Mary Drake. *Can She Bake a Cherry Pie? American Women and the Kitchen in the Twentieth Century*. Amherst: University of Massachusetts Press, 2000.

McGrath, Emma. "The Politics of Veganism." *Social Alternatives* 19.4 (October 2000): 50–60.

McHugh, Kathleen Anne. *American Domesticity: From How-to Manual to Hollywood Melodrama.* New York: Oxford University Press, 1999.

McIlwaine, Shields. *The Southern Poor White from Lubberland to Tobacco Road.* Norman: University of Oklahoma Press, 1939.

McLaughlin, Katy. "Yum, Grilled Fungus Franks." *Wall Street Journal* July 3, 2003: D1.

McWhiney, Grady. *Cracker Culture: Celtic Ways in the Old South.* Tuscaloosa: University of Alabama Press, 1988.

Medearis, Angela Shelf. *The African-American Kitchen: Cooking from Our Heritage.* New York: Dutton, 1994.

———. *A Kwanzaa Celebration: Festive Recipes and Homemade Gifts from an African-American Kitchen.* New York: Dutton, 1995.

———. *Ideas for Entertaining from the African-American Kitchen.* New York: Dutton, 1997.

Melina, Vesanto, and Brenda Davis. *Becoming Vegan: The Complete Guide to Adopting a Healthy Plant-Based Diet.* Toronto: Wiley, 2003.

Mendes, Helen. *The African Heritage Cookbook.* New York: Macmillan, 1971.

Metcalfe, William. *A Conversation on Abstinence from the Flesh of Animals as Food; Introductory to a Consideration of the Subject in Relation to the Habitual Reasoning of Men, Popular Opinion, Domestic Economy, and the Facts of Chemistry, Anatomy, Physiology, History, Morality, and Religion.* 1821. London: Whittaker, 1846.

Meyer, Connie. "Nothing Tastes Quite Like Mom's Home Cookin'." *Christian Science Monitor* March 27, 1995: 17.

Meyers, Miriam. *A Bite off Mama's Plate: Mothers' and Daughters' Connections through Food.* Westport, CT: Bergin & Garvey, 2001.

Mickler, Ernest Matthew. *White Trash Cooking.* East Haven, CT: Jargon Society, 1986.

———. *Sinkin Spells, Hot Flashes, Fits, and Cravings.* Berkeley, CA: Ten Speed Press, 1988.

Mickler, Trisha. *More White Trash Cooking.* Berkeley, CA: Ten Speed Press, 1998.

Miller, Bryan. "Cooking." *New York Times* June 1, 1996: BR13.

Miller, Lori. "Women's Collective Finds Ingredients for Success." *Washington Post* January 25, 1990: 11.

Miller, Marjorie Ann. *Introduction to Health Foods.* Los Angeles: Nash Pub., 1971.

Mitchell, Alice Miller. *Oriental Cookbook.* Chicago: Rand, 1950.

"Mix in a Little Magic." *Good Housekeeping* September 1955: 90+.

Moran, Victoria. *Compassion, the Ultimate Ethic: An Exploration of Veganism.* Wellingborough, Northamptonshire: Thorsons, 1985.

Morgan, Ann Howard. "Convenience Foods Are Convenient for Me and Every Modern Mother." *Parents' Magazine* April 1962: 61+.

Morr, Mary. "Food Mixes and Frozen Foods." *Journal of Home Economics* 43.1 (1951): 14–16.

Muddy Pond Mennonite Community. *A Collection of Favorite Recipes.* Monterey, TN: R. Habegger, 1981.

Musgrave, Sarah. "Vegans Have Fun, Too." *Gazette* (Montreal) December 13, 2003: G6.

Nagle, James J. "$71 Billion Food Consumed in U.S." *New York Times* January 2, 1957: 97.

Nash, Helen. *Kosher Cuisine.* New York: Random House, 1984.

Nathan, Joan. *Jewish Cooking in America.* New York: Knopf, 1994.

National Council of Negro Women. *The Historical Cookbook of the American Negro.* Washington, D.C.: Corporate, 1958.

———. *The Black Family Reunion Cookbook.* New York: Simon & Schuster, 1991.

———. *The Black Family Dinner Quilt Cookbook: Health Conscious Recipes and Food Memories.* New York: Simon & Schuster, 1994.

"Nature's Table: Bulgur." *Seventeen* September 1973: 30.

"Nature's Table: Good Foods of California." *Seventeen* March 1972: 156.

"Nature's Table: Seeds . . . Not Just for the Birds." *Seventeen* November 1971: 142.

Neuhaus, Jessamyn. *Manly Meals and Mom's Home Cooking: Cookbooks and Gender in Modern America.* Baltimore: Johns Hopkins University Press, 2003.

"New Foods that Make Cooking Easier." *Redbook* January 1969: 88+.

"A New Simplicity Touches Our Lives Today." *Woman's Home Companion* February 1956: 35–37.

Nickerson, Jane. "Books on How to Prepare Chinese Dishes Suggest Savory But Hard-to-Make Items." *New York Times* June 7, 1952: 163.

Nissenbaum, Stephen. *Sex, Diet, and Debility in Jacksonian America: Sylvester Graham and Health Reform.* Chicago: Dorsey, 1988.

"No Relief for Breadwinners." *New York Times* March 20, 1952: 43.

Novak, Karen. "Restauranteur Expands Vegan Cuisine from Stahstown to Oakland." *Pittsburgh Post-Gazette* August 26, 2004: D1.

Ogden, Annegret S. *The Great American Housewife: From Helpmate to Wage Earner, 1776–1986.* Westport, CT: Greenwood, 1986.

Oliver, Frank. *Chinese Cooking.* London: Deutsch, 1955.

Oliveri, Katie. "Keeping Up with Changing Tastes on a College Campus." *Boston Globe* August 22, 2004: C12.

"One Dish Dinner, Chinese-style." *Sunset* October 1954: 139.

Oriental Flavors. Seattle, WA: St. Peter's Sunday School, 1952.

Owen, June. "Food: Bountiful 1955." *New York Times* December 28, 1955: 26.

Palmer, Jerry. *Taking Humor Seriously.* London: Routledge, 1994.

Palmer, Phyllis M. *Domesticity and Dirt: Housewives and Domestic Servants in the United States, 1920–1945.* Philadelphia: Temple University Press, 1989.

Pan, Lynn. *Sons of the Golden Emperor: A History of the Chinese Diaspora.* New York: Kodansha America, 1994.

Parr, Jan. "Vegan Victory on Campus." *Vegetarian Times* April 1995: 19+.

Paterson, Jennifer, and Clarissa Dickson Wright. *Cooking with the Two Fat Ladies*. New York: Clarkson Potter, 1996.

————. *The Two Fat Ladies Ride Again*. New York: Clarkson Potter, 1997.

————. *The Two Fat Ladies Full Throttle*. New York: Clarkson Potter, 1999.

————. *Two Fat Ladies: Obsessions*. New York: Clarkson Potter, 1999.

Perez, Luis. "Grandma Fears for Vegan Toddler." *Newsday* September 8, 2004: A30.

"The Perils of Eating, American Style." *Time* December 18, 1972: 68+.

Perry, Sara. "Peg Bracken's Simple Ways Turn Strangers into Friends." *Oregonian* October 31, 1999: L18.

Petosa, Bruno. "Indulge the Bulge: Two Fat Ladies Love Butter and Cream." *Gazette* (Montreal) October 24, 1998: W4+.

Plath, Sylvia. *The Bell Jar*. London: Harper & Row, 1963.

Poe, Tracy N. "The Origins of Soul Food in Black Urban Identity: Chicago, 1915–1947." *American Studies International* 37.1 (1999): 4–33.

Pope, Mary. *Novel Dishes for Vegetarian Households: A Complete and Trustworthy Guide to Vegetarian Cooking*. London: Percy Lord, 1893.

Porter, Mrs. M. E. *Mrs. Porter's New Southern Cookery Book*. 1871. New York: Arno, 1973.

Porter, Margaret. Rev. of *Diet for a Small Planet*, by Frances Moore Lappé. *Library Journal* February 15, 1972: 691–692.

"Potato Favorites . . . Instantly!" *Better Homes and Gardens* April 1965: 105.

Prettyman, Quandra. "Come Eat at My Table: Lives with Recipes." *Southern Quarterly* 30.2/3 (1992): 131–140.

Princess Pamela. *Princess Pamela's Soul Food Cookbook*. New York: Signet, 1969.

Pritzer, Wendy. *Natural Foods: Eat Better, Live Longer, Improve Your Sex Life*. New York: Dafran House, 1971.

Proust, Marcel. *Remembrance of Things Past*. Vols. 1–3. New York: Viking Books, 1998.

Puente, Maria. "From Infomercials to 'Iron Chef,' Food Network Grows Up." *USA Today* March 3, 2003: 2D.

"Puttin' on the Grits." *Irish Times* October 19, 2002: 73.

Rafter, Nicole Hahn, ed. *White Trash: The Eugenic Family Studies, 1877–1919*. Boston: Northeastern, 1988.

Raloff, Janet. "Americans Eat Faster, and More." *Science News* June 12, 2004: 381–382.

"Raviolis . . . the Chinese Way." *Sunset* June 1953: 145–146.

"Reality Food: Menu, Recipes, Tips for an Organic Dinner." *Vogue* November 15, 1971: 72–73.

"Recipes that Go with Earth Week." *New York Times* April 19, 1971: 42.

"*Redbook*'s Timesaver Cookbook." *Redbook* October 1965: 97+.

"Respectable Vegetables." *Utne Reader* March/April 1992: 106–107.

Rev. of *Diet for a Small Planet*, by Frances Moore Lappé. *Publishers' Weekly* August 2, 1971: 66.

Rev. of *The I Hate to Cook Book*, by Peg Bracken. *Booklist* January 1960: 78.

Rev. of *The I Hate to Cook Book*, by Peg Bracken. *Bulletin from Virginia Kirkus' Service* January 15, 1960: 603.

Rev. of *Laurel's Kitchen: A Handbook for Vegetarian Cookery and Nutrition*, by Laurel Robertson, Carol Flinders, and Bronwyn Godfrey. *Publishers' Weekly* August 16, 1976: 116.

Richard, Lenz. *New Orleans Cookbook*. New York: Houghton Mifflin, 1940.

Richards, Janet, and Charles Richards. *Basic Chinese and Japanese Recipes, Incorporating Cooking with Fresh Ginger*. San Francisco: Regional Foods, 1958.

Ridley, Helen E. "Introduction." *The Frozen-Foods Cookbook*. Poppy Cannon. New York: Crowell, 1964. vii–viii.

Ripley, Eliza. *Social Life in Old New Orleans, Being Recollections of My Girlhood*. New York: Appleton, 1912.

Robbins, John. *The Food Revolution: How Your Diet Can Help Save Your Life and Our World*. Berkeley, CA: Conari, 2001.

Roberts, J. A. G. *China to Chinatown: Chinese Food in the West*. London: Reaktion Books, 2002.

Robertson, Jordan. "Vegans' Food Chain." *San Diego Union Tribune* June 18, 2004: C1.

Robertson, Laurel, Carol Flinders, and Bronwyn Godfrey. *Laurel's Kitchen: A Handbook for Vegetarian Cookery and Nutrition*. 1976. New York: Bantam, 1978.

Robertson, Robin. *Vegan Planet: 400 Irresistible Recipes with Fantastic Flavors from Home and around the World*. Boston: Harvard Common Press, 2003.

Roebuck, Julian B., and Mark Hickson III. *The Southern Redneck: A Phenomenological Class Study*. New York: Prager, 1982.

Root, Waverley, and Richard de Rochemont. *Eating in America: A History*. New York: Morrow, 1976.

Rothschild, Joan, and Alethea Cheng, eds. *Design and Feminism: Re-envisioning Spaces, Places, and Everyday Things*. New Brunswick, NJ: Rutgers University Press, 1999.

Russell, Melinda. *A Domestic Cook Book: Containing a Careful Selection of Useful Receipts for the Kitchen*. Paw Paw, MI: Printed by T. G. Ward, at the True Northern Office, 1866.

Samuels, Debra. "Food and Entertaining for Vegetarians." *Boston Globe* April 24, 2003: H6.

Sanchez-Klein. "Jessica Harris Brings It All Back Home." *Baltimore Sun* February 15, 1995: 1E+.

Sandomir, Richard. "Zoeller Learns Race Remarks Carry a Price." *New York Times* April 24, 1997: B7.

Sass, Lorna. *The New Vegan Cookbook: Innovative Vegetarian Recipes Free of Dairy, Eggs and Cholesterol.* San Francisco: Chronicle Books, 2001.

Saunders, Lelia. Rev. of *The I Hate to Cook Book*, by Peg Bracken. *Library Journal* 85 (October 1, 1960): 3444.

Scelfo, Julie. "Vegan Chic." *Newsweek* March 22, 2004: 68.

Schenone, Laura. *A Thousand Years Over a Hot Stove: A History of American Women Told through Food, Recipes, and Remembrances.* New York: Norton, 2003.

Schrambling, Regina. " 'The Fat Lady' Has a Few More Songs." *New York Times* November 7, 2001: F1.

Schultz, Dodi. "Health Foods May Be Anything But Healthful." *Science Digest* August 1979: 82–83.

Schwartz, Hillel. *Never Satisfied: A Cultural History of Diets, Fantasies, and Fat.* New York: Free Press, 1986.

Schweitzer, Ivy. "The Mammy and the Mummy: Cultural Imagery and Interracial Coalition." *Mothers and Daughters: Connection, Empowerment, and Transformation.* Ed. Andrea O'Reilley and Sharon Abby. Lanham, MD: Rowman & Littlefield, 2000. 121–139.

"The Secrets of the Chinese Cook." *Sunset* April 1957: 158+.

Sessions, Mina A. "The Feeble-Minded in a Rural County of Ohio." *White Trash: The Eugenic Family Studies, 1877 to 1919.* Ed. Nicole Hahn Rafter. Boston: Northeastern, 1997, 253–340.

Shange, Ntozake. *If I Can Cook, You Know God Can.* Boston: Beacon, 1998.

Shapiro, Laura. *Perfection Salad: Women and Cooking at the Turn of the Century.* New York: Farrar, Straus, and Giroux, 1986.

————. *Something from the Oven: Reinventing Dinner in 1950s America.* New York: Viking, 2004.

Sheraton, Mimi. Rev. of *Laurel's Kitchen: A Handbook for Vegetarian Cookery and Nutrition*, by Laurel Robertson, Carol Flinders, and Godfrey Bronwyn. *New York Times Book Review* December 5, 1976: 94.

Shigley, Sally Bishop. "Empathy, Energy, and Eating: Politics and Power in *The Black Family Dinner Quilt Cookbook*." *Recipes for Reading: Community Cookbooks, Stories, Histories.* Ed. Anne L. Bower. Amherst: University of Massachusetts Press, 1997. 118–131.

Sia, Mary Li. *Mary Sia's Chinese Cookbook.* Honolulu: University Press of Hawaii, 1956.

Simons, John, and Maria Mallory. "Kmart: Fuzzy's Not Funny." *U.S. News & World Report* May 5, 1997: 55.

Slatalla, Michelle. "Joined by the Hip: Food and TV." *New York Times* September 6, 2000: F1+.

Smedes, Susan Dabney. *Memorials of a Southern Planter.* New York: Knopf, 1968.

Smith, Christopher Holmes. "Freeze Frames: Frozen Foods and Memories of the Postwar American Family." *Kitchen Culture in America: Popular Representations of Food, Gender, and Race.* Ed. Sherrie A. Inness. Philadelphia: University of Pennsylvania Press, 2001, 175–209.

Smith, Dinitia. "Demonizing Fat in the War on Weight." *New York Times* May 1, 2004: 7.

Smith, Lutisha. *In the Kitchen with Lutisha: Cooking with a Mother's Love.* New York: First Books Library, 2003.

Smith, Zay. "Crazy Cows? Flue Birds? Time to Enter the Vegan." *Chicago Sun-Times* February 1, 2004: 18.

Snider, Arthur J. "Beware Back-to-Nature Fads." *Science Digest* September 1972: 48+.

Sobal, Jeffery, and Donna Maurer, eds. *Weighty Issues: Fatness and Thinness as Social Problems.* Hawthorne, NY: Aldine de Gruyter, 1999.

Sokolov, Raymond A. "The Food at the Heart of Commune Life." *New York Times* December 2, 1971: 60.

————. "Macrobiotic Cooking—Learning the Secrets of Yang and Yin." *New York Times* July 8, 1971: 41.

————. "Learning to Cook Natural Foods." *New York Times Magazine* June 25, 1972: 45.

Sokolow, Jayme A. *Eros and Modernization: Sylvester Graham, Health Reform, and the Origins of Victorian Sexuality in America.* Rutherford, NJ: Fairleigh Dickinson University Press, 1983.

Solomons, Noel W. "Diet and Long-term Health: An African Diaspora Perspective." *Asia Pacific Journal of Clinical Nutrition* 12.3 (2003): 313–330.

"Some G.I. Captives May Seem Pro-Red." *New York Times* April 13, 1953: 3.

"Speed in the Kitchen." *New York Times* October 30, 1952: 30.

Spencer, Colin. *The Heretic's Feast: A History of Vegetarianism.* Hanover, NH: University Press of New England, 1995.

"Spend & Save." *Ladies' Home Journal* June 1964: 106+.

Spindler, Amy. "Trash Fash." *New York Times* September 12, 1993: 10.

Sprankle, Judith K. *Working It Out: The Domestic Double Standard.* New York: Walker, 1986.

Stallybrass, Peter, and Allon White. *The Politics and Poetics of Transgression.* Ithaca, NY: Cornell University Press, 1986.

Starr, Kathy. *The Soul of Southern Cooking.* Jackson: University Press of Mississippi, 1989.

Stearns, Peter N. *Fat History: Bodies and Beauty in the Modern West.* New York: New York University Press, 1997.

Steil, Janice M. *Marital Equality: Its Relationship to the Well-Being of Husbands and Wives.* Thousand Oaks, CA: Sage Publications, 1997.

Steinle, Diane. "60s Classic Is Fresh for 90s." *St. Petersburg Times* March 24, 1994: ID.

Stepaniak, Joanne. *The Vegan Sourcebook.* Los Angeles: Lowell House, 1998.

————. *Being Vegan.* Los Angeles: Lowell House, 2000.

Stiers, Louise. "Company Supper with Chow Mein." *Farm Journal* May 1957: 114–115.

Stilwill, Lois. "The Pleasures of Convenience Foods." *Ladies' Home Journal* November 1963: 133.

———. "Instant Cook." *Ladies' Home Journal* January 1964: 132.

Strasser, Susan. *Never Done: A History of American Housework.* New York: Holt, 2000.

Takaki, Ronald T. *Democracy and Race: Asian Americans and World War II.* New York: Chelsea House, 1995.

Talbot, Margaret. "Getting Credit for Being White." *New York Times Magazine* November 30, 1997: 116–119.

Tausend, Marilyn. *Cocina de la Familia: More than 200 Authentic Recipes from Mexican-American Home Kitchens.* New York: Simon & Schuster, 1997.

Tchen, John Kuo Wei. *New York Before Chinatown: Orientalism and the Shaping of American Culture, 1776–1882.* Baltimore: Johns Hopkins University Press, 1999.

Theophano, Janet. "Home Cooking: Boston Baked Beans and Sizzling Rice Soup as Recipes for Pride and Prejudice." *Kitchen Culture in America: Popular Representations of Food, Gender, and Race.* Ed. Sherrie A. Inness. Philadelphia: University of Pennsylvania Press, 2001. 139–156.

———. *Eat My Words: Reading Women's Lives Through the Cookbooks They Wrote.* New York: Palgrave, 2002.

"These Chinese Dishes Are Classics." *Sunset* October 1957: 158+.

"They're All Quick—with a Mix." *Better Homes and Gardens* January 1950: 54+.

Thomas, Jeannie B., and Doug Enders. "Bluegrass and 'White Trash': A Case Study Concerning the Name 'Folklore' and Class Bias." *Journal of Folklore Research* 37.1 (2000): 23–52.

Tisdale, Sallie. *The Best Thing I Ever Tasted: The Secret of Food.* New York: Riverhead 2000.

Tong, Benson. *The Chinese Americans.* Rev. ed. Boulder: University Press of Colorado, 2003.

"Tortured to Confess, Fliers Say." *New York Times* September 6, 1953: 3.

"Treat Yourself to Mixes and Pre-Prepared Foods." *Parents' Magazine* October 1955: 62+.

Tucker, Katherine. "Dietary Patterns and Blood Pressure in African Americans." *Nutrition Reviews* 57.11 (1999): 356–358.

Turner, Bertha L. *The Federation Cook Book: A Collection of Tested Recipes by the Colored Women of the State of California.* Pasadena: n.p., 1910.

Turner, Patricia A. *Ceramic Uncles & Celluloid Mammies: Black Images and Their Influence on Culture.* New York: Anchor Books, 1994.

Two Fat Ladies. Performed by Jennifer Paterson and Clarissa Dickson Wright. Videocassette. Vols. 1–5. New River Media, 1997.

"Two Miami Dining Halls Serve Vegetarian/Vegan Fare." *Cincinnati Post* September 21, 2004: 32.

"Two Parades Mark City Loyalty Day." *New York Times* April 29, 1956: 56.

Urdaneta, Maria Luisa. *Deleites de la Cocina Mexican = Healthy Mexican American Cooking*. Austin: University of Texas Press, 1996.

Van Brunt, Lloyd. "About Men." *New York Times Magazine* March 27, 1994: 38.

Varner, Gary E. "In Defense of the Vegan Ideal: Rhetoric and Bias in the Nutrition Literature." *Journal of Agricultural and Environmental Ethics* 7.1 (1994): 29–40.

"The Vegan Society." September 5, 2004. <http://www.vegansociety.com>

"Vegan Victory." *Toronto Star* July 24, 2004: J14.

Voltz, Jeanne. *The Los Angeles Times Natural Foods Cookbook*. New York: Putnam, 1973.

Wandersee, Winifred D. *Women's Work and Family Values, 1920–1940*. Cambridge: Harvard University Press, 1981.

Warner, Mark. "Ham Hocks on Your Cornflakes: Examining the Role of Food in African-American Identity." *Archaeology* 54.6 (2001): 48–52.

Wasserman, Debra. *Simply Vegan: Quick Vegetarian Meals*. Baltimore: Vegetarian Resource Group, 1991.

Watts, Sara Hervey. "You Can Perform Magic with Mixes." *Country Gentleman* November 1953: 129–132.

W.C.T.U. Cookbook: Health and Comfort for the Home. Providence, RI: E. L. Freeman & Sons, 1889.

Webster, Cassandra Hughes, comp. *Mother Africa's Table: A Collection of West African and African-American Recipes and Cultural Traditions*. New York: Doubleday, 1998.

"The Week of Living (Almost) Organically." *Toronto Star* May 7, 2004: D16.

Wegars, Priscilla. Rev. of *Diet for a Small Planet*, by Frances Moore Lappé. *Library Journal* May 15, 1972: 1938.

Weiss, Gertrude S. "Time and Money Costs of Meals Using Home- and Pre-Kitchen-Prepared Foods." *Journal of Home Economics* 46.2 (1954): 98–100.

Weston, Elizabeth. "The Saving Graces of Convenience Foods." *McCall's* May 1965: 44.

"We've Been Asked: How Healthful Is Health Food?" *U.S. News & World Report* July 21, 1975: 64.

"What's So Great about Health Foods?" *Life* September 29, 1972: 45+.

Wheldon, Rupert H. *No Animal Food: Two Essays and 100 Recipes*. London: Daniel, 1910.

White, Deborah Gray. *Ar'n't I a Woman? Female Slaves in the Plantation South*. New York: Norton, 1985.

White, Joyce. *Soul Food: Recipes and Reflections from African-American Churches*. New York: HarperCollins, 1998.

"Whole Family in Kitchen." *New York Times* May 6, 1952: 33.

Whorton, James C. *Crusaders for Fitness: The History of American Health Reformers.* Princeton: Princeton University Press, 1982.

Wiener, Joan. "New Food Freaks." *Seventeen* March 1972: 134+.

Wiley, Mary Elizabeth, and Alexandra Field Meyer. "What America Needs Is a New Domestic Philosophy." *House Beautiful* April 1951: 104+.

"Will the Real Vegetarians Please Stand Up?" *Environmental Nutrition* 18.4 (April 1995): 8.

Williams-Forson, Psyche A. " 'Suckin' the Chicken Bone Dry': African-American Women, Fried Chicken, and the Power of a National Narrative." *Cooking Lessons: The Politics of Gender and Food.* Ed. Sherrie A. Inness. Lanham, MD: Rowman & Littlefield, 2001. 169–191.

Williamson, J. W. *Hillbillyland: What the Movies Did to the Mountains and What the Mountains Did to the Movies.* Chapel Hill: University of North Carolina Press, 1995.

Wilson, Jacqueline Zara. "Invisible Racism: The Language and Ontology of 'White Trash.' " *Critique of Anthropology* 22.4 (2002): 387–401.

Winders, Jamie. "White in All the Wrong Places: White Rural Poverty in the Postbellum U. S. South." *Cultural Geographies* 10.1 (2003): 45–63.

Wing, Fred, and Mabel Stegner. *New Chinese Recipes, Using Only Ingredients Easily Obtainable in Neighborhood Stores.* New York: Edelmuth, 1951.

Witt, Doris. *Black Hunger: Food and the Politics of U.S. Identity.* New York: Oxford University Press, 1999.

Wolf, Naomi. *The Beauty Myth: How Images of Female Beauty Are Used Against Women.* New York: William Morrow, 1991.

Wong, Gail. *Gail Wong's Authentic Chinese Recipes.* Honolulu: G. Wong, 1953.

Wong, Jade Snow. "Chinese Food Can Be Wonderful." *Holiday* May 1951: 94+.

Wong, K. Scott, and Sucheng Chan, eds. *Claiming America: Constructing Chinese American Identities during the Exclusion Era.* Philadelphia: Temple University Press, 1998.

Wood, Nancy Crawford. "The Magic of Mixes." *Ladies' Home Journal* April 1963: 90+.

Woods, Audrey. "Politically Incorrect 'Fat Lady' Served Up Comedic Anarchy: TV Chef Added Lots of Butter, Cream, and Wry Humour." *Ottawa Citizen* August 11, 1999: A9.

Woods, Sylvia. *Sylvia's Family Soul Food Cookbook: From Hemingway, South Carolina to Harlem.* New York: Morrow, 1999.

"Work Wonders with Packaged Potato Products." *Ladies' Home Journal* April 1967: 118+.

Wray, Matt, and Annalee Newitz, eds. *White Trash: Race and Class in America.* New York: Routledge, 1997.

Wright, Clarissa Dickson. "A Fat Lot of Good Dieting Ever Did Anyone." *Financial Times* (London) January 2, 2004: 15.

Wu, Cheng-Tsu. *"Chink!" A Documentary History of Anti-Chinese Prejudice in America.* New York: Word Pub., 1972.

Wynette, Tammy. *The Tammy Wynette Southern Cookbook.* Gretna, LA: Pelican, 1990.

Yaeger, Patricia. "Edible Labor." *Southern Quarterly* 30 (Winter–Spring 1992): 150–159.

Yim, Su-Jin. "Living La Vida Vegan." *Oregonian* September 5, 2003: E01.

"You Cook This Chinese Dinner Right at the Table." *Sunset* January 1957: 56–57.

Young, Myrtle Lum. *Fun with Chinese Recipes.* New York: Vantage, 1958.

Yung, Judy. *Unbound Feet: A Social History of Chinese Women in San Francisco.* Berkeley: University of California Press, 1995.

Zafar, Rafia. "The Signifying Dish: Autobiography and History in Two Black Women's Cookbooks." *Feminist Studies* 25.2 (1999): 449–469.

Zamir, Tzachi. "Veganism." *Journal of Social Philosophy* 35.3 (2004): 367–390.

Zhao, Xiojian. *Remaking Chinese America: Immigration, Family, and Community, 1940–1965.* New Brunswick: Rutgers University Press, 2002.

Zia, Helen. *Asian American Dreams: The Emergence of an American People.* New York: Farrar, Straus, & Giroux, 2000.

Index

chow mein, 39, 47, 48, 52, 53, 58
Civil Rights movement, 87, 125
Civil War, 107, 109, 153
class: and African Americans, 107–25;
and Chinese-American cooking,
52–53; and convenience foods,
21–22, 32, 37; and natural foods, 90,
102, 200; and white trash, 127–48
Cold War, 44–46
Colonel Higbee, 110
Coltrane, Scott, 72
Columbia Exposition, 109
Communism, 25, 42, 45, 51
Communist Control Act, 45
*Complete Vegan Cookbook: Over 200
Tantalizing Recipes* (Toomay), 151,
159, 161
convenience foods, 9–10, 190; and class,
21–22, 32, 37; and cooking literature,
18, 19; and cost, 35; and creativity,
19, 27–31, 36, 66, 69, 102; and
employment, 32–33; and gender
roles, 20–26, 31–32; and
international foods, 30–31; and
marketing, 21–23; and mass media,
17–18, 22–23; and modernity,
24–26, 36–37; and quality, 22–24,
36; and schools, 23–24; and speed,
31–35, 37; and status quo, 20; and
The I Hate to Cook Book, 77–79
*Conversation on Abstinence from the
Flesh of Animals as Food, A*
(Metcalfe), 154
cookbooks: and African Americans,
111–25; and Chinese Americans,
48–60; and convenience foods,
9–10, 18–37; and gender roles, 2–3,
10–11, 15; as literature, 2–3; and
natural foods movement, 11, 83,
86–104; and status quo, 6, 8; and
veganism, 13, 151, 156, 158–62;
and white trash, 12, 138–48; *see also*
political agendas in cookbooks

cooking culture: and African
Americans, 106, 113–25; and
Chinese Americans, 10, 48–60; and
competition, 72; and convenience
foods, 9–10, 18–37, 66, 69; and
creativity, 27–31, 37; and the
Internet, 2, 15, 168; and natural
foods, 11, 91; and race, 9, 11–12;
and television, 2, 13–15, 17–18,
21–22, 175–77; and *The I Hate to
Cook Book*, 66–80; and *Two Fat
Ladies*, 13–14; and vegans, 149–68;
and white trash, 12, 138–48
Cooking Light, 2
cooking mystique, 65, 196
cooperatives, 90
Cornell University, 42
Cowherd, Reverend William, 152
Crea, Joe, 118
creativity, 27–31, 64, 66, 68, 78, 102
Crescent Dragonwagon, 90
Crocker, Betty, 27, 29, 40, 145
cultural identity: and African
Americans, 111–25; and Chinese-
Americans, 43–44, 46, 49–52,
56–60; and cooking, 6, 10; and
white trash, 128–32, 136–48

Danielson, Florence H., 133
Darden, Carole, 115
*Date with a Dish: A Cook Book of
American Negro Recipes, A*
(De Knight), 122
Daughters of the Confederacy, 108
Davenport, Charles B., 133
Davis, Adelle, 85
Davis Milling Company, 110
Day, Doris, 40
Dean, James, 40
Deck, Alice A., 107, 110, 111
De Knight, Freda, 122
Denker, Joel, 51
Dickson, Clarissa, 13